T0189738

Smart Card Application Development Using Java

Springer-Verlag Berlin Heidelberg GmbH

Uwe Hansmann Martin S. Nicklous
Thomas Schäck Achim Schneider
Frank Seliger

Smart Card Application Development Using Java

Second Edition

With 98 Figures, 16 Tables
and a Multi Function Smart Card

 Springer

Uwe Hansmann
Martin S. Nicklous
Thomas Schäck
Achim Schneider
Frank Seliger

IBM Deutschland Entwicklung GmbH
Schönaicherstraße 220
71032 Böblingen, Germany

Additional material to this book can be downloaded from http://extras.springer.com

Library of Congress Cataloging-in-Publication Data
Smart card application development using Java: with 98 figures, 16 tables and a multi
function smart card/Uwe Hansmann ...[et al.]. – 2. ed.
    p.cm.
    Includes bibliographical references and index.
    ISBN 978-3-540-43202-9   ISBN 978-3-642-55969-3 (eBook)
    DOI 10.1007/978-3-642-55969-3
      1. Java (computer program language) 2. Smart cards – Programming I. Hansmann,
    Uwe, 1970–
QA76.73.J38 S597 2002
005.13'3–dc21   2002066929

ISBN 978-3-540-43202-9

http://www.springer.de

© Springer-Verlag Berlin Heidelberg 2000, 2002
Originally published by Springer-Verlag Berlin Heidelberg in 2002
Softcover reprint of the hardcover 2nd edition 2002

Cover design: KünkelLopka , Heidelberg
Typesetting: Camera-ready by the authors
Printed on acid-free paper – SPIN: 10866335   33/3142 GF 543210

Foreword

As we reach adolescence in the Internet era, we are now facing the dawn of the digital era – an era that will be marked not by PCs and servers, but by computational capability that is embedded in all things around us. The simple user interfaces of the browser – which seemed revolutionary a few short years ago – will be replaced by more natural interactions that are more convenient to daily life. Whether in work or play, we will be able to interact with information and applications in a highly personalized, yet adaptive way using whatever device they may be carrying. They will be able to interact with these capabilities using a variety of modes – traditional visual based methods, voice based systems and new emerging multimodal technologies combining different access methodologies in one transaction. In the not too distant future, the networks will introduce multi-lingual capabilities including dynamic translations and gaze recognition technologies that put context around where you are looking.

Applications are increasingly moving to the network – self-healing networks that are always on, fully connected. Access will be carried by service providers who in turn become the next generation of utility – much like electricity did a century before. This access will be managed across an interconnected web of wireless networks (both short and long range), broadband wireline networks and traditional dial up networks. Many business model issues and perhaps regulatory issues will have to be solved as this comes to pass, but it will happen. The next steps are so clear that they must.

As these networks emerge and these devices come to fruition, we are facing a dilemma. How can we create a secure transactional capability across this new frontier? As devices increasingly become commodities, how can we transition security information from one device to the new one, without leaving the old device open to break in?

The unfortunate incidents on September 11th, 2001 have reminded us that security systems are fragile and must be rethought. New methods of identification must be developed – more secure, more robust than the last generation and easy to use. New advances in technologies, like smart cards, are paving the way to these new systems combining means of high security and privacy at the same time. Identification schemes need to be portable and totally reliable. Whether the application is embedded in SIM cards for Mobil phones, credit or debit cards, corporate or national identification cards, the next steps are clear.

Michael D. Rhodin
Vice President, Pervasive Computing
IBM Corporation

February 2002

Foreword 1 to the First Edition

Until recently, most books on smart cards needed to be divided into two distinct categories: One for North American readers, and the other for readers from all other parts of the world. The reason being that while the rest of the world has deployed hundreds of millions of smart cards for applications as diverse as telecommunications, banking, pay-television, health-care, or transportation, North America has deployed relatively few.

This book marks the beginning of a new era when smart cards have outgrown their European cradle, and have attracted the talent and creativity of "heavyweights" in the US information technology industry. Its authors are employed by IBM and the technology they describe is based on a programming platform initiated by Sun Microsystems. This is a clear signal that smart cards are coming of age.

Why this sudden interest by American companies in a technology that they have admittedly ignored or misunderstood for quite a long time? The answer has a lot to do with "e-words", company names ending in "dot com" and, above all, the promise of a new digital economy where consumers are connected pervasively to the Internet and happily spending their money online.

Consumers are increasingly surrounded by Web-aware appliances. As a result, personal computers will begin to fade as the primary point of access to the Internet. They will not go away, of course, but cellular phones, set-top boxes, video games, and even cars will outnumber them as network-connected consumer devices.

Dear reader – and consumer, are you going to identify yourself to your car, your TV set top box, and your phone by punching in passwords all day long? Not very likely.

If you own a GSM or PCS phone, a smart card chip is already hidden inside your handset to provide strong authentication to the network operator. If you watch satellite TV, chances are that your set-top box uses a smart card to hold your subscription rights securely. And in a couple of years, your car will recognize you by your smart ignition key, which will hold your preferences for seat and mirror adjustments, and favorite radio stations.

Granted, you will not spend your day inserting plastic cards into slots either. Smart card technology will remain mostly hidden from you, seamlessly integrated into the products of your everyday life.

This book explains how such integration is possible. It teaches us about developing smart card applications in "Internet time", meaning in weeks instead of months. It shows us the merits of using open, inclusive, proven standards developed by industry consortia to advance the state of the technology. It is about crossing the chasm between the early adopters of smart card technology (mostly European and Asian telecommunication operators and banks) and the incumbent deployers of information infrastructure technology (mostly American IT companies).

It is somewhat ironic that you can find many of the technical foundations of this book somewhere on the World Wide Web because of the very principles guiding the authors in their development work. However, this book goes beyond the basic technology foundations: You will find here a wealth of detailed diagrams as well as examples and information on design rationales and tradeoffs. Smart cards remain a relatively under-documented subject and it was indispensable that the OpenCard^{SM} and Java^{TM} technologies explained here, be preceded and integrated with a detailed explanation of existing smart card hardware and software platforms, as well as existing smart card standards.

Like with most other technologies, the devil is in the details. You will find here the tools to chase the devil out of successful implementations of smart card capable products.

Patrice Peyret
Director, Sun Microsystems Inc.
Consumer & Embedded Platforms

August 1999

Foreword 2 to the First Edition

Computers that understand voice and handwriting ... intelligent cars
... computers that are as small as a walkman – these aren't pictures
of the future, but reality. The theme behind this is e-business, and a
wide variety of e-business products, technologies and services demonstrate its leading role on the way to e-society. And pervasive
computing is a key factor. It refers to the idea of computer intelligence in everyday devices that give customers convenient access to
data and services, and the ability to conduct e-business at any time,
from any location. In the next five to ten years there will be over one
million businesses and one billion people using one trillion mobile
and network devices to communicate worldwide.

In the new world of pervasive computing, relevant, customized
information will always be within easy reach, ready to be acted on
immediately. This convenient access and ability to take action will
be provided to users by a new generation of smart devices – embedded with powerful microprocessors – that connect to the network for
data and services.

These devices – smartphones, screenphones, personal digital assistants, kiosks, smart machines and other Internet appliances – will
be simple and intuitive to use. Processes that now take a number of
commands to run on a PC will require only the push of a button, a
spoken request, or a hand-written command.

A number of technology innovations are helping to make sure
this happens. For example, IBM's record-setting, high-capacity
miniature hard drives and the extension of its leading virtual machine and compiler implementations into the space of embedded
computers are steps towards reusing applications across different
devices, such as embedded computing devices and smart cards.

In this networked world, smart cards will play a major role. The
smart card is the ultimate device for carrying data, it is extremely secure, and it has a familiar shape, that of the widely used and known
credit card. The power of a smart card, and with the possibility of an
integrated cryptographic engine at that, is tremendous.

The key characteristics for smart cards in today's world are security, ease of use, mobility, and multi-functionality.

They are thus geared/predestined to become the next major IT platform. And they are going to revolutionize the business world over the next few years. Many smart-card applications are today being implemented – from citizen ID cards to health cards, electronic purse cards, and network access cards. It is widely accepted that nearly all organizations will sooner or later need to assimilate smart cards into their routine business processes.

This book is the first to describe – besides the pure smart card technology – the complete end-to-end system approach. The complete scenario, from the standards involved to the programming capabilities required, is dealt with, and in a way that is easy to understand.

This book complements the smart-card application suite. It was written to enable readers to take over an active role in the software development of smart-card applications without the necessity of having to go into the bits and bytes of the card itself.

I'd like to thank the authors for this new approach in addressing smart-card-related technology, and I wish all the readers much fun in developing their first application!

Sabine Schilg
Business Line Manager
IBM Pervasive Computing Solutions

August 1999

Table of Contents

XII ■ *Table of Contents*
    ■
    ■

XIV   ■   *Table of Contents*
       ■
       ■

Preface

About This Book

This book is a guide for the rapid development of smart card applications using Java. It provides you with basic information that you need about smart cards and how they work. It explains concepts and patterns for the use of smart cards in e-commerce applications and gives a foundation of the required security techniques. It shows in detail how to develop applications that use smart cards by guiding you through examples, which we present step by step.

In today's world, smart cards play an increasingly important role. We encounter them as credit cards, loyalty cards, electronic purses, health cards, and as secure tokens for authentication or digital signature. The smart card itself is a secure computing device for storing all kinds of information and executing commands using this information. Its small size makes the smart card the ideal carrier for personal information like customization profiles, medical emergency information, secret keys, and passwords.

A growing number of application owners and developers will enable their applications for the use of smart cards. Particularly electronic commerce over the Internet will increasingly involve smart cards. In the past, the integration of smart cards into e-commerce software had been a cumbersome and difficult task. Recent developments in standards and framework offerings have made this task easier and more efficient. To be platform independent and executable in any web browser, new software is frequently written in Java. Consequently, it is desirable to access a smart card in the same platform independent way.

Since 1997, a Java framework for smart card usage has been developed and published by an industry consortium. The OpenCard^{SM} Framework plays an important role in the development of applications that use smart cards. This book places emphasis on the use of the OpenCard Framework for smart card application development in

Java. This second edition now covers the currently latest version of the Open Card Framework: Version 1.2.

You can find all the material that you need to get started with the OpenCard Framework on http://www.opencard.org/. The samples of source code presented in this book are available for downloading on http://www.opencard.org/SCJavaBook/. The smart card provided with this book will help you to quickly get your first hands-on experience.

The Audience of This Book

This book assumes a technical audience. If you are a software architect, technical project manager, application designer, or application developer, this book can help you with your work.

Software Architects and Project Managers

For you, this book gives you an overview of state-of-the-art smart card technology and shows you how smart cards can be quickly integrated into your software.

Application Developers

You will learn how to rapidly enable your applications for the use of smart cards. You will also learn some typical patterns of smart card usage and how to trade off various desirable properties in making your design decisions. We assume that the reader possesses a basic knowledge of Java.

No Need to Read the Whole Book

Most of us no longer have the time to read an application development book cover to cover. Therefore, we have broken this book into chunks that may be read in almost any sequence. In the following, we give an overview of this book.

Marginal notes aid navigation
To allow for fast access to sections of interest or to sections that you have already read and would like to review, we have included eye-catchers at the margins. You can think of the marginal notes as subheadings, which together with the headings form the fine-grained structure of the book.

Index
The index at the back should help you to quickly find the related text using standard smart card terms.

This book has three main parts and a supplementary section:

- "Part I, Smart Card Introduction and Overview",
- "Part II, OpenCard Framework",
- "Part III, Smart Card Application Development Using OCF", and
- "Part IV, Appendixes".

Are you interested in smart card technology in general? To concentrate on the technology of smart cards, we suggest you to read Part I in detail.

Are you interested in developing an application that uses smart cards? To concentrate on smart card application development, we suggest you to read Parts II and III in detail and to use Part I as a reference to look up the questions that might arise.

Smart Card Introduction and Overview   **Part I**

We set the stage by providing background information on smart cards. We give an overview of basic smart card technology and of the most common applications that use smart cards.

What Makes the Smart Card "Smart"?   **Chapter 1**

We describe the different types of smart cards, explain their features, and give some recommendations on when to use which type. We present the benefits of smart cards and their advantage over magnetic stripe cards. We explain how new applications benefit from storing information securely on a smart card and delegating operations on this data to the smart card. We also explain why the smart card's portability, security, and low cost have been so important for its success.

We provide you with a basic knowledge of smart card hardware and the associated terminology. This will enable you to understand the implications of smart card hardware for the software and for the overall system.

Introduction to Smart Card Software   **Chapter 2**

We point out the distinctions between the on-card part and the off-card part of an application. We explain the standard communication mechanisms and protocols that link both parts. In the case of multiple application smart cards, the card operating system must meet special requirements. We briefly explain the most important smart card platforms and operating systems designed to support multiple applications, including Java Card, Multos, and Smart Card for Windows.

Chapter 3 **Smart Cards and e-business**

Smart cards are widely used in e-business as purses (like Geld-Karte, Mondex, Moneo, Proton, or Visa Cash), and as personal devices for secure access. Smart cards are ideal for digitally signing electronic orders or digital contracts. Furthermore, smart cards are used to protect the privacy and integrity of e-mails. Other applications include loyalty programs, some of which work with smart cards to authenticate the customer and to administer bonus points.

We briefly outline how these systems work. Some of the concepts you encounter here are patterns that you will come across repeatedly in applications using smart cards.

Chapter 4 **Cryptography**

Cryptography is used for the secure storage and transfer of data, especially if smart cards are used as security tokens. We explain the background of cryptography and give a short overview of the different standards, algorithms, and protocols used.

Chapter 5 **Smart Card Readers and Terminals**

To enable an application to communicate with a smart card, a smart card reader device is required. We give an overview of the different types of smart card readers, from simple devices with no computing power of their own to complex devices that are also able to execute complete command sequences autonomously.

Chapter 6 **Smart Card Standards and Industry Initiatives**

Depending on the application, various standards and specifications from industry initiatives may be relevant. We introduce some of the standards and specifications with wide scope, established by ISO, EMV, Global Platform, and PC/SC. Java Card and Multos, the industry initiatives specifying card platforms, were already covered in Chapter 2.

Part II **OpenCard Framework**

Parts II and III concentrate on the development of applications that use smart cards. We base the development on Java and on the OpenCard Framework (or "OCF" for short), the industry standard for smart card access in a Java environment. In Part II, we cover the OpenCard Framework's goals, concepts, architecture, and components in depth.

Introduction to OpenCard Chapter 7

We give a brief overview of the history of OpenCard and cover the OpenCard Consortium, the driving organization behind the OpenCard Framework. We explain the scope of OpenCard.

As an introduction to the OpenCard Framework, we explain its objectives and give a high-level overview of its architecture, layers, and components.

The Utility Classes Chapter 8

Starting with this chapter, we explain the architecture, layers, and components of the OpenCard Framework in depth, including some of the design considerations.

In Chapter 8, we cover the core definitions and all utility classes of OCF. These are used throughout the framework and are available to the applications as well.

The Terminal Layer Chapter 9

We cover the bottom layer of OCF, which provides all the support for driving the devices that perform the communication with the smart card. Most of the material in this chapter is important to anyone who works with OCF; some of it helps smart card reader developers in creating the drivers required to have their devices supported by OCF.

The Service Layer Chapter 10

The service layer provides all the support for encapsulating details of the smart card and its operating system and for offering a high-level interface to the application program. We explain the service layer in depth. Most of the material in this chapter is important to anyone who works with OCF; some of it helps smart card developers in creating the components required to offer an OCF-based high-level application program interface for their cards.

The OCF Security Concept Chapter 11

We cover the security concepts in OCF and explain how they interlock with the security concepts of Java and with the diverging implementations found in the different web browsers. In web-based client-server applications using a smart card on the client side, the application needs to access the smart card from within a Java applet running in a standard web browser. We explain the security measures and the details to consider with the most common web browsers.

OCF offers several classes that provide help in integrating smart cards with various security mechanisms into the framework. We discuss these classes, which are relevant for smart card developers and application programmers.

Part III   Smart Card Application Development Using OCF

To demonstrate the application of the concepts and techniques that we explained in Part II, we develop simple example applications in Part III. In addition, we present parts of the architecture, design, and code of more complex and more advanced applications.

Chapter 12   Using OCF

First, we explain how to setup and configure OCF. Then we develop two sample applications, starting very simple and moving on to the more complex.

You will learn what steps are necessary to enable an application for the use of smart cards. You will appreciate how Java and OCF make the programming task easy. The complete source code of our example applications is available on the web.

Chapter 13   OCF and e-business

We demonstrate the use of OCF in a classical client-server application. The scenario is an Internet stockbroker application, in which the stock orders are digitally signed by the client's smart card. We also present the case of a distributed payment system, in which OCF is used in a servlet for accessing a smart card on the server side.

Chapter 14   Java™ Card and OCF

Java Cards are smart cards that allow the on-card software to be developed in Java. Developing on-card programs in Java takes advantage of the known benefits of Java. The Java Card's interpreting environment helps to provide multiple applications on the card without unintended interference.

As communication with on-card applets requires using the same low-level protocol as with other smart cards, OCF can be used advantageously to deal with this communication on a higher level.

Chapter 15   Card and Application Management

As soon as software is widely used and successful, it results in new requirements that lead to upgrades. The deployment of updates and extensions is a challenge in its own right. We discuss how OCF uses Java to help you meet this challenge. We show how you can download, for example, a new Java Card applet from a central server onto your customer's Java Card. We also explain how a computer or terminal could be enabled to support new or updated versions of smart cards without manually installing software on that device.

OCF for Embedded Devices   Chapter 16

For embedded devices and for computers with very limited resources, such as PDAs, screen phones or smart card terminals, some of the flexibility and complexity of OCF is not needed. For these environments, a trimmed-down version of OCF is a better fit. We describe this version of OCF in-depth in this chapter.

Appendixes   Part IV

The Card   Appendix A

Along with the book, you received a smart card that enables you to immediately start practicing what you read. The examples that we present in Chapter 12 "Using OCF", and which you can download from http://www.opencard.org/SCJavaBook/, work with this card. We give basic information about the card, an IBM Multi-Function Card, and describe the data layout that we gave this card.

Useful Web Sites   Appendix B

The OpenCard Framework documentation and reference implementation, the Java development kit, Java extension packages, smart card reader drivers, and the Java Card specification are examples of helpful material that you can immediately download from the web.

In this appendix, we share with you references to web sites, which we found relevant to developing smart card applications in Java. Of course, we cannot guarantee that all of the links will correctly work for as long as this book is available.

Bibliography   Appendix C

In this appendix, we reference the sources that we used. In addition, we point to material that is very helpful for learning more about those areas that are not the focus of this book.

Glossary   Appendix D

The glossary briefly explains some of the most important terms.

Index   Appendix E

The index helps you locate terms used and explained in this book.

About the Authors

Uwe Hansmann is now managing development projects in IBM's Pervasive Computing Division. He represents IBM in various industry groups, like the SyncML Initiative. He was Secretary and Board member of the OpenCard Consortium and the Open Services Gateway Initiative. Uwe received a Master of Science from the University of Applied Studies of Stuttgart in 1993 and an MBA from the University of Hagen in 1998. He joined IBM in 1993 as software developer and led the technical marketing support team for IBM Digital Library before joining IBM Smart Card Solutions in 1998. From 1999 on he is leading IBM's effort on synchronization, especially SyncML. Uwe published various articles and papers in the areas of smart cards, synchronization, and pervasive computing and is co-author of the book "Pervasive Computing Handbook" (Springer 2001).

Scott Nicklous is currently development manager for smart card technology in IBM's Pervasive Computing Division. He joined IBM in 1984 as software development engineer with the Financial Systems group at the IBM development laboratory in Böblingen, Germany. While at IBM, Scott has been involved as developer and team leader in numerous projects, mainly in the financial sector, including banking machine and image processing system development. He joined IBM Smart Card Solutions in 1997 to lead the OpenCard Framework development team in Böblingen.

Thomas Schaeck started at IBM in 1996 after his graduation in Computer Sciences from the University of Karlsruhe. He worked in various development projects related to smart cards, including internet payments, a digital signature solution, and the OpenCard Framework. He is now working as an architect in the WebSphere Portal Server development. Thomas published various papers in the areas of smart cards and pervasive computing and is a co-author of the book "Pervasive Computing" (Addison-Wesley 2001).

Achim Schneider is currently development manager for Smart Card Solutions in IBM's Pervasive Computing Division. He joined IBM in 1989 as software development engineer with the MERVA software development group at the IBM program product development centre in Sindelfingen, Germany. While at IBM, Achim has been involved as developer and team leader in numerous projects in the financial sector, including banking network solutions. He joined the Smart Card Solutions team in 1996 where he developed parts of the

Smart Card ToolKit. The current product set of the IBM Smart Card Solutions team in Böblingen include the IBM MultiFunction card family, MONEO smart cards for the French market and VISA Smart Credit/Debit smart card solutions as well as consulting and personalization support for customer projects.

Frank Seliger is currently security architect in IBM's Pervasive Computing Division. In this role, he has worked on the architecture of the OpenCard Framework. In 1978, Frank joined IBM, where he has been active in various areas of software and firmware development. Since 1990, his focus has been on Object-Oriented software. He worked on the IBM C++ collection class library that is shipped with all IBM C++ compilers. As consultant in the IBM Object Oriented Technology Center, he coached Object-Oriented development projects inside and outside of IBM. Together with his technology center colleagues he captured his experience in "Developing Object-Oriented Software – An Experience-Based Approach", Prentice Hall 1997.

Acknowledgements

To work on the OpenCard Framework was a unique opportunity that helped us gain and broaden our experience in smart card technology, security technology, and object-oriented framework design. Without that opportunity we could not have written this book. We would like to thank the International Business Machines Corporation and, in particular, its Pervasive Computing Division for having provided us with that opportunity.

Numerous people furnished us with in-depth reviews of the book, supported us, or provided us with their invaluable expertise. We are indebted to Peter Bendel, Alexander Busek, A. J. Cave, Fernand De Decker, Hermann Engesser, Gabi Fischer, Dorothea Glaunsinger, Yolanda Gu, Klaus Gungl, Mike Hamann, Horst Henn, Stefan Hepper, Reto Hermann, Dirk Husemann, Kyle Ingols, Thomas Kohn, Christophe Muller, Ute Niedermeier, Silke Niemann, Patrice Peyret, Gregor Reichle, Mike Rhodin, Sabine Schilg, Michael Schilling, Jo Stark, Peter Trommler, and Dirk Wittkopp.

Part I
Smart Card Introduction
and Overview

"The learning and knowledge that we have,
is, at the most, but little compared with
that of which we are ignorant."

Plato (B.C. 427–347)

1 What Makes the Smart Card "Smart"?

In this chapter, we describe the different types of smart cards, explain their features and benefits, and give some recommendations on when to use which type. We also introduce the smart card hardware in this chapter. Since the focus of this book is on the software side, we will provide only a basic introduction to hardware terminology and concepts. If you have worked with smart cards before, you will probably want to skip this chapter.

1.1 What is a Smart Card?

Some of us already use one or more smart cards in daily life. The smart card can be a phone card, a card carrying our health insurance information, or an electronic purse. The latter allows us to store digital "money" and to use this money later to pay for a ticket or buy a drink from a vending machine.

The smart card itself is a device, which is able to store data and execute commands. It is a single-chip microcomputer with a size of 25 mm^2 at most. This microcomputer is mounted on a plastic card of the size of a standard credit card. Plastic cards have a long tradition.

The plastic card started its career in the early 1950s when Diners Club introduced the first credit card. This card had the name of the cardholder printed on the front. It was used to confirm that the organization that issued the card had enough confidence in the cardholder to allow her to buy goods or services on credit at selected hotels or restaurants. It was now easier to go on business travel without worrying about the amount of money that might be needed to pay the bills. Showing the credit card at hotels or restaurants was sufficient and the amount would be charged later to the traveler's account at home.

The first cards

Later, cards with embossed printing were introduced. The embossing made it possible to take an imprint of the cardholder information instead of copying it down manually. A few years later, the magnetic stripe, which carries the account information and the name of the ˌcardholder, was introduced. This made the card machine-readable so the information could be electronically processed. Still, one problem remained: Everybody with the necessary equipment can read and write the data on the magnetic stripe. This led to a fraud problem.

The first smart card

In 1968, a patent for an identification card with an integrated circuit was filed, and the smart card was born [RAN00]. The smart card is a secure, tamper-resistant device. The data stored on the card can be secured with a secret (usually a password), which is shared between the cardholder and the smart card. Only the person knowing the secret can use the card and the information stored on it.

Furthermore, with the ability to execute programs and commands, the smart card became able to encrypt and decrypt information.

Figure 1.1: Magnetic Stripe Card and Smart Card

The first trials in Europe

The success of the smart card in Europe started in the early eighties. Between 1982 and 1984, Carte Bancaire (the French Bank Card Group) had the first pilot running. Together with Bull, Philips, and Schlumberger, Carte Bancaire launched trials in the French cities of Blois, Caen, and Lyon. The trials were a great success and had only minor problems [TOW02]. One improvement that resulted from these trials was the integration of a magnetic stripe onto the smart card to maintain compatibility with existing systems.

Following these trials, French banks launched the use of smart cards for banking. This was the first mass rollout of smart cards in the banking industry.

Since the eighties, the smart card industry has grown. German banks issued over 52 million GeldKarte smart cards to their customers [EPSO02]. GeldKarte is an electronic purse that we will explain in Chapter 3.1.1 "GeldKarte".

Today every mobile phone that complies with the GSM standard contains a smart card that authenticates the owner. GSM is widely used in Europe and other regions.

1.1.1
The Benefits of Smart Cards

A smart card is a portable computer. Usually it has the shape and size of a credit card. A smart card can be made physically tamper-resistant. Therefore, it can be used as a highly secure storage for all kind of confidential information, such as secret keys. Security and portability are two reasons to use smart cards.

Physical improvements

In the case of an electronic purse, the card can store the current balance and can tightly control increasing or decreasing it. Smart card based electronic purses can reduce the cost of cash handling.

Usage examples

An important characteristic of a smart card is that the information on it cannot be copied. A credit card's magnetic stripe can easily be copied and then be misused. This could never happen with a smart card-based credit card. Therefore, smart cards are recognized as the next generation financial transaction card [VIS02].

In a building access system, the card can be used to store the data required to open a door. The same data can later authenticate the employee to his computer. Or it can be used for payment in the company's cafeteria.

In home-banking applications, the card can be used as a secure token to authenticate the user over a public network between the user's computer and the bank's system. This is more secure than using today's passwords[1].

In a multi-company loyalty scheme, the card can store the loyalty points that the customer already earned.

In a mass-transit system, the card can replace paper tickets. The fare can be calculated based on the distance. This can be done at the time the customer leaves the public transport system, and the fare

---

[1] We will explain the advantage of smart cards for securing network and server access in Section 3.2.2 "Network- and Server-Login".

can be deducted from the card on the spot. Using a contactless card, the traveler could even leave the card in her pocket.

With all these benefits of the smart card as a secure and portable computer, we will see smart card usage grow year by year.

1.2
Smart Card Hardware

In this chapter, we touch upon the general concepts of smart card hardware and give an overview of the technology. We do not cover hardware technology extensively. We explain just as much as you probably need for smart card programming in Java. You can find more on smart card hardware and technology in the excellent book by Rankl & Effing [RAN00].

1.2.1
Memory Cards and Microprocessor Cards

In the early days of the smart card, the card was not really smart, because it had no microprocessor. Such cards are called memory cards. Memory cards are able to store limited information, such as the name of the cardholder. The software in the host computer[2] can then retrieve this information.

Figure 1.2: Memory Cards and Microprocessor Cards

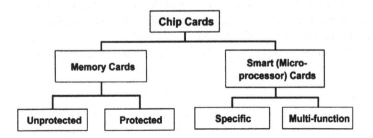

Depending on the security requirements of the stored data, the memory access can be protected. For example, the memory of a prepaid phone card is protected to prevent unauthorized reloading.

Unprotected memory cards are used in some applications that have no particular security requirements (see [RAN00]).

---

[2] "Host computer" here refers to the computer as host to the smart card. This can be any computer: a PC, a larger machine, or a smaller device.

"Smart" cards are chip cards with microprocessors. These smart cards can be divided into smart cards for a single specific application and multi-function smart cards.

1.2.2
Contactless Cards

The host computer has to communicate with the processor on the smart card to exchange information and commands. Communication can take place either through the contacts on the card or via wireless ("contactless") transmission. A hybrid smart card combines both technologies and is able to communicate with the host system using either method.

Contactless smart cards are often used in situations requiring fast transactions or where only a limited amount of data has to be exchanged. Examples are public transport systems or access control for buildings.

Contact cards are more difficult to use than contactless cards. With a contact smart card, the cardholder has to take care that he inserts the smart card into the reader in the right way and with the right orientation. Also, the contacts are occasionally the cause of failures if they are damaged, worn, or just not sufficiently clean.

Advantages of contactless cards

On the other hand, contactless cards also have some disadvantages. The power for the processor must be transmitted as an electromagnetic wave, which limits the maximum power consumption of the processor and therefore the processor capabilities. Also, the combination of analog and digital technologies makes contactless smart cards more expensive than comparable contact smart cards.

Disadvantages of contactless cards

Though today several mass-transit and access control systems work with contactless smart cards [Ampel98], [Chamb99], the technology is not as widely used as contact smart cards. In the near future this may change. Contactless cards may also be used for payment systems.

1.2.3
The Computer on the Smart Card

As we explained earlier, the most important characteristic of a smart card is that it contains a computer with CPU and memory. Today's smart cards have approximately the same computing power as the first IBM PC.

The chip of a smart card (see Figure 1.3) consists of a microprocessor, ROM (Read Only Memory), EEPROM (Electrical Erasable

Programmable Read Only Memory), and RAM (Random Access Memory). An EEPROM requires a larger surface than a PROM of the same size. This makes EEPROM more expensive and lets EEPROM size become an important factor for the price of a smart card.

Memory cards have only ROM and EEPROM. They do not contain programmable logic. The EEPROM can be secured by a hard-wired key, which is checked on every access.

Figure 1.3:
Example of a
Smart Card Chip
and its
Components

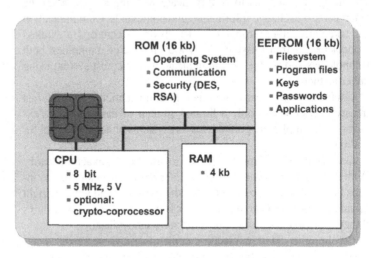

CPU Today, most smart cards have an inexpensive 8-bit microprocessor, but in high-end cards we can find a 16-bit or 32-bit processor.

Cryptographic An optional cryptographic coprocessor increases the performance
coprocessor of cryptographic operations. By performing signature operations on the card itself, the user's private key never needs to leave the card.

ROM The information stored in the ROM is written during production. It is the same for all chips of a series. It contains the card operating system and maybe also some applications.

EEPROM The EEPROM is used for permanent storage of data. Even if the smart card is unpowered, the EEPROM still keeps the data. Some smart cards also allow storing additional application code or application specific commands in the EEPROM.

RAM The RAM is the transient memory of the card and keeps the data only as long as the card is powered.

1.2.4
Mechanical Contacts

A contact smart card has up to eight mechanical contacts, which are used to supply power and a clock signal to the card and to transmit data. The ISO standard 7816-2 [ISO02] specifies the position, the minimal size, and the usage of the contacts.

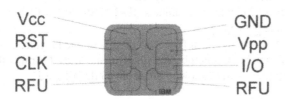

Figure 1.4:
Mechanical
Contacts of a
Smart Card

Two out of the eight contacts are reserved for future use (RFU) and six are actually used[3]. The six active contacts are:

- **Vcc** is used to supply voltage to the chip. In general, the voltage is between 4.5 V and 5.5 V. In the future we will see lower voltage rates around 3 V.

- **RST** is used for the reset signal to reset the address counter and the microprocessor. A reset without removing power is called "warm reset". A "cold reset" takes place if the power is removed and reapplied.

- The external clock signal, from which the microprocessor clock is derived, is supplied to the **CLK** contact.

- **GND** is used for ground connection.

- The **Vpp** connector is used for the high voltage signal, which is necessary to program the EEPROM. Newer smart cards have the capability to generate this high voltage themselves, so that they do not use the Vpp contact.

- **I/O** is used to transfer data between the smart card and the reader device in a half-duplex mode. The protocols for this communication are also specified in ISO 7816.

---

[3] Several types of cards today only have actually six contacts, for example the phone cards in Germany. This is less expensive to produce and the lifetime of a prepaid phone card is short enough not to conflict with potential future use of these two contacts.

1.2.5
The Size of a Smart Card

Several forms and sizes were specified for plastic cards. The two most important forms for smart cards are ID-1 and ID-000.

The form ID-1 has the size of a credit card and is used for most of the applications.

The form called ID-000 is mostly used in mobile phones and for Security Access Modules in terminals. ID-1 cards do not fit inside modern mobile phones.

Figure 1.5 shows the form ID-1 and ID-000 in one graphic, centered on the chip. Some smart cards actually come in ID-1 form with the ID-000 form scored to allow to break out an ID-000 card.

Figure 1.5: The Size of the Smart Cards ID-000 and ID-1

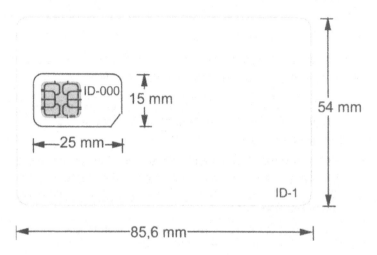

The main reason for the size and shape of the smart card is to make it geometrically compatible with magnetic stripe cards. This allows for using the same card either as smart card in new applications or as magnetic stripe card in legacy applications.

For applications where the compatibility to standard magnetic stripe cards is not an issue, physically secure small cryptographic units are available in other forms like a ring or button (for example Dallas Semiconductor's iButton [IBtn02]) or as a token directly attachable to the universal serial bus (for example Aladdin's eToken [Ala02]).

1.2.6
Hardware Security

The objective of smart card chip design is to provide high physical security for the data stored in the card. The processor and the memory are combined in the same chip. This makes it difficult to tap the signals exchanged between the processor and the memory.

The design of a smart card chip considers many more possible threats [RAN00]. These include slicing off layers of the chip to optically read out data, manipulating the voltage or clock to make the processor fail, attacks using high temperature or X-rays, and several others.

Sophisticated counter measures are applied to guard the chip against the various attacks. For example, passivation layers are added to prevent analysis in combination with slicing off layers of the chip. Address lines and the memory cells of the chip are arranged in unusual patterns to make the physical examination harder. Furthermore, some chips have the capability to detect if the layer above the chip was removed, as it would occur if somebody were to examine the chip. Chips can detect unusual variations in the clock or in the voltage and react with shutdown of the operation.

Some newer techniques to spy on the information stored on the card try to do this by manipulating or observing the power supplied to the card. Newer versions of smart cards have been made resistant to these types of attacks.

1.2.7
The Manufacturing Process

Usually the following eight steps are necessary to produce and issue a smart card [GUT98]:

- **Fabrication of the chip itself.** This is done using the standard semiconductor manufacturing process.
- **Making a module.** The chips on the wafer are tested and the good ones are marked. The wafer is sawn into individual chips. The single chip is connected to the golden contact plate to make a module.
- **Fabrication of the plastic card.** PVC is often used as the material for the card. All text and graphics, which are common for a series of cards, are printed on the front and back of the card during this step.

- **Module insertion**. A hole is made into the plastic and the module is inserted.

- **Initialization**. The data files and programs that are common for a series of cards are loaded into the EEPROM of the smart card.

- **Personalization**. During this step, the cardholder-specific information is loaded into the smart card's EEPROM and printed on the front and/or back of the card. Data that is typically loaded into the card during personalization include the name of the cardholder, the number of his bank account, or his private key. The printing during personalization usually includes the name of the cardholder and sometimes also his picture.

2 Introduction to Smart Card Software

In this chapter, we introduce the concepts of smart card software development. We assume that you are familiar with application software development and that we need to cover here only the smart card specifics. We explain the distinction between the on-card and the off-card part of an application and we cover the interaction between both parts. We give an overview of the software development for both parts.

This chapter serves as a foundation for Part II of this book, where we will cover the development of smart card software in Java.

2.1 Smart Card Application Development Process

Usually a smart card application consists of the following two parts:

- Off-card application
- On-card application

The off-card part of the application is the part that resides on the computer or terminal connected to the smart card through a smart card reader device. The OpenCard Framework (OCF), for example, is a framework that supports off-card application development using Java. We will cover the development of the off-card part using OCF in more detail in Part II of this book.

Off-card

The on-card part of an application is stored in the chip of the smart card. This part can consist of data and maybe executable code. If the on-card part has executable code, this code is executed by the smart card operating system and can use operating system services.

On-card

Most manufacturers of smart cards offer toolkits or software development kits that support the development of the on-card part of the application.

Most smart cards provide functions to encrypt and decrypt data. These functions can be used to make the smart card and the communication with the smart card notably secure.

File system cards   The majority of current smart cards have a file system integrated into the operating system. A file system on a smart card supports the storage and retrieval of all kinds of data and is useful for many types of applications.

For most types of current smart cards, development of on-card executable code is not in the hands of the application developers. The development of such code can only be done by the card operating system developers. The code must be integrated into the mask for the ROM of the smart card before the smart card is manufactured.

Recently developed card operating systems enable application developers to create and download on-card application code on their own. The most important ones of these operating systems are Java Card, Multos, and Smart Card for Windows.

2.2
Communication with the Card

The protocol stack of the communication between the smart card and the host has several layers. On the top layer, the communication takes place between the off-card part of an application and its corresponding on-card part. The commands and data exchanged have a meaning only for the particular application.

The next lower layer is the layer of the Application Protocol Data Units (APDUs). The format of the APDUs is independent of the application, but the contents and meanings are application-specific.

One layer below that, we encounter protocols with names such as T=0 and T=1. We briefly introduce these protocol layers in the following sections.

2.2.1
APDUs

Application Protocol Data Units are used to exchange data between the host and the smart card. ISO 7816-4 [ISO02] defines two types of APDUs: Command APDUs, which are sent from the off-card application to the smart card, and Response APDUs, which are sent from the smart card to reply to commands.

There are several variants of Command APDUs. Each Command APDU contains:

Command APDU

- A class byte (CLA). It identifies the class of the instruction, for example if the instruction is ISO conformant or proprietary, or if it is using secure messaging.

- An instruction byte (INS). It determines the specific command.

- Two parameter bytes P1 and P2. These are used to pass command specific parameters to the command.

- A length byte Lc ("length command"). It specifies the length of the optional data sent to the card with this APDU.

- Optional data.

- A length byte Le ("length expected"). It specifies the expected length of the data returned in the subsequent Response APDU. If Le is 0x00[1], the host side expects the card to send all data available in response to this command.

CLA, INS, P1, and P2 constitute the header of the Command APDU. This header has a fixed form. Lc, optional data, and Le constitute the body of the Command APDU. This body can have several variations, upon which we will not elaborate here. You will find more information in ISO 7816-4 or in [RAN00].

Command APDU

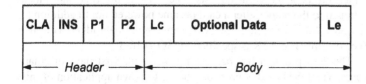

Figure 2.1:
Command
APDU and
Response APDU

Response APDU

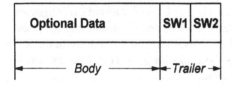

---

[1] Here and in the following, we use Java syntax for expressions like this one.

A Response APDU contains:

■ Optional data.

■ Two status word bytes SW1 and SW2. They contain the status information as defined in ISO 7816-4.

The length of the optional data in the Response APDU is as specified by the preceding Command APDU. Should an error occur, no optional data might be returned in spite of the specified length.

The content that you will hopefully find most often in the status word bytes SW1 and SW2 is 0x9000, for successful execution.

If you are using the OpenCard Framework, the framework will do most of the APDU handling for you. Nevertheless it is good to understand what actually happens when OCF communicates with the card. If you ever need to run a trace, this knowledge will help significantly.

2.2.2
T=0 and T=1

The protocols T=0 and T=1 are the two most-used variants of half-duplex asynchronous protocols defined in ISO 7816-3.

With T=0, each character is transmitted separately, while with T=1, blocks of characters are transmitted.

ATR   Most modern smart card readers (see Chapter 5 "Smart Card Readers") are capable of transmitting with either one of these protocols. From the card's answer to reset (ATR), the reader can find out which protocol the card requests. The ATR is the first data block returned to the reader after a card became powered up. In addition to the protocol information, the ATR can contain data identifying the type of card. The ATR is specified in ISO 7816-3.

T=0   The T=0 protocol has been in use since the first days of smart cards. The GSM card is probably the best-known application of this protocol. Its advantage is that it has simple and space efficient implementations. The price to pay for that simplicity is the incomplete separation of the transport layer from the layer above.

To retrieve data from a smart card, two command exchanges are necessary. In the first, the host issues the command and the smart card returns the length of the response that it will return. In the second (GETRESPONSE), the host asks for the expected number of response bytes and the card returns these.

The T=1 protocol can send a command and receive the response in the same exchange. It cleanly separates the application layer from the transport layer and is suitable for secure messaging between the host and the card.

T=1

One of the details that increase the complexity of asynchronous transfers is the error handling, especially the prevention of endless waiting. For this reason, a block waiting time (BWT) is specified, which indicates how long it is reasonable to wait for a response block. The BWT appropriate for a card is among the protocol information that the card returns in the ATR.

Block waiting time

For some commands, the smart card needs more time than typical, for example for complex cryptographic computations. To prevent the host from giving up waiting for the response too early, the card sends a preliminary response asking for a wait time extension. The card and the host communicate on a wait time extension using so called "S-blocks", while the standard command and response exchange is made with "I-blocks".

Waiting time extension

You will encounter the BWT, I-blocks, and S-blocks again in Section 9.2.2 "The opencard.opt.terminal.protocol Package". For a complete and excellent coverage of these protocols please see [RAN00].

2.2.3
TLV Structures

For the encoding of data objects on the smart card, ASN.1 BER TLVs are very popular. ASN.1 BER stands for Abstract Syntax Notation One basic encoding rules. This is a way of describing data objects, which is specified in ISO 8824 and ISO 8825. In this scheme, every data object is described as "TLV" or "Tag-Length-Value" with a tag that identifies the type of the object, a length of the contents, and the contents (value) itself.

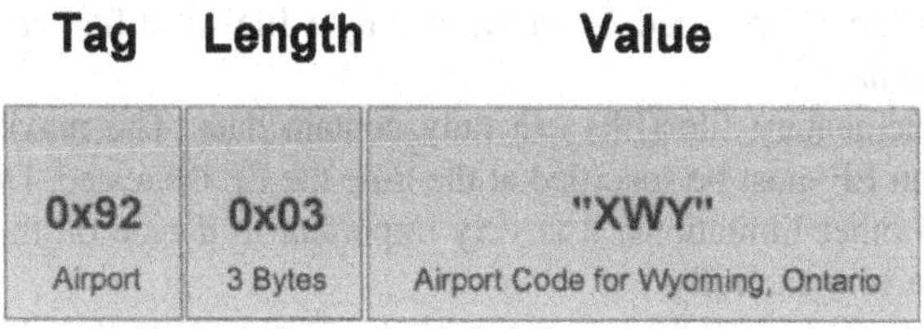

Tag	Length	Value
0x92	0x03	"XWY"
Airport	3 Bytes	Airport Code for Wyoming, Ontario

Figure 2.2: Example of a Simple TLV

TLVs allow for adding of new object types without breaking existing programs. TLVs can be nested: The value can be a TLV.

2.3
Smart Card Operating Systems

In this section we first cover the well-established file system cards and then concentrate on the new operating systems, which support independent development and download of custom application code. The new operating systems, Java Card, Multos, and Smart Card for Windows, are the primary candidates for multi-application scenarios.

2.3.1
File System Smart Cards

ISO 7816-4 defines the smart card file system. Such a file system is built based on the following three components (see Figure 2.3):

- Elementary file (EF)
- Dedicated file (DF)
- Master file (MF)

Figure 2.3:
Example of a
Smart Card File
System

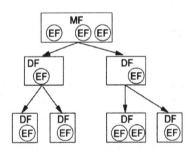

Each file is specified either by a 2-byte file identifier or by a symbolic name.

Elementary file
(EF)
An elementary file (EF) can only contain data. The maximum size of an EF must be specified at the time the EF is created. Due to this and other limitations, it is very important to decide on the file structure very carefully.

Dedicated file
(DF)
A dedicated file (DF) is comparable to a directory in the file systems, which we know from UNIX or PCs. A DF can contain EFs and other DFs. DFs are used to separate the data of different applications. Each application usually has its own DF. Based on this concept it is possible to build a directory structure like in UNIX or on a PC.

The master file (MF) is the root of the file system. Like a DF, it contains EFs and DFs. There is only one MF per smart card. Elementary files in the MF are normally used to store data and keys, which are accessed by different applications on the card. According to ISO 7816-4 the identifier of the MF is 0x3F00 on every ISO-compliant file system smart card.

Master file (MF)

The file system of a smart card has the following specific file types:

- Transparent
- Fixed Record
- Variable Record
- Cyclic Record

Transparent	Fixed Records	Variable Records	Cyclic	*Figure 2.4: Smart Card File Types*

With a transparent file, reading and writing is done as when accessing a memory range. To access data in a transparent file, the file identifier, the offset within the file where the reading or writing should start, and the length of the data have to be specified.

Transparent file

A record file with variable or fixed record length is a structured file. The content is structured in records, as the name suggests. In a fixed record file, all records have the same length. Within a variable record file, the length of the records can be varying. On one hand, this can save space on the smart card because only the necessary record length is allocated. On the other hand, a variable record file needs some space to record each record's length. Data within the file is in both cases accessed by specifying the record number.

Record file

The cyclic file is structured like a record file with fixed length. A write operation always writes to the next record; a read operation always reads the last written record. If all allocated memory is filled,

Cyclic file

the cyclic file automatically wraps and overwrites the record that was written first. Such a file is often used for logs.

ISO 7816-4 file commands ISO 7816-4 specifies a number of commands for a file system, like:

- Select File
- Read Binary
- Write Binary
- Update Binary
- Append Record
- ...

Before any other operation on a file can be performed, the file must be selected. Read/Write/Update Binary is used for transparent files. The equivalent operations for record files are Read/Write/-Update/Append Record.

Access conditions Access to data in files (EFs) is controlled by access conditions. Before a certain operation can be performed on a file, the access conditions for the specified operation and file must be satisfied. These access conditions are not specified in ISO 7816-4 and vary considerably between current operating system implementations.

Examples of some access conditions specified for IBM Multi-Function Cards, are:

- **Always**: The specified operation can be performed on the specified file without satisfying any access condition.

- **Protected**: A message authentication code (MAC) that matches the command and was generated with a secret key secures the specified operation on the specified file. The key required for the message authentication code could be different for each operation on the same file.

- **External Authentication**: Before the specified operation can be performed on the specified file, the card tests if the off-card application shares a common secret with the card.

The use of message authentication codes and external authentication are typical patterns that you will often encounter in smart card software. You will learn more about these patterns and others in Chapter 4 "Cryptography".

2.3.2
Java Card

The Java Card platform allows the on-card application to be written in Java. This brings the main advantages of Java to on-card software development. In addition, it provides a good basis for multi-application cards, where on the same card more than one application is supported. Java Card applications can still be loaded onto the card, even if the card was already issued and is in use by the customer.

The Java Card specification is owned by Sun, extensions and improvements to it are discussed and contributed in the Java Card Forum [JCF02]. The following discussion is based on the version 2.1.1 of the Java Card specification, which was released in May 2000 on http://www.javasoft.com/javacard/.

The on-card executable code consists of byte codes that are interpreted by the Java Card Runtime Environment, which controls the execution of the different applications while making sure that these applications do not interfere. The goal is that Java Card applets run in any Java Card. This goal is not fully achieved yet because current implementations still differ slightly from the current specification and from each other.

Strictly speaking, Java Card is a platform but not a smart card operating system. This platform is carried by an operating system, which is not directly accessible by the applications. The applications are written against the interfaces of this platform in the same way, in which they would use operating system services otherwise.

An on-card application is called "card applet". It has an application identifier (AID) as specified in ISO 7816-5. As we explain in Section 6.1 "ISO Standards", the AID is a unique identifier for applications. It consists of two parts, with the first part being globally registered for the owning company.

It should not come as a surprise that the Java language subset that can be used on a card has limitations that are not known from the Java language for PCs or servers. Some of the differences between the Java Card specification [JC00] and the specification of full Java are:

Limitations of JavaCard

Dynamic class loading is not supported. Garbage collection is not mandatory. There is no SecurityManager class – security policies are implemented by the JVM directly. The JVM does not support multiple threads. Objects cannot be cloned. Java.lang is significantly different, for example is no String available. The basic types char, double, float, and long are not available, the int keyword and 32-bit integers are only optionally supported .

Nevertheless can you use a common Java compiler to compile Java Card sources to byte code. Instead of the standard JDK classes, you must use the Java Card framework during compilation. The resulting byte code cannot be executed on the card directly, for performance reasons, it must first be converted and statically linked.

The software stack of a Java Card is shown in Figure 2.5. The Java Card Runtime Environment (JCRE) has thefollowing interfaces: The Card Executive manages the card and is the communication link between the card applet and the off-card code. The Java Virtual Machine (JVM) executes the byte code of the applet and of the library functions it uses. The Java Card Framework provides the library functions. They form the standard Java Card API.

The operating system kernel and the Java virtual machine (JVM) are native code, the layers above it are Java byte code.

Figure 2.5:
Software Stack
of a Java Card

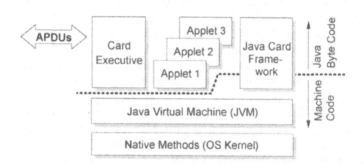

We will cover the development of Java applications that can be loaded onto a Java Card in Chapter 14 "Java Card and OCF".

2.3.3
Multos

Multos is one of the multi-application smart card operating systems that allow the download or update of an application on the card after it was issued. Multos is currently available in Version 5, which was released in October 2000. The industry consortium Maosco owns the Multos specification [MUL02].

A Multos smart card provides an ISO compliant file system interface and in addition an execution environment for custom applications. Application developers can create these custom applications using a new language called MEL (Multos Executable Language).

Additionally developers can use C or Java, which is then converted to MEL using a compiler. Support for Visual Basic is planned.

Multos specifies a common operating system with an API that is called the Application Abstract Machine (AAM). This ensures that after the creation of a new Multos application, this application can be downloaded to every Multos smart card without any additional processing.

The AAM sits on top of the Multos operating system and is hardware independent. It interprets the application written in MEL and translates it into operating system specific commands, which it then executes.

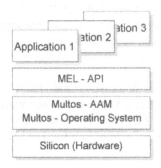

Multos for example is in use as one of the operating systems carrying the Mondex purse system, which we explain in Section 3.1.2 "Mondex". For more information on Multos, please see Maosco's homepage: http://www.multos.com/.

Figure 2.6:
The Multos
Operating
System

2.3.4
Smart Card for Windows

In October 1998, Microsoft announced that it would enter the market for smart card operating systems with a new product called Smart Card for Windows.

In November 1999, Microsoft releases the first version of this new smart card operation system, followed by Version 1.1 in June of 2000.

The card is a combination of a traditional ISO 7816-4 compliant operating system and a programmable platform. The core provides a file system, access control, I/O, cryptographic services, an API, and a selection of ISO commands. An optional runtime environment allows the addition of custom-developed applications.

Microsoft provides the developers with all components needed to write the application. The components with dotted lines in Figure 2.7 are optional.

With the Smart Card for Windows product, Microsoft enables other companies to create a card operating system using a Windows-based smart card toolkit for Visual Basic. Using this toolkit, the developer selects the desired operating system components and then creates a mask that can be loaded onto a card.

The command set is customizable. The first version of the Smart Card for Windows product provided ISO and EMV commands; GSM commands were introduced with Version 1.1.

The file system of a Smart Card for Windows is based on a reduced version of the DOS FAT file system. The number of partitions and the partition size can be set during creation.

An extensive list of cryptographic services is available for the developer to select.

The internal API is language-neutral. The first version of the Runtime Environment is a Visual Basic interpreter; the support of C++ is planned. This Runtime Environment provides the flexibility and advantages known also from Java Card and Multos.

Figure 2.7:
Smart Card for
Windows

3 Smart Cards and e-business

In recent time, e-business and m-business (mobile e-business) have become buzzwords that are often encountered in the media. Right now, a lot of companies and businesses are transforming into e-businesses and expanding to m-businesses to improve their internal efficiency, to improve the link to their suppliers and to reach new markets via the Internet.

Security issues are critical for the success of e-business. As e-business may provide millions of people with the power to move trillions of dollars in goods or money by a few mouse-clicks, security of e-business transactions is a top priority.

Smart cards can be used to assure security in a lot of e-business scenarios. They can be used to securely store money, to allow for spending this money on the net, for secure authentication of users or for generating digital signatures for electronic contracts, just to name a few examples.

In this chapter, we give an overview of the various uses of smart cards for e-business. We start by explaining some of the new challenges that appear when business is moved from traditional stores to the Internet. Then we introduce the concepts to meet these challenges with electronic purse cards, secure access systems, encryption, digital signatures, electronic tickets, and loyalty applications. We give examples of existing systems that apply these concepts.

The use of the Internet is increasing at a phenomenal rate. About 25 years ago, its predecessor, the ARPAnet was only used for the exchange of information between scientists around the world. About 15 years ago, the first version of the HTTP protocol was specified and the World Wide Web (WWW) started its growth. Today, the Internet is widely used. Every company has its own corporate web site providing all kinds of information for its customers, employees, business partners, and suppliers.

In the last several years the Internet was also discovered as a huge market with billions of customers around the world. The Internet enables companies to sell to customers around the world with minimal investment. This is frequently called e-commerce. We consider electronic commerce a subset of e-business[1]. In the last few years, companies are more and more integrating their suppliers into their own production and business processes by using the Internet as the communication platform. This is often called business-to-business (b2b). The examples that we will discuss in the following are mainly e-commerce applications, but the concepts are common to all e-businesses.

Electronic commerce has advantages for both the supplier and the customer. It also brings new challenges that traditional stores do not face:

Authentication
- A merchant must know the identity of the customer. For some kinds of business it is not sufficient that the customer authenticates himself by the use of a password. In these cases an electronic version of today's identity or credit card is required. The recipient of a message or an order should know the identity of the sender and should also be sure that the data wasn't altered during its transmission. This challenge is met using various cryptographic methods to authenticate persons or messages.

Non-repudiation
- It is often necessary to assert that a particular person sent an order or message and that no other person could possibly have sent it. In traditional business the personal signature is used to assert this, in cases of high importance combined with a witness of the signing act. In e-business, this challenge is met using digital signatures based on public key cryptography.

Privacy
- In most cases the exchange of data between the merchant and the customer should be kept in secret. No unauthorized party should be able to read or copy such a communication. This challenge is met using encryption.

Payment
- Another issue for e-business is the method to pay for the goods or services. Today, electronic shopping malls usually require the customer to enter his credit card number. This is not ideal for two reasons: First, the customer must trust that his credit card information is kept in confidence and not abused. Second, credit card transactions incur a cost that might be out of proportion for low cost goods like individual newspaper articles. A replacement for cash is desirable in these cases.

---

[1] The term "e-business" is more general than e-commerce. It includes also applications like supply chain management and other business-to-business flows.

Smart cards can help to address all these challenges. They can be used to authenticate persons and transactions, to get secure access to data or services, and to protect the privacy of communication. Smart cards are a central element for digital signatures and for electronic purses.

In this chapter we cover security mechanisms for e-business with a focus on smart card based schemes. In [Smith97] you can find a detailed coverage of all major security mechanisms used to protect communication in the Internet.

3.1
Electronic Purses

The most promising types of digital money are based on smart cards. Several payment systems either use smart cards today or have announced plans to do so in the near future.

For security reasons, today's credit card payments usually require on-line transactions. Having a permanent online connection or establishing a connection for every payment transaction involves costs that can be too expensive for the payment of small amounts (sometimes referred to as "micropayment"). For the payment of small amounts, purse systems based on a smart card provide a secure, reliable, and inexpensive solution. Electronic purse cards are also an attractive alternative to cash in areas where cash handling is an expensive task, for example, in vending machines.

As an electronic purse, the smart card stores the actual balance. To prevent unauthorized manipulation of this balance, the smart card requires the commands to be authenticated. Increasing and decreasing the balance is secured by the use of two different cryptographic keys.

To load money into the card, a load key is required, which is usually owned by the bank.

To draw money from the card and to transfer it to the merchant's account, again a key is required. The merchant's terminal has this required key. It keeps it safely inside a "Security Access Module" (SAM). This SAM is often a second smart card, which is permanently inserted in the terminal.

These security mechanisms prevent unauthorized persons from increasing or decreasing the balance of an electronic purse card.

The concept of digital tokens provides an alternative way of implementing digital money. This concept does not require a smart card as a secure purse carrier, but it has the disadvantage that the payment needs an on-line connection.

Digital tokens versus smart card based purses

Digital tokens can be held on computer hard disks and manipulated with the standard mechanisms provided by the operating system. These tokens provide some resistance to simple fraud attempts. Every token has a unique number and is digitally signed by the issuer. The receiver of a token can verify its signature.

When a merchant transfers a digital token to the issuer to get the money credited to his bank account, the issuer of the token also does some verification. The issuer again verifies the token's signature, checks if a token with this number has been issued, and if this token has not yet been spent.

While not being connected to the issuer's system, a merchant cannot be sure that a digital token is not a copy of a token that was already spent. In contrast, systems based on smart cards do not require that a merchant is connected to the issuer's system while accepting a payment.

Many electronic purses – all incompatible to each other

Currently there are more than 40 different electronic purse systems in use or in trial operations. Some of the more widely known systems are listed in Table 3.1. Cards are valid for one system only and cannot be used to pay in any other system. Money cannot be directly transferred from a card of one system to a card of a different system. It does not help the attractiveness of electronic purses if the cards of one system are accepted in just one country. Especially with the Euro now being the currency for 300 million people in twelve European countries, consumers will hardly prefer a great selection of incompatible electronic purses to cash in a common currency.

A new initiative, the Common Electronic Purse Specification (CEPS) attempts to lay the foundation for a global system of compatible individual electronic purse systems [CEPS00].

Table 3.1: Electronic Purse Systems Worldwide [EPSO02]

Name of Purse	Country	Purse System Initiator	Million Cards Issued
Chipknip	Netherlands	Dutch banks	14.0
Danmont	Denmark	PBS Danmont	. 0.6
GeldKarte	Germany	ZKA	52.0
Mondex	49 countries	Mondex	1.0
Moneo	France	French banks / public transport sector	10.0
Proton	25 countries	Proton World	35.0
Quick	Austria	Austria Card	4.8
Visa Cash	19 countries	Visa	8.0

In the following we briefly introduce selected electronic purse systems as well as CEPS.

3.1.1
GeldKarte

In 1993, the "Zentraler Kreditausschuß (ZKA)", the organization of German banks regulating payment systems, chose a proposal from Deutsche Telekom, GAD, and IBM for a multifunction chip card with a payment function. Later, the ZKA bought the rights for this specification, which is the base for today's GeldKarte.

In 1996, the first GeldKarte trial started in the town of Ravensburg in southern Germany with 60,000 smart cards and 600 merchants. Within 6 months 6.2 million DM (about 3.1 million dollars) were spent.

At the end of this trial in Ravensburg, the ZKA decided to introduce the GeldKarte in all parts of Germany. So far, about 52 million GeldKarte cards have been issued to customers. The customer is not charged for GeldKarte payment transactions. Nevertheless, only two to three percent of the issued cards are actually in use[2].

A GeldKarte stores the following information: Card serial number, identification number of the issuing bank, bank account number, activation date, expiration date, balance, maximum amount to credit, maximum amount to debit, sequence number of credit transaction, sequence number of debit transaction, log of the latest 15 debit transactions, log of the latest 3 load transactions.

Data on a GeldKarte

There are two types of GeldKarte: Cards associated with a bank account can be loaded in an ATM-like loading station. During this load process the amount is transferred from the customer's bank account into the purse.

Cards associated with an account

Cards that are not associated with a bank account are sometimes called "white cards". The advantage of the white GeldKarte is its anonymity. Although we do not expect this to happen with the GeldKarte today, it would be feasible to build a relationship between the amount paid with the card, the owner of the card, and the goods or services the owner paid for. This would not at all be feasible with a "white" GeldKarte. Privacy versus recording of personal data and preferences is in many countries an important issue for the wide acceptance of a system.

White cards

At the CeBIT '99 fair in Hanover several companies already showed solutions in which a GeldKarte was used to pay over the

---

[2] The ZKA counts as active and in use every card which has been used for payment or loading at least once a month.

Internet. These pilots used standard smart card reader without the enhanced security required by the ZKA. Currently several of these systems are going into production. The reader required for Geld-Karte payments over the Internet must have an integrated display and PIN-pad. This type of readers is also called "class-3 reader".

3.1.2
Mondex

In the early 1990s, the National Westminster Bank (Natwest) in Great Britain developed the Mondex system together with British Telecom.

The first trial started in July 1995 in the English town of Swindon with 40,000 cards issued and 1,000 merchants participating.

Card-to-card   A unique feature of the Mondex system is the direct card-to-card transfer of money. In the other purse systems like GeldKarte or Visa Cash, every payment is a transaction that eventually involves a central server. The direct transfer of money from one Mondex card to another Mondex card is done with a so-called Mondex 'Wallet', a device of the size of a pocket calculator, in which both cards are inserted. However, currently this card-to-card transfer is only interesting from the technical point of view. In most rollouts the issued cards are intentionally disabled for direct card-to-card transfer because of legal reasons.

Loading and   Another interesting point of Mondex is that British Telecom also
unloading at   provides public pay phones that can be used to load and unload the
payphones   purse card. Going to the nearest pay phone for loading money onto the electronic purse might often be more convenient than going to a bank's ATM.

An alternative   The Mondex system is similar to cash money, not only in regard
to cash   to the capability of direct transfer. No fee is charged for an individual Mondex payment – in the same way as there is no fee for cash payments. Mondex payments do not allow the recording of who paid where for what and are therefore as anonymous as cash payments. The downside of the anonymity is that digital money on a lost card is irretrievably lost – in the same way as the cash in a lost traditional purse is lost forever.

Today, Mondex has systems in about 49 countries in the world [MNDX02]. The latest Mondex cards are based on the MULTOS card operating system (see Section 2.3.3 "Multos").

3.1.3
Proton

Proton is an electronic purse system developed in Belgium by Bank-sys, a Belgium organization specializing in electronic fund handling and security. Today 4,000,000 Proton electronic cash cards are in use by customers in Belgium with 23,000 terminals installed. Worldwide, Proton systems are in use or in trial in 25 countries with a total number of 35 million issued cards.

American Express, Banksys, ERG (a public transport smart card systems company in Hong Kong), Interpay Nederland (the issuer of 14 million Dutch Chipknip banking cards), and Visa International created Proton World in 1998 to further promote Proton. In October of 2001 ERG acquired the shares owned by the other members of the consortium and is now the solely owner of Proton World International.

The Proton system platform cannot only be used for payment, but also for security controls, loyalty schemes, or social security cards. For example, a health care system will be based on Proton: "Mutuelle", a Belgian state-held health insurance company issued during 1999 a health card that uses the Proton platform and also includes a Proton purse. In summer of 2001 a government multi-purpose card was rolled out in Malaysia, which included Proton [PRO02].

Proton World provides a complete solution for an electronic purse including host-systems, terminals, cards, and implementation and support services. The purse cards can be loaded at ATM's, public pay phones, and smart phones [PRO02].

The first Proton cards based on CEPS were demonstrated in October of 2001 during "Cartes" trade show in Paris.

3.1.4
Visa Cash

In 1995, Visa International introduced an electronic purse system called Visa Cash. Today Visa Cash is used in several trials and implementations around the world. It is also being used for electronic payments on the Internet.

Visa International has about 20,700 member banks and is the world's largest credit card organization. These member banks have issued around 561 million Visa credit cards that are accepted at approximately 13 million places around the world. This credit/debit card acceptance infrastructure forms a good base for a chip-based purse as an add-on to the Visa credit card.

Visa Cash cards can be reloadable or disposable, associated with an account or not associated with an account. Reloadable Visa Cash cards can be loaded. Disposable Visa Cash cards can only be bought with prepaid value on it. With a reloadable Visa Cash card that is associated with a bank account, the customer can transfer money from his account to his card and vice versa. In the case of reloadable cards that are not associated to a bank account, the funds can be obtained from cash or any account and be loaded onto the card.

The merchant has to pay a transaction fee that is usually a percentage of the transaction amount. There is no transaction fee for the customer.

Trials   Together with local banks, Visa International has trials running in several countries around the world. The first trial started in 1995, when Bank of America issued about 2,000 Visa Cash cards to employees of Visa International. These cards are used at Visa's headquarter at vending machines and in its cafeteria. During the 1996 Olympic Games in Atlanta, three large local banks issued about two million Visa Cash cards to visitors and citizens of Atlanta. The cards were used at merchants, Olympic venues, and in the public transit system of Atlanta.

Components   A Visa Cash system consists of the following three components:

- Service Payment Terminals,
- Concentration Points, and a
- Clearing and Administration System.

Service   A Service Payment Terminal is the interface to the customer. It is
Payment   used to pay with a Visa Cash card at a merchant's site. A Service
Terminal   Payment Terminal has a smart card reader and a display.
Concentration   The Concentration Point is operated in the background. It calls
Point   each Service Payment Terminal in regular intervals (or gets called from the Service Payment Terminals) and collects payment records for later processing in the Clearing and Administration System.

Clearing and   The Clearing and Administration System is the last stage in the
Administration   background operation. It processes all payment records, transfers the
System   money to the merchant's bank accounts, and controls the loading of cards.

All payment transactions are done off-line. The Service Payment Terminal creates a record for each transaction. The record is later transferred to the Clearing and Administration System via the Concentration Point.

Activation and loading of a reloadable Visa Cash card is always done as an on-line transaction. The Clearing and Administration System ensures that the card is valid.

3.1.5
Common Electronic Purse Specification

Since 2002, the Euro replaces national bank notes and coins in twelve European countries. This common European currency will create additional momentum to merge the electronic purse systems that are not interoperable. Consumers will expect that they can use their electronic purse in the same way they could use the Euro in all participating countries.

Europay International (the organization behind Europe's Euro-card), Visa International, Visa Spain, and the ZKA (the owner of Germany's GeldKarte specification) founded the Common Electronic Purse Specification (CEPS) Group. Mondex is notably not a member of this group. The CEPS group works on defining a common standard for electronic purse systems, which can be used and are compatible worldwide. Organizations from 22 countries, representing more than 90 percent of the world's electronic purse cards, have agreed to implement CEPS. The specifications were finalized in August of 1999 and during 2001 the first cards supporting CEPS were available.

It is natural that CEPS tries to accommodate existing specifications and systems as much as possible. For the chip cards, CEPS is based on the EMV specifications (see Section 6.2 "ICC Specifications for Payment Systems"). In addition, CEPS specifies the card-to-terminal interface, the terminal application for point-of-sale and load-transactions, and the data elements and recommended message formats for transaction processing. It also provides functional requirements for the various electronic purse scheme participants. For enhanced security, CEPS requires the use of public key cryptography.

3.2
Authentication and Secure Access

The challenge of identifying a person on the local computer, or on the other end of a communication session, or in the role of the sender of a message, is a recurring theme in e-business. Here the smart card plays an important role as a secure device with cryptographic capabilities.

The most common alternatives to smart card-based schemes for authentication and secure access are based on passwords or pass-phrases. Passwords can be stolen or forwarded freely. Therefore, many companies look for schemes that are based on smart cards or on biometric methods. We give an overview of smart card-based authentication in the following.

Usually the smart card itself requires the owner to authenticate himself with a password. This is sometimes referred to as "two-factor" authentication, combining "what you have" (the physical smart card) with "what you know" (the password needed to use the smart card). Two-factor authentication can provide a higher level of security than authentication on a password or on a hardware token alone.

3.2.1
Workstation Access

The most common way of securing the access to a workstation is user authentication before starting a user session. Some systems do not even start loading the operating system without authentication.

Both variants can be combined with an additional function that locks the session after a specified time without activity and then re-quires authentication before the session can be resumed.

For standard workstation operating systems like UNIX variants or Windows 2000, there are numerous products on the market to provide secure workstation access based on smart cards. In most of these products, smart card authentication uses standard crypto-graphic mechanisms. The cryptographic computations are performed by the smart card, which also holds the secrets needed for the authentication. We describe these cryptographic mechanisms in de-tail in Section 4.2 "Smart Card Cryptographic Protocols".

3.2.2
Network- and Server-Login

Authentication is required to work with a remote server, to access data on a server, or to use a private network. It is obvious that the more secure the authentication mechanisms are, the better protected the servers, the data, and the private networks are. In all of these cases the authentication is usually based on a challenge-response protocol with asymmetrical keys, as we describe in Section 4.2.

The authentication can go in two directions. Either the server needs to prove its authenticity to the client, or the client needs to prove its authenticity to the server, or both. Therefore either the server, or the client, or both must securely keep a private key. For the client key the portable smart card is ideal. It can securely store the private key and execute the required cryptographic algorithms with it.

The server also can use a smart card for the private key. However, one of the advantages of the smart card, its portability, is less of an issue at servers. Therefore it is common to use other cryptographic hardware at the server side.

After the one-way or mutual authentication succeeds, a trusted communication between both sides can be established. Now the issue of protecting this communication arises.

3.2.3
Secure Communication

A common way to protect the communication between client and server is by establishing a secure session, where all communication is encrypted using a symmetrical key. This symmetrical key, often called "session key", is exchanged between the session partners by using public key cryptography. This exchange is typically combined with authentication of the partners. An example of such a scheme is SSL and its successor TLS (see Section 4.3 "TLS and Smart Cards"). A smart card is ideal to host the private key for authenticating the client to the server in a SSL connection.

As we have seen, in a secure session the data is encrypted immediately before it is transmitted and decrypted directly after it is received. Alternatively, the data can be permanently stored in an encrypted form, and sent and received unchanged. In this case, decryption takes place before the data is used.

In all of these schemes the key that is required for the decryption can be stored in a smart card. Because a smart card usually is not powerful enough to efficiently decrypt large amounts of data, the smart card passes the decryption key to the host computer, which then performs the decryption.

A more secure variant is to use a changing decryption key, which itself is kept in encrypted form. The smart card then decrypts the decryption key. In this way the smart card only decrypts a few bytes and yet its decryption key is not exposed.

So far we have looked at communication between a client and a server. For communication between two clients we need a different form of protection. One type of client-client communication that we all use is e-mail. An individual e-mail is stored and forwarded across many nodes. To protect its privacy, the e-mail client of the sender encrypts the data and the e-mail client of the receiver decrypts them.

Established schemes for encrypting and decrypting e-mail use public key cryptography (for example PGP [PGP02]). On the sender's side the data is encrypted using the public key of the receiver, and on the receiver's side it is decrypted using the receiver's private key. If the receiver stores his private key on a smart card, it will be always with him and still be kept secure.

3.3
Digital Signatures

If we order some goods or services, we often have to sign a contract on paper to testify that we placed the order and are liable to pay for it. If we make the same deal over the network instead, we need the electronic equivalent of signing on paper: a digital signature. Such a digital signature must guarantee that a person cannot repudiate his or her order or statement.

The different methods for a digital signature are based on an asymmetrical key pair. The signing person has a private key, which cannot be accessed or used by anybody else. The public knows a second key, which is associated to the private key. This key is called the public key. Only the unique owner of the private key can sign an order or a statement, while everybody can check the signature using the corresponding public key.

Certificates   The public key is distributed in a certificate, which contains the owner's name and public key. In addition, the certificate has an expiration date. How do we know that the public key in the certificate is not manipulated? A trusted authority digitally signed the certificate. To check the certificate signature we need the public key of the signer, which is in the certificate of the signer. This certificate is also signed by a trusted authority. The recursion can go on until we arrive at the "root certificate", which is something that we trust because it was distributed through a trusted channel, like for example shipped with the web browser.

Until now, digital signatures were mainly used for private business. Recently, first trials set out to use digital signatures for electronic forms filed with public authorities. Filling out an on-line form can speed up the process considerably compared to calling an office for a form, waiting for the mail with the blank form, and finally mailing the completed form. Therefore we expect that digital signatures will become increasingly popular in the public as well as the private sector.

For digital signatures it is crucial that the private key remains absolutely private. If any person could copy another person's private key, the digital signature would no longer be unique to the owner. Therefore the private key has to be stored in a very secure place where nobody could possibly copy it and where nobody but the owner can use it.

The most secure place to store such a private key is a cryptographic hardware unit, often called "crypto token". A smart card can be considered the most convenient and most portable cryptographic hardware unit. Modern smart cards are able to perform the signing operation inside the card. At the same time they do not provide any function to export the private signature key to the outside. Legislation in some European countries requires that the signature key must be generated on the smart card. In combination with the requirement that there must be no way to export the signature key, this makes it highly unlikely that any additional copies of a signature key could exist.

3.4
Other Uses of Smart Cards in e-business

The Internet as a ubiquitous network leads to new opportunities in various areas of commerce. We have seen examples of how the smart card can help to protect the data and communication on the net.

On the other hand, we can think of the smart card as an extension of the network. It allows the owner to load data onto the card while connected to the net and to later use this data at off-line devices.

In the following we present some applications of smart cards, in which the smart card is used at times connected to the network and at other times off-line.

3.4.1
Electronic Ticketing

Electronic Ticketing is a typical application where the card receives data from the net for later use. Consumers can put a ticket for a flight, a bus ride, or an event onto their smart cards. These transactions can take place at ticket vending machines, at kiosks, or at the consumers' PCs or Internet screen phones. In the latter case, an obvious path for the transaction is a web browser running a Java applet that communicates with the ticketing server through the Internet and with the smart card through the local software stack and attached hardware.

In the theater or bus or at the gate, it is often not practical or cost effective to have the device receiving the electronic tickets connected to the ticketing server. With an online device the server could detect and prevent fraud attempts, like using the same ticket more than once. Having no online connection, we need a smart card to prevent fraud. A smart card with its cryptographic function and secure data storage can prevent the copying or forging of tickets (see our discussion on electronic purse cards and digital tokens in Section 3.1 on page 37). Therefore a smart card allows the secure use of electronic tickets with devices that are currently off-line. Requiring a permanent network connection for all collecting devices in trains, at airports, or at theater entries would make electronic ticketing too expensive in most cases. For these applications the use of smart cards is attractive.

Especially contact-less smart cards are very convenient for users. With contact-less smart cards users can pass for example a gate to a subway without pulling the smart card out of his pocket and the ticket is automatically checked while he passes the gate.

3.4.2
Loyalty Programs

Customer loyalty programs, in which more than one single store participates, often require a high administrative effort or significant resources for network connections and computing.

If we look at the loyalty program of a group of partner airlines today, all information must be consolidated between the participating companies. Often it takes weeks before loyalty points are credited to a frequent flyer's account.

Or, if we planned to create a loyalty system in a city or shopping mall with hundreds of different shops participating, would we want to set up a central server, to which all shops are connected and which stores a record for each transaction in each shop? This might require considerable resources.

Instead it might be less effort and cost to store each customer's amount of loyalty points on the customer's own smart card and to consolidate the sum of all credits and debits in a shop. Such a system based on smart cards might be less complex, faster, and easier to use than a centralized system.

3.4.3
Growth Expected

In this chapter we have discussed several ways in which smart cards help to protect or enable e-business solutions. E-business itself and the use of smart cards for e-business are expected to grow at enormous rates over the next years. We would not be surprised if you read this book because you are up to developing a new type of solution not discussed here. The goal of this book is to provide you with concepts and patterns that support working with smart cards in Java, the premium language for development of e-business solutions.

4 Cryptography

In this chapter, we will give a brief introduction to cryptography, focusing on aspects that are important in conjunction with smart cards. We start by a short overview of the predominant cryptographic algorithms. Then we present commonly used cryptographic protocols for authentication and secure transmission of data and give some examples on how these protocols are used in the smart card area. Finally, we give an example for usage of smart cards to support cryptographic software on a PC. It shows how to use smart cards for private-key operations required by TLS (Transport Layer Security, the successor of SSL 3.0).

This will give you a reasonable understanding of cryptographic algorithms and protocols relevant in the smart card domain. If you are seeking more comprehensive and detailed information, we recommend the excellent book "Applied Cryptography" by Bruce Schneier [SCH96].

4.1 Cryptographic Algorithms

In this section we give an overview on the most relevant cryptographic algorithms in the smart card environment.

There are two important classes of cryptographic algorithms that we want to present – symmetric algorithms and asymmetric algorithms. While symmetric algorithms use the same key for encryption and decryption of data, asymmetric algorithms use two keys – what one key encrypts, the other one decrypts.

4.1.1
Symmetric Cryptographic Algorithms

Symmetric cryptographic algorithms are fast and can be used to encrypt and decrypt large amounts of data. However, the fact that the same key has to be used for encryption and decryption causes a problem when symmetric algorithms are to be used to ensure privacy of communication. The sender and receiver of a message must use the same key i.e. the receiver and only the receiver must know the key of the sender to ensure privacy of the transmission. Each receiver must know the keys of all potential senders to be able to decrypt all incoming messages. Evidently, the geometrically growing number of required keys is impractical if the number of entities in the network is big. The solution for this problem is a combination of asymmetric and symmetric algorithms, as described in section 4.1.3.

As this is a smart card book, we only present symmetric algorithms that are relevant for smart cards. For information on algorithms not described here or for more details, you may refer to [SCH96].

4.1.1.1
DES

The Data Encryption Standard was developed in a program to protect computer and communications data, initiated by the National Bureau of Standards (NBS) and the National Institute of Standards and Technology (NIST) in 1972. The first request for proposals was issued in 1973, but none of the submissions met the requirements. A second request was issued in 1974 and this time, the NBS received a promising proposal from IBM, which became DES.

The DES algorithm is a block cipher, i.e. an algorithm that divides the data to be encrypted into blocks and operates on one block at a time. DES uses a block size of 64 bits and a key size of 56 bits. Actually, DES keys are represented by 64 bits, but the least significant bit of each byte is used for parity checking only and ignored by the algorithm.

The fundamental building block of DES is a substitution followed by a permutation, called a round. DES has 16 rounds i.e. 16 substitutions and permutations are applied to each 64-bit block of data. Because of its repetitive nature, DES can be easily implemented in hardware.

The key size of 56 bits used in the DES algorithm is quite small. Given today's powerful computers, the DES algorithm offers only mediocre security. At RSA '99, a DES challenge was announced where the 56-bit key was broken in less than 24 hours, although more than the average of 50 percent of the key space had to be searched by a network of many cooperating computers.

4.1.1.2
Triple DES

Triple DES is based on DES, but uses 112-bit keys. The key is divided into two 56 bit keys, K_1 and K_2. The data to be encrypted is first encrypted under K_1, then decrypted under K_2 and encrypted once again under K_1. This is also known as the encrypt-decrypt-encrypt (EDE) mode. To decrypt, the cipher is decrypted using K_1, encrypted using K_2 and decrypted using K_1 again.

Triple DES offers a very high level of security. Brute force attacks like against DES are not feasible, because the key space to be searched grows exponentially with the size of the key, i.e. finding a 112 bit key by exhaustive search takes 2^{56} times more time than finding a 56-bit key.

4.1.1.3
DES Encryption Modes

There are several different DES modes that are often used in conjunction with smart cards. The simplest mode is the Electronic Code Book (ECB) mode. ECB mode encryption means that the encrypt-operation is applied to each single 64-bit block of plaintext, as shown in the following Figure 4.1:

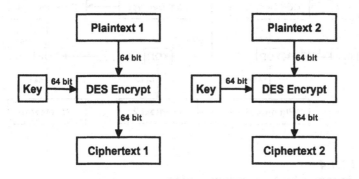

Figure 4.1:
DES ECB Mode
– Each 64-bit
Block is
Separately
Encrypted

The decrypt-operation is applied to each single 64-bit block separately, obtaining the original plain text block.

The Cipher Block Chaining (CBC) mode chains the result of each DES operation to the subsequent operation, as shown in Figure 4.2. The first operation is chained to an Initial Chaining Value (ICV), in most cases a random 64-bit block or a block of 64 zero bits. The first block of plaintext is XORed with the ICV and the result is encrypted, obtaining the first ciphertext block. Each following data block is XORed with the result of the previous DES operation, the result is encrypted to obtain the next block of ciphertext.

Figure 4.2:
DES CBC Mode
Encryption

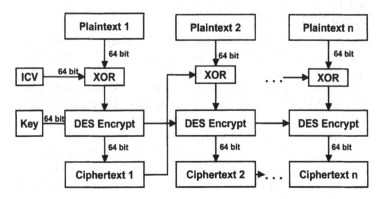

CBC mode decryption first applies the decrypt operation to each single cipher text block and then applies a XOR operation with ICV for the first block, with the result of the previous operation for all subsequent blocks (see Figure 4.3).

Figure 4.3:
DES CBC Mode
Decryption

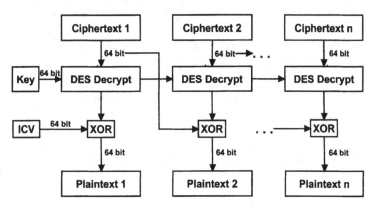

4.1.1.4
Message Authentication Codes

DES cannot only be used for encrypting data, it is also possible to use the DES algorithm for calculating Message Authentication Codes (MACs). A MAC ensures data integrity and can also be used for authentication. Here we present MAC calculation according to ANSI X9.9.

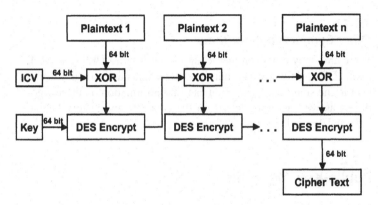

Figure 4.4:
DES CBC Mode
MAC
Calculation

You may realize that the result is equal to the last ciphertext block obtained from CBC encryption. This means that given a DES CBC implementation, a MAC can be obtained by encrypting the relevant data and taking the last 64-bit block of the cipher text.

4.1.1.5
AES

The Advanced Encryption Standard (AES) is the successor of the Data Encryption Standard. Many algorithms have been proposed for the new standard and had to go through an extensive selection process. Out of five finalists, the NIST chose the Rijndael algorithm designed by Joan Daemen and Vincent Rijmen.

Rijndael is a block cipher with variable block length and key length that allows using keys with a length of 128, 192, or 256 bits to encrypt blocks with a length of 128, 192 or 256 bits. All nine combinations of key length and block length are possible in Rijndael and it is possible to extend both block length and key length to multiples of 32 bits.

Choosing from these options, the Advanced Encryption Standard specifies a block size of 128 bits and key lengths of 128, 192, or 256 bits, the other options are not adopted in the standard. The AES algorithm can be implemented very efficiently in software on a wide range of processors as well as in hardware. For detailed information about the AES algorithm, see [AES01].

4.1.1.6
Other Symmetric Algorithms

There are many other symmetric algorithms besides DES, like RC4, RC5, IDEA, Skipjack etc., but these algorithms are virtually irrelevant in the smart card area. You can find information on these algorithms as well as more details on the concepts and history behind DES and Triple DES in [SCH96].

4.1.2
Public-Key Algorithms

The basic idea that led to public key algorithms was that keys could come in pairs of an encryption and a decryption key and that it could be impossible to compute one key given the other. This concept was invented by Whitfield Diffie and Martin Hellman [DIF76], and independently by Ralph Merkle [MER78].

Since then, many public-key algorithms have been proposed, most of them insecure or impractical. All public-key algorithms are very slow compared to secret key algorithms. The well known RSA algorithm for example takes about 1000 times longer than DES when implemented in hardware, 100 times longer in software to encrypt the same amount of data. However, public-key algorithms have a big advantage when used for ensuring privacy of communication: Public-key algorithms use different keys for encryption and decryption. The private key may only be known to its owner and must be kept in secret. It may be used for generation of digital signatures or for decrypting private information encrypted under the public key. The public key may be used for verifying digital signatures or for encrypting information. It needs not to be kept secret, because it is infeasible to compute the private key from a given public key. Thus, receivers or signers of messages can post their public key to a directory, where everybody who wants to send a message can look it up. Each entity in the network only needs to store its own private key and a public directory can store the public keys of all entities, which is practical even in large networks.

4.1.2.1
RSA

The RSA algorithm was invented by Ron Rivest, Adi Shamir, and Leonard Adleman [RIV78], [RIV79]. It is based on the difficulty of factoring the product of two large prime numbers. RSA uses key pairs, where the public key consists of a modulus m and a public exponent e and the private key consists of the same modulus m and a private exponent d.

The two keys are generated from two randomly chosen large prime numbers, p and q. To assure maximum security, the lengths of these numbers should be equal. The modulus m is computed as the product of the two primes:

$$m = pq$$

Next, an encryption key e is chosen so that e and (p-1)(q-1) are relatively prime. The decryption key d is chosen so that

$$ed = 1 \ (mod \ (p\text{-}1)(q\text{-}1)) \ or \ d = e^{-1} \ mod \ ((p\text{-}1)(q\text{-}1))$$

Let x be the plaintext with the same size as the modulus and y be the ciphertext. Then the formulas for encryption and decryption are as follows:

$$y = x^e \ mod \ m$$

$$x = y^d \ mod \ m$$

More details on the mathematical background of the RSA algorithm can be found in [COR89].

As the problem of factoring two large prime numbers is very hard to solve, it is infeasible to compute the private key from the public key if the primes multiplied to obtain the modulus are big enough. Today's smart cards usually offer key sizes between 512 and 1024 bits. A modulus size of 512 bits is not considered very secure. A modulus size of 1024 bits is considered to offer a reasonable level of security for applications like digital signatures and encryption for documents.

4.1.2.2
DSA

The National Institute of Standards and Technology (NIST) proposed the Digital Signature Algorithm (DSA) in 1991 for use in the Digital Signature Standard (DSS). The security of the algorithm relies on the difficulty of computing discrete logarithms in a modulus whose length defines the key size. The algorithm was designed by the NSA, which along with the proposed key size of only 512 bits led to criticism regarding its security. In 1994, the standard was issued with a variable key length from 512 to 1024. The DSA algorithm works as follows:

p = a prime with 512 to 1024 bits, a multiple of 64 bit.

q = 160-bit prime factor of p-1.

$g = h^{(p-1)/q} \bmod p$, where $h < p-1$ such that $h^{(p-1)/q} \bmod p > 1$.

$x < q$.

$y = g^x \bmod p$.

p, q and g are public and can be common across a community of users. x is the private key and y is the public key. H is a one-way hash function. The Digital Signature Standard specifies the Secure Hash Algorithm (SHA-1), see [SCH96]. The sender of a message m performs the following operations:

Generate a random number $k < q$.

Generate $r = (g^k \bmod p) \bmod q$ and $s = (k^{-1} (H(m) + xr)) \bmod q$.

r and s are the signature and are sent along with the message. The receiver verifies the signature by performing the following calculations:

$w = s^{-1} \bmod q$

$u_1 = (H(m) * w) \bmod q$

$u_2 = (rw) \bmod q$

$v = ((g^{u1} * y^{u2}) \bmod p) \bmod q$

The signature is verified if $v = r$. We will not present the proofs here, they can be found in [NIST94].

4.1.2.3
Elliptic Curve

Elliptic curves were first proposed for use in public-key cryptosystems in 1985 [KOB87, MIL86]. Algorithms using Elliptic Curves are faster than RSA or DSA and require smaller key sizes for the same level of security. Elliptic Curves over the finite field $GF(2^n)$ are especially interesting, because they allow for efficient implementations.

The advantages of Elliptic Curves make them good candidates for use on smart cards, because the computations can be conducted even on smart cards without a cryptographic coprocessor and the small key sizes save valuable space in the smart card's memory. However, the Elliptic Curve Algorithm is supported by few of today's smart cards. Virtually all e-business products on the market, like Web Servers, Certificate Authorities, middle-ware, cryptographic libraries, SSL implementations etc., already support RSA and DSA, so that smart cards must support these algorithms to be usable in existing public-key infrastructures. Support of RSA and DSA on smart cards requires a cryptographic coprocessor and a persistent memory size of at least 8 Kbytes anyway, so that not needing a coprocessor in not a real advantage in many cases.

4.1.3
Hybrid Algorithms

As mentioned above, symmetric algorithms are fast but have the disadvantage of being impractical in networks connecting many entities. Asymmetric Public Key Algorithms on the other hand are practical in such networks, but have the disadvantage of being slow.

However, the advantages of both can be combined while avoiding the disadvantages. Hybrid Algorithms use randomly generated session keys for symmetric algorithms used for the symmetric bulk encryption. Then, the session key is encrypted using an asymmetric algorithm. The fact that the asymmetric algorithm is slow doesn't matter in this case, because only the session key is encrypted using that algorithm. Most of today's software uses such a combination of secret-key and public-key algorithms.

4.2
Smart Card Cryptographic Protocols

In this section we give some examples of cryptographic protocols – protocols including cryptographic operations for establishing trust between involved entities – in the smart card area. The most important protocols are external authentication, internal authentication and secure messaging.

4.2.1
External Authentication

External authentication means the authentication of an external entity to the smart card. The smart card and the external entity conduct a challenge-response protocol like the one shown in Figure 4.5.

The external entity obtains a challenge – typically a random number – from the smart card and encrypts it with a key shared between the card and authentic external entities.

1. The external entity requests a random number r from the smart card by sending an appropriate command to the smart card.

2. The smart card creates a random number r, stores it and returns it in the response to the external entity.

3. The external entity uses a cryptographic key corresponding to a cryptographic key in the smart card to encrypt r. It sends an authentication command containing the encrypted random number to the card.

4. The smart card receives the authentication command and decrypts the encrypted random number contained in that command. If the result is equal to the stored random number r, the smart card assumes that the external entity is authentic.

Figure 4.5: Authentication of an External Entity to a Smart Card

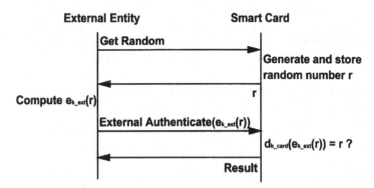

The cryptographic algorithms used can be symmetric algorithms like DES or public-key algorithms like RSA or DSA. In case of symmetric algorithms, the external entity and the smart card must share a secret key. If public-key algorithms are employed, the external entity uses the private key corresponding to the public key to be used for validation on the smart card.

4.2.2
Internal Authentication

Internal authentication means the authentication of a smart card to an external entity. The smart card and the external entity conduct a protocol like shown in the Figure 4.6.

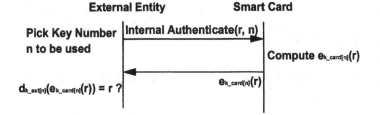

Figure 4.6:
Authentication of
a Smart Card to
an External
Entity

1. The external entity sends an authentication command containing a random number r and the key number n specifying the key to be used by the smart card.

2. The smart card encrypts the random number r received from the external entity using the authentication key with the number n and sends back the encrypted random number.

3. The external entity decrypts the encrypted random number using the cryptographic key corresponding to the cryptographic key that was used in the smart card. If the result equals r, the external entity assumes that the card is authentic.

If a symmetric algorithm is used, the external entity and the smart card must share a secret key. If a public-key algorithm is employed, the external entity uses the public key, corresponding to the private-key used on the smart card.

4.2.3
Secure Messaging

There are several different concepts of secure messaging which are employed in smart cards. Messages can be protected by a Message Authentication Code (MAC) or protected by a MAC and also encrypted. For calculation of the MACs or encryption of the transferred data, secret keys shared by the external entity and the smart card can be used directly or session keys can be established. There is a broad spectrum of possible schemes. In this book, we will only present some examples, without claiming full coverage of schemes.

4.2.3.1
Protected Mode Operations

The first scheme we want to explore is a very simple one, where the smart card and the external entity accessing the card share a common key, which is used for calculating a Message Authentication Code (MAC) over the transmitted data. The purpose of a MAC is to ensure integrity and authenticity of transferred messages. Figure 4.7 shows how this scheme works when reading data from a smart card with a file system:

Figure 4.7: Secure Messaging in Read-Operations

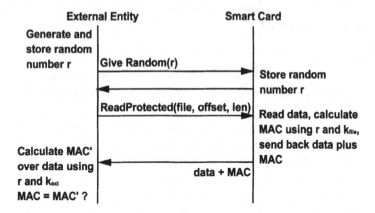

1. The external entity generates a random number r and gives it to the smart card as a challenge by sending an appropriate command.

2. The smart card stores the random number r and sends back a response indicating that it now has a random number to be used in a subsequent command.

3. The external entity sends a command to read data of a given length, from a given file, starting at a given index in protected mode.

4. The smart card receives the read command and gets the desired data from the file in the smart card's persistent storage. The smart card uses the key k_{file} and the random number r to calculate a MAC over the data. It sends the data and the MAC back to the external entity in the response.

5. The external entity receives the data read and the MAC from the smart card. It calculates a MAC over the received data, using the key k_{ext} - that must match the key k_{file} - and the random number r generated in step 1. Only if both MACs are equal, the data is accepted.

A similar method can protect data sent to the card, as shown in Figure 4.8.

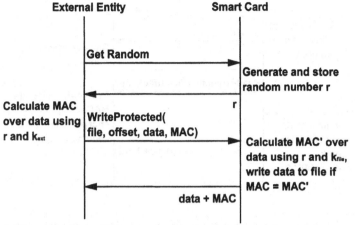

External Entity   Smart Card

Get Random

Generate and store
random number r

Calculate MAC
over data using
r and k$_{ext}$

r

WriteProtected(
file, offset, data, MAC)

Calculate MAC' over
data using r and k$_{file}$,
write data to file if
MAC = MAC'

data + MAC

1. The external entity requests a random challenge from the smart card by sending an appropriate command to the smart card.

2. The smart card generates a random number r, stores it and sends back a response containing r.

3. The external entity computes a MAC over a part of the write command's APDU header and the data to be written to the smart card. For the computation, it uses the random challenge r received from the smart card and a key k_{ext} that matches the key k_{file} protecting the file on the card. It constructs the entire command from the APDU header, the data and the MAC and sends it to the smart card.

4. The smart card receives the write command. It calculates a MAC over the relevant part of the command APDU header and the contained data, using the random number r and the key k_{file}. If that MAC equals the MAC contained in the command, the data contained in the command is actually written to the smart card's persistent memory.

4.2.3.2
Protected and Encrypted Mode Operations

Now we take a look at reading and writing data in encrypted mode. Usually, the smart card or the external entity first calculates a MAC, then appends it and encrypts the data plus the MAC. Figure 4.9 shows the read operation:

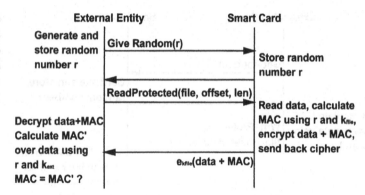

*Figure 4.9:
Secure
Messaging and
Encryption of
Data Read from
a Smart Card*

1. The external entity generates a random challenge r and gives it to the smart card by sending an appropriate command.

2. The smart card stores the random number r and sends back a response indicating that it now has a random number to be used in a subsequent command.

3. The external entity sends a command to read data of a given length, from a given file, starting at a given index in the encrypted mode.

4. The smart card receives the read command and gets the desired data from the file in the smart card's persistent storage. The smart card uses the key k_{file} and the random number r to calculate a MAC over the data. The smart card additionally encrypts the data and the MAC using the same key k_{file} for encryption and the random number r as initial chaining value (for DES-CBC) and sends back the cipher to the external entity in the response.

5. The external entity receives the data and the MAC from the smart card as ciphertext. First, it decrypts the received ciphertext using the key k_{ext} that matches the key k_{file} and the random number r. Then it calculates a MAC over the received data, using the key k_{ext} and random number r to verify the authenticity of the data.

Figure 4.10 shows the write operation in the enciphered mode.

1. The external entity requests a random challenge r from the smart card by sending the appropriate command to the smart card.

2. The smart card generates a random number r, stores it and also sends r back in the response.

3. The external entity computes a MAC over a part of the write command APDU header and the data to be written to the smart card using the random number r and the key k_{ext}. This key must match the key k_{file} that protects the file on the card. Then, the external entity encrypts the relevant part of the APDU, the data and the MAC and constructs the entire command from the clear part of the APDU header and the ciphertext.

4. The smart card receives the write command. It decrypts the cipher contained in the command using the random number r and the appropriate key k_{file}. It calculates a MAC over the relevant part of the command APDU header and the contained data using the same key k_{file} and random number r. If that MAC equals the MAC contained in the command, the data is actually written to the smart card's persistent memory.

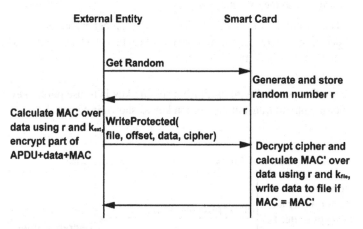

Figure 4.10:
Secure
Messaging –
Data Written to a
Smart Card is
Protected by a
MAC and
Enciphered

There are other variants of the schemes presented above. Some cards offer the possibility of establishing a session key, either by key derivation or by generating and transferring a session key using a public-key for encryption of the session key. Figure 4.11 shows how key derivation works.

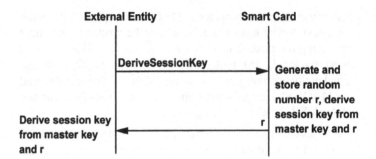

Figure 4.11: Secure Messaging – Establishing a Session Key Using Key Derivation

1. The external entity sends a command to establish a session key to the smart card.

2. The smart card generates a random number r, uses it to derive a session key from a given master key and sends back the random number r to the external entity.

3. The external entity receives the random number r and uses it to derive a session key from a master key that it shares with the smart card as a common secret.

Another possibility to establish a session key is to use public-key cryptography to transmit the session key as shown in Figure 4.12.

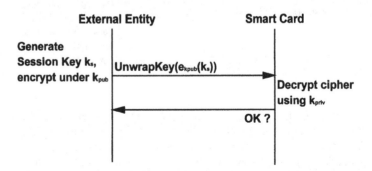

Figure 4.12: Secure Messaging – Establishing a Session Key Using a Public Key

1. The external entity generates a session key, encrypts it using a public key k_{pub} matching a private key k_{priv} in the smart card and sends it to the card.

2. The smart card decrypts the session key using the appropriate private key and indicates success.

4.3
TLS and Smart Cards

TLS is the abbreviation for Transport Layer Security, the successor of SSL 3.0. The current version is TLS 1.0, which is still very similar to SSL 3.0 (see [DIE99]). The primary goal of TLS is to provide privacy and data integrity of messages exchanged between two communicating parties over an untrusted network – like the Internet. In addition, TLS also allows for mutual authentication of the communicating parties.

The TLS protocol consists of several layers. The lowest layer is the TLS Record Protocol that assures privacy and reliability of connections and is used for encapsulating higher-level protocols, like the TLS Handshake Protocol. This protocol provides connection security that ensures that the peer's identity can be authenticated using public key cryptography and that the negotiation of a shared secret is secure and reliable.

When TLS is used to secure client-server communication, in most cases the handshake protocol only conducts server authentication: During the handshake protocol, the server transmits its certificates to the client. The client validates the server certificates and extracts the public key from one of the certificates. This key is used to encrypt the session key for further communication.

However, for e-business applications additional client authentication is often required to ensure that only authorized people can access certain services or information. TLS allows for optional client authentication: During the handshake protocol, the server can send a Certificate Request that requires the client to send its certificate and a Certificate Verify message to the server. The server can authenticate the client by validating the obtained certificate and using the public key from that certificate to verify the client's signature contained in the Certificate Verify message.

Client authentication in TLS requires a private key and a certificate at the client; its security relies on the security of the private key of the client. To achieve maximum security and mobility, the private key and the certificate for authentication can be stored on a smart card with a cryptographic coprocessor. Such a card can generate the digital signature for the Certificate Verify message on-card, so that the private key never has to leave the secure storage of the smart card. An additional advantage of using smart cards for client authentication is that the user is not bound to a particular PC that holds the authentication credentials; she can use the smart card with the authentication credentials in various devices.

5 Smart Card Readers and Terminals

To write and read data to a smart card or to execute a command on a smart card, it is necessary to have a physical connection with the card. To make the connection with a contact card, it has to be inserted in a smart card acceptance device. In this chapter we give an overview of the different types of card acceptance devices.

There are a wide variety of acceptance devices available on the market. We can distinguish two groups:

Readers and Terminals

- Readers and
- Terminals.

The smart card reader is basically a connector between the smart card and the device communicating with the card. In contrast to this, a terminal is a computer on its own and can operate standalone without being attached to another device.

A reader can usually also write data to a card. Nevertheless, for brevity we will in this book always refer to this reading and writing device as a "reader". Other names that you will encounter for these devices are "read/write unit", "contact unit", "acceptance device", or "interface device (IFD)".

What we call a reader has many other names

5.1 Smart Card Readers

Smart card readers often have their own housing and are connected to the serial-, parallel-, or USB-port of a computer. Other reader types are integrated in a keyboard or fit into a PCMCIA slot. Another reader type has the size of a 3.5" diskette and is inserted into a diskette drive to be connected to the computer.

*Readers can
have a display
and a PIN-pad*

In addition to the card slot and the computer interface, a smart card reader can also have a display and a PIN-pad (see Figure 5.1). The main use of the PIN-pad is to enter a PIN (Personal Identification Number), which is sent to the smart card to identify the card owner.

Most readers have only one slot for a smart card. For special applications like a medical patient card, which can only be accessed upon authorization through a doctor card, the reader can have a second card slot.

*Figure 5.1:
Smart Card
Readers
(TOWITOKO)*

To operate cards with an additional cryptographic coprocessor, the reader needs more electrical power than it can draw from the serial port. Some readers therefore have an external power supply. Other readers tap the computer's power through a special connector, which is plugged between the keyboard and the computer. PCMCIA compatible readers can draw sufficient power directly from the PCMCIA interface.

*Readers come
with different
application
programming
interfaces*

Readers come with different software support. Almost every reader has some sort of support for Microsoft's Windows operating systems. Many of them conform to the PC/SC specification (which we discuss in Section 6.3 "PC/SC"), while others have only proprietary software support and are not compliant to any standard. A proprietary programming interface might not be a problem if the application only has to work with one single type of reader and if the application developer is not familiar with any standard reader API. In all other cases, a proprietary interface requires additional work and learning for the application developer.

Not only the application developer has advantages from an application written against a standard reader API. Customers have a choice between readers that support this standard API. They can replace one reader with another compatible device without changing a single line of code in the application code.

*OpenCard
Framework, the
Java API*

For developing smart card applications using the Java language and execution platform, the natural choice of standard API is the OpenCard Framework, about which you will learn almost everything in this book. When developing with Java, you should look for a smart card reader with support for the OpenCard Framework.

The OpenCard Consortium maintains a list of readers that can be directly plugged into the OpenCard Framework on http://www.opencard.org/index-devices.shtml/.

5.2
Smart Card Terminals

The advantage of a smart card terminal over a smart card reader attached to a computer is a tighter control of the smart card access. A terminal can be sealed to prevent tampering with the hardware. The software installation can be tightly controlled by special schemes, which could not be applied to a general-purpose computer.

Figure 5.2: Smart Card Terminal (Intellect IPT 2000/2010)

Such a secure and protected system is desirable for payment transactions, for example. For a payment transaction, the customer wants to be certain that no manipulation of hardware or software would draw more money from the card than he authorized. Before a terminal can be used for a specific electronic purse scheme, the issuer of this purse scheme usually requires an inspection of the terminal hardware and software. This certification focuses primarily on security against fraud and misuse.

Some purse schemes require a special smart card for the merchant, which is inserted in one of the slots of the terminal. In these schemes, the money is transferred from the customer's card to the merchant's card, or the merchant card authenticates the terminal to the customer's card.

Merchant cards

Often, a merchant accepts payment from more than one purse scheme. To use a separate terminal for each scheme accepted would increase the cost and take up more desk space. Therefore it is common that terminals have one slot for the customer's card and four or

Terminals can have several card slots

more slots for the merchant's cards. With such a terminal, the merchant can accept several different electronic purses with a single device.

A terminal is a computer on its own, with a processor and memory. Today a high-end payment terminal typically has a 32-bit processor and up to several megabytes of memory. Some terminals can even be programmed in Java.

For maintenance or to add new features to a terminal, it is often necessary to download software or software updates to these devices. Such a download will change the system after it was certified. Therefore additional security mechanisms in combination with certification of the downloaded software must be established.

Magnetic stripe technology
Most of the payment terminals are not only capable of executing smart card transactions, they can also perform credit and debit transactions based on data read from a magnetic stripe.

Terminal form factors
Terminals are available in different enclosures. The most common kind is a tabletop device, which you might have seen at your gas station or local grocery store. A tabletop device is mainly used for payment or credit transactions made while the customer visits the merchant. When the merchant visits the customer, e.g. to deliver a pizza, the merchant preferably uses a portable payment terminal. Portable terminals can perform off-line transactions. Some are also capable of using mobile data networks for on-line transactions. Many terminals can also be extended with additional features like ticket printers.

Self service terminals
In the same way we can draw cash from an ATM, we can load an electronic purse at an unattended load device. Using this kind of unattended terminal is very similar to using a traditional ATM. In addition to loading an electronic purse, this type of terminal can often be used to change passwords, to check the card balance, to print statements, to lock or unlock the purse card, to pay bills, and more.

5.3
Biometric Identification

Often, it is not sufficient just to have the card (identification through "something that you possess"). Most of the systems require the user to identify himself as the rightful holder of the card. The most common additional cardholder identification is to enter a password or a Personal Identification Number ("something that you know").

Passwords and PINs are not very user-friendly and not completely immune to misuse and fraud. The cardholder can forget them and bystanders can steal them. Therefore, various biometric identification techniques ("something that you are") are increasingly applied instead of passwords and PINs. You can find an excellent overview of the current state of biometrics in the book from Jain, Bolle, and Pankanti [Jain99].

6 Smart Card Standards and Industry Initiatives

Standards like ISO 7816 and industry initiatives like EMV or Open-Card are necessary to ensure that smart card aware applications, cards, and card readers are built to uniform specifications. Without standards, interoperability is not possible. A smart card application or a card itself would be usable only in a very limited environment. But smart cards, readers, and applications developed and manufactured according to standards also work with devices developed by another company in a different part of the world.

In this chapter we will give a brief overview of some standards and industry initiatives important for developing a smart card application.

6.1 ISO Standards

The International Organization for Standardization (ISO) also develops and maintains standards for smart cards. Of these, ISO 7816 "Identification cards – Integrated circuit cards with contacts" is the most important for working with chip cards that have electrical contacts.

Today ISO 7816 has nine parts:

Physical characteristics: *ISO 7816-1*
Part 1 defines the physical dimensions of contact smart cards and their resistance to static electricity, electromagnetic radiation, and mechanical stress.

ISO 7816-2   Dimensions and location of the contacts:
Part 2 defines the location, purpose, and electrical characteristics of the contacts (see also Section 1.1.4 "Mechanical Contacts").

ISO 7816-3   Electronic signals and transmission proto-cols:
Part 3 of ISO 7816 defines the voltage and current requirements for the signals at the electrical contacts defined in Part 2.

Part 3 also specifies the ATR (answer to reset, see Section 2.2.2 "T=0 and T=1").

In addition, Part 3 defines the asynchronous half-duplex character transmission protocol T=0 (see also Section 2.2.2 "T=0 and T=1"). Smart cards with proprietary protocols, like the German health card or the German phone card, carry the designation T=14, which indicates that the protocol is a variant not specified in ISO 7816-3.

ISO 7816-3
Amendment 1   Protocol type T=1, asynchronous half-duplex block transmission protocol:
Amendment 1 to Part 3 adds the half-duplex block transmission protocol T=1 (see also Section 2.2.2 "T=0 and T=1").

ISO 7816-3
Amendment 2   Protocol type selection:
Amendment 2 to Part 3 defines a revision of the protocol type selection mechanism.

ISO 7816-4   Inter-industry commands for interchange
Part 4 is the most important part of ISO 7816 from an application developer's point of view. It defines a set of commands to provide access, security, and transmission of card data, like for example a command to read, write, and update data.

Unfortunately, the smart card manufacturers implement only parts of this standard and in addition to this add proprietary features to the commands of their smart cards. Also, error handling is different for almost every card family.

The application developer has to take the hexadecimal codes and combine them to form a command. This makes such a command difficult to develop and to understand.

ISO 7816-5   Numbering system and registration procedure for application identifiers:
In Part 5 the form of an Application Identifier (AID) is defined. The AID consists of two parts: The first one is a Registered Application Provider Identifier (RID). The RID is 5 bytes long and unique

to a vendor. The second part has a variable length with up to 11 bytes, and the vendor can use it to identify a specific application.

Registration of identifiers:

Amendment 1 to Part 5 defines the process for obtaining an RID. The purpose of RIDs is to uniquely identify the provider of an application on the smart card.

Inter-industry data elements:

Part 6 defines the data elements and the TLV tags (see Section 2.2.3 "TLV Structures") for industry applications. It also defines the appropriate TLV structure and the procedures to read these structures.

Registration of IC Manufacturers:

Amendment 1 to Part 6 defines the process for registering IC Manufacturers.

Inter-industry commands for Structured Card Query Language (SCQL):

Part 7 adds new commands to the ones defined in Part 4, like for the smart card access using SQL, the structured query language known from relational databases.

Inter-industry security architecture:

Part 8 defines a detailed security architecture for smart cards.

Additional inter-industry commands and security attributes:

Part 9 adds news commands to the ones defined in Part 4, as well as additional security attributes to those defined in Part 8.

Electronic signals and answer to reset for synchronous cards:

Part 10 defines the behavior of synchronous smart cards. Note that Part 3 defines the protocol for asynchronous cards.

6.2
EMV ICC Specifications for Payment Systems

In June of 1996, Europay, MasterCard International, and Visa International (EMV) published EMV'96: ICC Specifications for Payment

Systems, also known as EMV. These specifications for a smart card infrastructure are derived from standards set by the International Organization for Standardization (ISO) for integrated circuit cards (ISO 7816). Since 1999, the EMV specifications are maintained by EMVCo, a company jointly formed and owned by Europay, MasterCard, and Visa. In December 2000, this new company released EMV 2000 Version 4.0. EMVCo is also responsible for the EMV Level 1 and 2 Type Approval process.

Europay, MasterCard, and Visa attempt to ensure correct operation and interoperability of smart cards in the payment system business sector. To attain this goal, the EMV specification states the minimum functionality required by smart cards and terminals.

Europay, MasterCard, and Visa require the testing and approval of cards and terminals, which are to be used for a credit card transaction done with an Eurocard, MasterCard, or Visa card. Through compliance with the EMV specifications, these major credit card organizations want to ensure interoperability across every terminal or card that is sold to the financial industry.

The EMV 2000 specification consists of four books, specifying the card, the security and key management, the application, and the terminal. The card specification consists of two parts:

EMV 2000 Card Part 1

Electromechanical Characteristics, Logical Interface, and Transmission Protocols:

Part 1 defines the electrical and mechanical characteristics of a smart card and a terminal. The specifications for the card are based on ISO 7816 with some variations. The terminal part of the specification attempts to ensure that a smart card with the characteristics also defined in this part of EMV can be processed without any damage to the card.

The card section also defines all stages involved in a card session, from insertion of the card into the terminal device through the execution of the transaction to the removal of the card from the terminal.

EMV 2000 Card Part 2

Files, Commands, and Application Selection

Part 2 defines data elements and commands that apply to the exchange of information between the smart card and the terminal device. In particular, it covers the data elements for financial interchange and their mapping onto data objects, the structure and referencing of files. It also covers the structure and coding of messages between the card and the terminal to achieve application level functions.

Additionally Part 2 defines the way in which an off-card application can select the appropriate on-card application in the case of a multi-application card. It defines the logical structure of data and files within the card that is required for this application selection. In addition, it specifies how the terminal has to process this data.

6.3
PC/SC

PC/SC, with full name **Interoperability Specification for ICCs and Personal Computer Systems 1.0** [PCSC02], covers the use of smart cards with personal computers. In eight parts, this specification spans the entire range from the physical characteristics required from smart cards and readers to the layer of application programming. The specification is based on and is compatible with ISO 7816. The focus is on the interoperability of smart card (called **Integrated Circuit Card** or **ICC**) and smart card reader (called **Interface Device** or **IFD**) and on the cooperation between the reader and the PC operating system.

The PC/SC Workgroup was formed in May 1996. The companies that drove the PC/SC specification 1.0 are: CP8 Transac (Bull), Gemplus, Hewlett-Packard Company, IBM, Microsoft Corporation, Schlumberger SA, Siemens Nixdorf Informationssysteme AG, Sun Microsystems, Toshiba, and Verifone. Most members are today offering PC/SC compliant products, particularly smart card readers of all kinds. Today the core members of the PC/SC workgroup are Apple, Bull, Gemplus, Hewlett-Packard, Infineon, Intel, Microsoft, Schlumberger, and Toshiba.

The eight specification parts of PC/SC 1.0 (see Figure 6.1) are:

Introduction and Architecture Overview
Part 1 explains the goals of the PC/SC specification and gives an overview of the PC/SC architecture and of the structure of the specification.

PC/SC 1.0
Part 1

Interface Requirements for Compatible IC Cards and Interface Devices
Part 2 specifies physical characteristics of the card and the reader hardware, as for example voltages. The lower transport protocol levels are specified here, including their error handling rules. Further, we find here the specification for the expected answer to reset (ATR).

PC/SC 1.0
Part 2

PC/SC 1.0
Part 3

Requirements for PC-Connected Interface Devices

Part 3 specifies the characteristics of the Interface Device Subsystem. To let the higher layers of PC/SC communicate with the **Interface Device (IFD)** in a device independent way, an **IFD Handler** adapts the IFD to a common programming interface. The IFD must provide basic functions like sending commands to the card or checking for card insertion. Optionally it can have various other capabilities, such as powering up or down the card inserted, or getting a user authentication with a PIN pad, keyboard, fingerprint scanner, etc.

PC/SC 1.0
Part 4

IFD Design Considerations and Reference Design Information

Part 4 gives help and guidelines for the design of the IFD Subsystem's inner protocols.

PC/SC 1.0
Part 5

ICC Resource Manager Definition

The **ICC Resource Manager** is the central component of a PC/SC system. It controls all IFDs, as well as the off-card resources providing the card's application-programming interface (called ICC Service Provider, see Part 6), and the interface to cryptographic functions (the Crypto Service Provider, also defined in Part 6).

The ICC Resource Manager is a privileged component. It should offer the same degree of security as the base operating system.

PC/SC 1.0
Part 6

ICC Service Provider Interface Definition

Part 6 specifies the ICC Service Provider and the Crypto Service Provider interfaces. These two interfaces are the primary interfaces the application developer will use.

The **ICC Service Provider (ICCSP)** must maintain the context of the communication with the card. Optionally, the ICCSP may offer classes for access to the files on the card and for the authorization functions needed to access the card.

The **Crypto Service Provider (CSP)** is optional. If cryptographic functions are needed for the access to the card, these functions are localized in the Crypto Service Provider. Such functions often fall under export restrictions for cryptography components. Keeping it localized allows for better control. For the CSP the interfaces are specified for key generation, key management, key import/export, digital signature, hashing, and bulk encryption services.

The ICC Service Providers need to be registered together with the card and interfaces they support. This enables the system to identify

and fetch the appropriate ICCSPs for a particular card. For the identification of the card, the ATR or parts of it are used.

Application Domain/Developer Design Considerations

PC/SC 1.0
Part 7

Part 7 contains advice for the application developer on how to use
the interface provided by the ICC Resource Manager to obtain information on the card readers installed, how to wait for insertion of a
particular card, and for other common tasks.

Recommendation for Implementation of Security and Privacy ICC Devices

PC/SC 1.0
Part 8

Part 8 contains advice on how to handle identification, authentication, and secure storage and how to achieve information integrity,
traceability, and confidentiality in a smart card solution. In the section on cryptographic services, it also offers an excellent overview
of the current cryptographic methods.

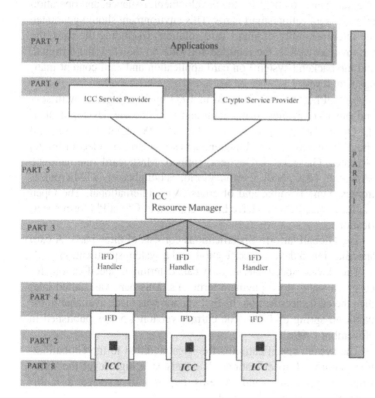

Figure 6.1:
Layers of the
PC/SC
Architecture and
the Eight Parts
of the
Specification

Implementations of PC/SC   Microsoft has provided implementations of the PC/SC 1.0 specifications on the Windows 95 and Windows NT 4.0 platforms and has released this implementation to the World Wide Web. For Windows 98, the implementation is shipped as part of the installation package. In Windows 2000, as well as in Windows XP, the resource manager is part of the operating system.

PC/SC 2.0 was originally scheduled for 2000, but currently no date is foreseeable. An update on the status on PC/SC 2.0 and a list of planned items can be found on the PCSC Workgroup homepage on http://www.pcscworkgroup.com. This list was published as part of a white paper in 1999.

6.4
GlobalPlatform

In the mid 90s, Visa started its Open Platform activities to specify an integrated environment for the development, issuance, and operation of multi-application smart cards. This environment should guarantee the interoperability of smart card solutions (including the card, the terminal, as well as the required software on the card, the terminal, and the backend system) on card application and card content management level.

GlobalPlatform was founded in 1999 by Visa together with several other companies to maintain and continue the development of the Open Platform specifications. In early 2002 GlobalPlatform had about 45 members including companies like British Telecom Ignite, Gemplus, Giesecke & Devrient, Infineo, Mastercard International, Microsoft, NEC, NTT, Proton World, Schlumberger, STMicroelectronics, Sun, Toshiba, and of course Visa International. The Open Platform specifications have been renamed to GlobalPlatform specifications.

The GlobalPlatform Specifications consists of three parts: A card specification, a device specification, and a system specification.

The device specification, also called terminal specification, focuses on stand-alone payment terminals. This part was started later than the card specification. Its first version was made available to the public in spring of 1999. The current version 1.5 was published in November 1999.

The system specification is the latest addition to the GlobalPlatform family of specifications. It covers at a high level the infrastructure, processes, and systems required to manage a multi-application card and its content.

The card specification defines an initial personalization process and standard ways for customizing the card after it has been issued ("post-issuance"). A goal of the specification is to provide the card issuer with tight control of the card and of the process of loading new applications onto the card.

The first versions of the card specification were based on the Java Card specification and extended that specification to add new features. After the announcement of the Smart Card for Windows, Visa announced plans to open the specification to base on more card operating systems and platforms. Version 2.1 was released in June 2001 and can be based on a Java Card or on a Smart Card for Windows.

A GlobalPlatform card has the following five high level components:

- The Runtime Environment – A secure multi-application card runtime environment. The Card Manager is build on top of it and uses its services.

- The GlobalPlatform API – It provides services for increased security, like the ability to open a secure channel for communication with the off-card part of the application. Additionally it provides card management functions, allows the card to verify the cardholder, and can be used to personalize the card.

- The Card Manager – It enables the issuer to maintain control of the card and its content, after the card was issued to a customer. The Card Manager also makes sure that a command sent to the card is processed by the proper application. The Card Manager consists of the Open Platform Environment (OPEN), the Issuer Security Domain (ISD), and the Cardholder Verification Method (CVM).

  - OPEN performs application selection, command dispatch, and performs card content management. It implements the GPSystem class API.

  - ISD is the on-card representative of the issuer. It loads and installs applications using OPEN. It implements the SecureChannel interface for its respective applications.

  - CVM implements a global PIN to support cardholder verification that all applications can use. It implements the CVM interface.

- Security Domains – They enable the applications of various providers to share space on a card without compromising the security of any particular provider or application. Each Security Domain implements the SecureChannel interface for its respective applications.

- Card Content – The applications, which are loaded onto the card with an Executable Load File.

Part II
OpenCard Framework

"Sit down before fact as a little child,
be prepared to give up every preconceived notion,
follow humbley wherever and whatever abysses nature leads,
or you shall learn nothing."

Thomas Huxley (1825–1895)

7 Introduction to OpenCard

7.1
The History of the OpenCard Framework

The history of the OpenCard Framework begins in 1997 with the introduction of the Network Computer. Companies like Sun, Oracle, and IBM worked on Network Computers to combine the advantages of a desktop computer with the low administration and maintenance cost of a terminal. The first Network Computers already contained smart card readers, and since Java is the language of choice on Network Computers, the idea of a Java framework for smart card access was born.

The beginning

Until recently, writing a smart card application was quite a difficult job mastered by a few specialists only. These specialists knew the APDUs and the protocols needed to drive smart cards as specified by the respective smart card operation systems.

In 1997, the first meeting of what later became the OpenCard Consortium was held. Computer manufacturers, solution providers, card manufacturers, and card reading device manufacturers met to work on a Java framework for smart card access. This framework was named "OpenCard Framework" or "OCF" for short.

For the reference implementation of a framework, researchers and developers from IBM took the lead in close cooperation with developers from Bull, Gemplus, Schlumberger, and Sun.

In September 1997, version 0.9 of OCF was published on the newly created OpenCard homepage http://www.opencard.org/.

OCF 0.9

During the spring 1998 CardTech/SecurTech conference and trade show, OCF version 1.0 was released to the public. The six industry leaders Bull, Gemplus, IBM, Schlumberger, SCM Microsystems, and Sun demonstrated the interoperability achieved by using the OpenCard Framework: The same application was shown on different hardware platforms, with different operating systems accessing the data on a smart card using readers from different manufac-

OCF 1.0

turers. All this was accomplished without having to change the application.

OCF 1.1   During the second half of 1998, the OCF reference implementation was improved with respect to code size and performance. It became available as OCF version 1.1 in October.

OCF 1.1.1   In May 1999, version 1.1.1 of OCF was published. In addition to a few minor corrections, this version contains support to run OCF in the newer versions of the web browsers from Netscape and Microsoft without using the Java Plugin technique.

OCF 1.2   In December 1999, OCF version 1.2 was published. This version incorporates many changes in response to Requests for Comments (RFC) from OpenCard Consortium members. Major enhancements include an easy to use installer package, improvements in various component packages, and Java Card support. In this book we work with OCF version 1.2.

Although the idea of the framework started in 1997 with Network Computers in mind, today the OpenCard Framework is used in all kinds of computers. Its range goes from large computers and network computers all the way down to small and embedded devices, like for example a Screen Phone or a payment terminal.

7.2
The OpenCard Consortium

During the 1998 CardTech/SecurTech conference and trade show, eleven of the companies supporting and working on the OpenCard Framework came together at the Inaugural Meeting of the OpenCard Consortium.

Figure 7.1:
The Members
of the OpenCard
Consortium

The purpose of the consortium is to produce the OpenCard Framework specification, to extend it, to foster its acceptance, and to assist in its use. This is done to promote and accelerate smart card interoperability at the point of card use, and to simplify application development [OCC99].

Purpose of the consortium

The founding members of the OpenCard Consortium are Bull, Dallas Semiconductor, Gemplus, IBM, Liberate Technologies (formerly Network Computer Inc.), Schlumberger, SCM Microsystems, Sun, UbiQ Inc., and Visa International.

Founding members

In the fall of 1998, 3-G International and Siemens joined the consortium. In spring of 1999 American Express and Toshiba also joined the consortium.

The OpenCard Consortium has a management board and a technical committee.

Organization

The management board is the main steering committee of the consortium. It also elects the officers of the OpenCard Consortium: the chair, the treasurer, and the secretary.

The technical committee is responsible for the evolution of the OpenCard Framework.

7.3
The Objectives of the OpenCard Framework

When looking at smart card applications from the point-of-view of application developers, at least three parties with a crucial role can be identified:

- Card Terminal Vendors: The card terminal vendors provide the actual card readers (also called "card acceptance devices", or, in OCF parlance "card terminals"). Each vendor carries a more or less broad spectrum of card terminals, ranging from the very simple units to more sophisticated models (featuring perhaps displays, Pin pads, or even biometrics input devices). Unfortunately, card terminal vendors have not yet agreed on a common standard interface. They still provide a number of APIs that are not compatible.

Card terminal vendors

- Card Operating System Providers: There are also numerous competing companies offering various different card operating systems and APIs. This results in a variety of commands and response codes.

Card OS providers

■ Card Issuers: These are the actual entities which issue smart cards to customers. The card issuers decide if and where to place what card-resident applications on the cards they issue.

The goal is to reduce dependence upon each of these parties (as well as upon the platform providers). Ultimately, different kinds of card terminals and various brands of smart cards should be usable for the same application.

Objectives of Thus, we can identify the following objectives of OCF: To pro-
OCF vide stable interfaces and function separation between

■ card terminal vendor dependent parts,

■ card operating system dependent parts, and

■ card issuer dependent parts.

In addition, OCF tries to be easy to use and expandable.

7.4
The Advantages of Using OCF

The architectural model of OCF makes a distinction between application and service developers on one hand and card and terminal providers on the other, offering significant advantages to all.

Benefits for Application- and service developers benefit from the OpenCard
application and Framework as follows:
service
developers ■ Vendor independence: Developers can choose cards and terminals from different suppliers.

■ Asset protection: Extensibility of the architecture enables developers to participate in future developments in smart card technology at low cost by migrating at the level of the API.

■ Improved time-to-market: Developers profit from shorter development cycles by programming against a high-level API.

■ Lower development cost: Developers save the extra cost of porting their applications to different platforms and benefit from using the high-level API of OpenCard Framework instead of dealing with low level programming.

Card and terminal providers benefit from OpenCard Framework in these ways:

- Increased clientele: Providers gain access to new market segments reaching many customers.

- Improved competition: Providers can compete in terms of functionality and are less vulnerable to the predominance of a single vendor.

- Less development effort: Providers inherit functionality provided by the framework. This improves their productivity.

Thus, using the OpenCard Framework becomes mutually beneficial for both developers and providers. Application- and service implementers writing to these interfaces can deploy their solutions in many different settings without having to change a single line of code. Providers adhering to these interfaces make their components directly usable for application- and service developers, thus gaining easy access to a rapidly growing market.

7.5
The OCF Architecture

In the remainder of this chapter, we give an overview of the concepts and the architecture of the OpenCard Framework. In the chapters that follow, we cover the framework in depth by explaining the utility classes, the terminal layer, the service layer, and the security concept.

7.5.1
A Note on Notation

For explaining OCF, we make heavy use of class diagrams in UML notation. Therefore, let us now recap the UML notation for those notational elements that we use in this book.

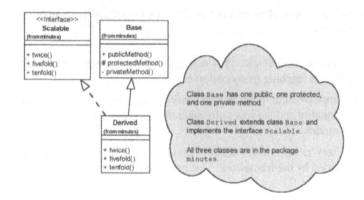

The "Unified Modeling Language" was proposed by Booch, Rumbaugh, and Jacobson and officially adopted as an OMG standard [UML97], [BOOCH97].

Classes Classes are shown as boxes with up to three sections. The top section contains the name and optional "stereotypes" (classifications, like for example "<<Interface>>"). In the middle section the attributes are listed, and in the bottom section the methods.

Visibility The visibility of methods and attributes is indicated by a character preceding the name, + for public, - for private, and # for protected. If no character precedes the name, the method or attribute has package visibility.

Static attributes are preceded by a $ character in addition to any visibility adornment characters.

Methods If the function signature of a method is given, it has the following form: methodName(TypeOfArg1, …) : ReturnType.

Associations The static relations between classes are shown as connecting lines. Unspecified associations are solid lines without arrows. A solid line with a closed arrowhead denotes inheritance (Java keyword extends). The direction of the arrow is from the extending class to the extended class – the direction of increasing generality. A dotted line with a closed arrowhead denotes a realize relationship (Java keyword implements). Optionally the role (often the name of the attribute used to implement the association) is shown.

Multiplicity Optionally, the multiplicity (0..1, 1, 0..*, *, 1..*, 1..6, …) can be specified at the connection.

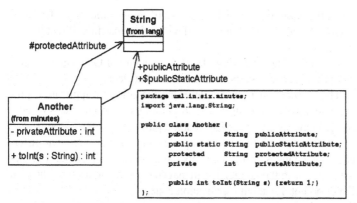

Figure 7.3:
Example Class
Another *in*
UML Notation
*and Source
Code*

We will use following terminology for classes: An **object** is an **instance** of a **class**. A class can be considered the blueprint for all objects of the same kind.

7.5.2
Architecture Overview

A reference implementation of OCF has been developed as a set of Java packages and classes. This reference implementation is publicly available on the web free of charge http://www.opencard.org .

One of the main objectives of the OCF architecture is to make the parts of a smart card solution, which are typically provided by different parties, independent of each other. These parties are shown in Figure 7.4. OCF's architecture allows each party to contribute software that corresponds to its portion of the complete solution.

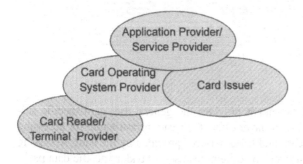

The application provider creates the off-card and sometimes the on-card applications seen by the end user of the smart card solution. The card issuer is responsible for card initialization, personalization, and issuing. The card operating system provider creates the basic operating system on which the on-card application runs. The card reader provider contributes the devices that interface directly with the smart cards.

Figure 7.5 shows the high-level architecture of OCF and the party that provides each component (horizontal layers).

The application provider develops the off-card application program seen by the end user. This program uses the interfaces offered by OCF and the CardServices that are plugged into the framework to communicate with the on-card application. This ensures that differences or changes in the card operating system, in the card reader software, or in the application management scheme used by the card issuer do not impact the application code.

The card issuer is responsible for the application management layer. This layer manages the coexistence of the various application functions (assuming a multi-application smart card) and of the application data on the same card. Application management schemes are found in ISO 7816-4,5 and in EMV 2000 4.0.

Figure 7.5:
The OpenCard
Framework
Architecture

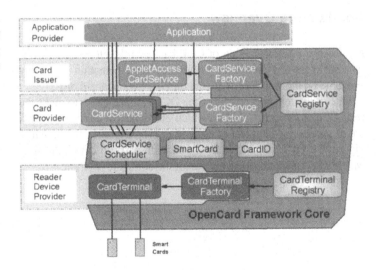

The card developer provides the general-use, card-specific services. The on-card layer offers the basic infrastructure for accessing data on the card and using services provided by the card. Accessing these basic services often requires use of vendor specific data packets.

Traditional &
programmable
cards

For traditional smart cards, the developer of the card operating system usually provides the application-specific executable code on the card. With modern, easily programmable cards such as Java Card and Smart Card for Windows, the application provider as well as the card operating system provider can develop the on-card application. Activating on-card executable code requires use of application specific data packets, regardless of the application provider.

The OCF `CardService` encapsulates the card operating system and on-card application dependencies, shielding the application from changes in those components.

CardService

A `CardService` that provides a standard way to access files on an ISO file system card is an example of a general-purpose component. Internally, this component would use basic services provided by the smart card vendor. A digital signature `CardService` is another example of a general-purpose component. Both of these are typical services that could be provided be the card vendor.

CardService examples

The application management components, discussed in the previous layer, also consist of `CardService` modules. Since the card issuer determines the application management scheme for a card, the card issuer is the logical source for these components.

With programmable cards, the APDUs sent to the card are not determined by the card operating system, but by the on-card application. Here, a single `CardService` developed by the application provider could be used regardless of the card provider. An example of this is seen with the Java Card. The APDUs and data needed by the application are determined by the card-resident applet.

Each card acceptance device, or card reader, has its own communication protocol. The **terminal layer** encapsulates these device differences. In this framework layer, the card reader provider can supply a `CardTerminal` implementation to drive his specific card reader hardware.

CardTerminal

We will now return to Figure 7.5 to address the OCF architecture in more detail. The OpenCard Framework core covers the right side of the figure. We will now discuss the core abstractions, the `CardServiceScheduler`, `SmartCard`, `CardID`, and the two registry classes.

The class **SmartCard** is the central abstraction. A `SmartCard` object has a **CardID** that contains the information identifying the card type. Contained in the `CardID` is the **answer to reset (ATR)** response from the card. The `SmartCard` is the primary object used by the application program. To obtain `CardService` modules for the card, an application uses the `SmartCard` object to request them.

SmartCard

A `CardService` encapsulates the implementation details of the application or function it supports and of the card operating system on which it can run. `CardServices` can draw on other `CardServices`. For example, a `PurseCardService`, which needs to access card files, can use the `FileSystemCardService` available for the card.

CardService

CardService-
Factory

All knowledge about the availability of CardServices is encapsulated in a **CardServiceFactory** for a family of services. The use of such factories is a standard object-oriented design pattern. The same developer usually provides the CardServiceFactory and associated CardServices.

CardService
Registry

The system-wide **CardServiceRegistry** keeps track of the installed CardServiceFactory objects. When a CardService with a particular interface is requested from OCF, the CardServiceRegistry calls every registered CardServiceFactory until an appropriate CardService has been created. The new CardService object is connected to the SmartCard object with which it will be used.

While we can have many CardService and CardServiceFactory objects in a system, there is always only a single CardServiceRegistry.

The CardService calls any cryptographic functions needed to access the card. Again, the CardService knows the most about the security mechanisms and protocols needed for the specific card operating system.

Card-
Service-
Scheduler

A CardService object communicates with the smart card through the **CardServiceScheduler**, which is also a class provided by the OpenCard Framework core. The CardServiceScheduler synchronizes concurrent accesses to one card from different applications. Consequently, there is exactly one CardServiceScheduler object for every SmartCard.

CardTerminal

The main abstraction in the terminal layer is the **CardTerminal**. An OCF CardTerminal provides the interface for smart card reader devices ranging from simple card readers with no intelligence to highly sophisticated, programmable payment terminals with several slots and user interface support. To support a hardware device, a CardTerminal implementation must be provided.

A CardTerminal supports one or more slots. Each slot is designated by a slot number. This allows exact modeling of real card terminals with more than one slot for card insertion. Such multi-slot terminals are used in the health industry, for example, to allow a patient data card and the authorization card of the doctor to be inserted at the same time.

CardTerminal
Factory and
CardTerminal
Registry

As we have previously discussed, a CardServiceFactory creates a CardService. The CardServiceRegistry administers all CardService and CardServiceFactory objects. Looking at the terminal layer, we find similar mechanisms: A CardTerminal object is created by a **CardTerminalFactory**, and keeping track of all known CardTerminals is the responsibility of the **CardTerminalRegistry**.

The application management layer consists of the `CardService` and `CardServiceFactory` classes for application management. An `ApplicationManagementCardService` can interpret the application management scheme used by the card (typically controlled by the card issuer). Using information from the card, the service can list, select, install, and delete on-card applications.

Application Management CardServices

Industry initiatives in specific business domains have agreed on application management schemes (for example EMV'96). Until these agreements are accepted across all domains, exchangeable application management card service objects will protect the application writers from differences and changes in the application management scheme.

OCF offers an optional separate component to encapsulate the file system of a smart card as specified in ISO 7816-4. Here we find a `CardFile` abstraction with attributes like **TRANSPARENT**, **LINEAR_FIXED**, **LINEAR_VARIABLE** and **CYCLIC_FIXED** along with support classes such as **CardFilePath**, **CardFileInput-Stream**, **CardFileOutputStream**, **CardFileReader** and more.

FileAccess- and FileSystem-CardServices

OCF has its own event objects, the most important of which are the `CardTerminalEvents`. A `CardTerminal` creates these events on card insertion and removal. They are delivered to registered `CTListeners` by the terminal via the `CardTerminalRegistry`. Each `CardTerminalEvent` carries a reference to the terminal and to the slot, which allows starting or closing down the communication with the card inserted or removed respectively.

Events

For diagnostic tracing, OCF defines the TracerEvent. **Tracer** objects create these events and `TracerListener` objects can register to receive them for filtering and post-processing. Since `TracerListener` objects can run in independent program threads, they can do arbitrarily complex filtering and formatting without impacting the threads being traced.

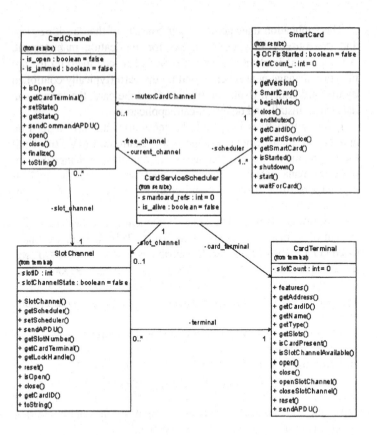

Figure 7.6: CardChannel, SlotChannel and Related Objects

SmartCard and
CardChannel

There are a number of objects governing the interaction between the terminal layer and the service layer. We want to take a closer look at these (see Figure 7.6) because they are essential for the control of concurrent smart card access as it will occur in typical multi-application card scenarios. This brief overview will give you an idea of how the OCF layers interact without going into detail on the individual classes – this will be saved for later sections.

CardTerminal

Let's start from the slot in which the smart card is inserted. A CardTerminal object can support one or more slots. Each slot represents one physical slot in the card reader. For every slot, there can be at most one SlotChannel. The association between slot and SlotChannel is set up when the SlotChannel is opened. The CardServiceRegistry creates a CardServiceScheduler object and opens the SlotChannel when the application requests a CardService from the SmartCard object for the first time.

After a card has been inserted and OCF has prepared the communication path, we have for that card exactly one `SlotChannel` and one `CardServiceScheduler` object. We have one or more `SmartCard` objects (typically one for each thread desiring access) and one or more `CardChannel` objects (one for each logical channel supported by the card).

SlotChannel, SmartCard

Maybe you wonder why we need a `CardChannel` at all, and why there should be more than one `CardChannel` per `SlotChannel`? The `CardChannel` represents the logical path to the card. ISO 7816 has a concept of logical channels to a card that allows up to four separate communication sessions. With the `CardChannel` mechanism, OCF is ready to support this ISO 7816 concept as soon as the first real smart card can support it.

CardChannel

Having whetted your appetite with a general overview of the OpenCard Framework, we will move on to take an in-depth look at the packages and classes making it up.

8 The Utility Classes

This chapter covers some support classes that are used throughout the OpenCard Framework. These classes define constants and exceptions that provide a foundation for the rest of the OpenCard classes. The utilities also provide service classes offering useful functionality such as string handling and property loading. These classes are used by the framework but are also available to the OpenCard application programmer.

We will cover three packages: `opencard.core`, which contains constant and exception definitions, `opencard.core.util`, which contains standard utility classes, and `opencard.opt.util`, which contains optional utility classes.

OpenCard utilities

8.1
The OpenCard Core Definitions

Figure 8.1 shows the classes contained in the `opencard.core` package.

The class `OpenCardConstants` is an interface having no methods. It defines constants such as the names of the properties that are used for configuring the framework.

Constants and base exceptions

The `OpenCardException` class is the base for all checked OpenCard exceptions. The base exceptions in the OpenCard service and terminal sub-packages – `CardServiceException` and `CardTerminalException` - are derived from this base class.

The `OpenCardRuntimeException` is the base class for all unchecked OpenCard exceptions. When a runtime exception is thrown it indicates a possible programming error in the application.

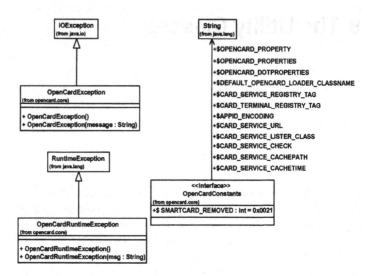

8.2
The Core Utility Classes

Core utilities The core utility classes are essential for tracing, accessing system resources, and automatic configuration of the OpenCard Framework. These classes, shown in Figure 8.2, are primarily contained in the opencard.core.util package.

8.2.1
Hex String Processing

HexString The **HexString** class provides a number of static methods that manipulate hex-coded strings – i.e. strings encoded in such a way that each string character represents one hex digit.

The **dump** (...) methods convert binary data stored in a byte array into a string format suitable for printing or display. This overloaded method can convert either the entire byte array or only a sub-array from binary to string format.

The **hexify** (...) methods convert integers and short integers from binary to string format.

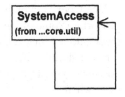

HexString
(from opencard.core.util)
+ dump()
+ hexify()
+ hexifyShort()
+ parseHexString()
+ parseLittleEndianHexString()

SystemAccess
(from ...core.util)

OpenCardPropertyLoadingException
(from opencard.core.util)
+ OpenCardPropertyLoadingException()

<<Interface>> TraceLevels
(from opencard.core.util)

<<Interface>> OpenCardConfigurationProvider
(from opencard.core.util)
+ loadProperties()

Tracer
(from opencard.core.util)

Figure 8.2: The OpenCard Core Utility and Trace Support Classes

The **dump** (...) and **hexify** (...) methods are frequently used within **toString** (...) methods of OpenCard classes and when preparing data for tracing.

The **parseHexString** (...) method accepts a string of hex digits as input and returns the corresponding byte array. Similarly, the **parseLittleEndianHexString** (...) method accepts a hex-coded string as input and returns a byte array with the digit order reversed. If the input string contains data in little-Endian (low-order digit first) format, the output byte array will be a positive integer in big-Endian format. This method is useful when preparing data for BigInteger computations.

8.2.2
The Configuration Provider

The configuration provider classes shown in Figure 8.2 provide the basic support for automatic configuration of the OpenCard Framework.

The simplest way to bring up the framework is through use of the **SmartCard.start()** method. SmartCard is a class from the opencard.core.service package, which will be covered in Section 10.1, "The CardService Layer Components". The **start()** method uses the properties settings along with a configuration provider to set up the CardTerminal and CardService support.

Configuring OCF

The OpenCard Framework is designed to run on a wide variety of platforms. Some of the target platforms, for instance Network Computers, do not have a concept of a file system. Since the possibilities for data storage differ widely across the target platforms, it was not possible to write a general configuration loader that would work everywhere.

Loading properties The **OpenCardConfigurationProvider** interface contains a single method – **loadProperties()**. This method adds configuration data for OpenCard to the system properties. This interface must be implemented to obtain configuration data according to the capabilities of the platform.

If an error occurs during property loading, an **OpenCardPropertyLoadingException** should be thrown.

The opencard.opt.util package provides an implementation of the OpenCardConfigurationProvider interface that reads the properties from a file. This sample implementation is covered in Section 8.3.1.

8.2.3
The Tracer

Figure 8.3:
Trace Support
Classes

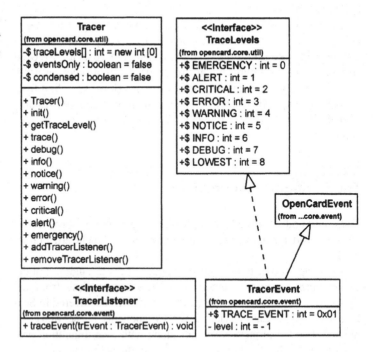

Provisions for debugging are present in all OpenCard Framework implementations. These are made up of classes from both the open-card.core.util and opencard.core.event packages as shown in Figure 8.3.

The **Tracer** class provides a standard method for capturing debug output. OpenCard classes use the Tracer to record significant events. When OpenCard applications also use the Tracer, the application trace information is captured along with the OpenCard trace information. This makes it easy to determine which application actions led to a specific error condition.

Tracer

8.2.3.1
Using the Tracer Class

Each class instrumented for tracing must create a Tracer object. The Tracer object can be created for each class instance, but it is often more convenient and less costly in terms of performance to create a static object that is used by all instances of the class.

The Tracer constructor requires the name of the class being traced. The Tracer object uses this information at runtime to determine whether trace information should be recorded, as we will see below.

After a Tracer object has been constructed, the programmer can call the trace methods from within the application methods.

The tracer provides a concept of trace level that can be used to categorize the trace information according to severity. The trace levels were modeled on those defined for the Linux syslog() facility (see http://www.linuxhq.org/). They are defined in the **Trace-Levels** interface of the core utility package.

Trace Level

The programmer specifies the trace level by calling the corresponding method of the Tracer class. The following table shows the severity level definitions along with the corresponding Tracer method names.

Level	Definition	Method
EMERGENCY = 0;	System is unus-able.	**emergency()**
ALERT = 1;	Action must be taken immediately	**alert()**
CRITICAL = 2;	Critical condition	**critical()**
Error = 3;	Error condition	**error()**

Table 8.1: Trace Level Definitions

WARNING = 4;	Warning condition	warning()
NOTICE = 5;	Normal but sig-nificant condition	notice()
INFO = 6;	Informational	info()
DEBUG = 7;	Debugging information	debug()

Trace method definitions

There are two methods defined for each trace method name. Both methods require a parameter that specifies the name of method being instrumented and a parameter that specifies the message to be in-serted into the trace stream.

```
public void debug(java.lang.String method,
    java.lang.String message)

public void debug(java.lang.String method,
    java.lang.Throwable throwable)
```

The methods differ in their specification of the message parame-ter. The first method requires a simple string parameter, while the second requires a Throwable object as parameter. In the latter case, the trace text is extracted from the Throwable object.

In addition to the trace methods, the Tracer provides a method that allows the application to query the active trace level. Sometimes a considerable amount of data manipulation must be performed to prepare a string of trace data. The programmer can use the getTra-ceLevel() method to avoid this data manipulation when tracing is not activated.

8.2.3.2
Trace Output

Each time a trace method is called, the Tracer creates a data record containing the information provided by the calling code. The record includes the trace level, name of the method causing the trace, trace message, the Throwable object causing the trace (optional) and thread performing the trace.

TracerEvent, TracerListener

The Tracer posts this record as a **TracerEvent** to all registered **TracerListener** classes (see Figure 8.3). The TracerEvent class from the opencard.core.event package provides acces-sors for all of the trace record fields. The TracerListener, also from opencard.core.event, is an interface containing one method – **traceEvent(...)**. This method is called for each TracerEvent that occurs.

The `Tracer` maintains a static list of all registered listeners. The `addTracerListener()` method adds a new listener to the list, while the `removeTracerListener()` method removes a listener.

Optionally, the trace record is also written to the `System.out` stream. Writing to this stream can be suppressed by setting the `OpenCard.trace.eventsOnly` Boolean system property to true.

8.2.3.3
Activating Trace Output

The `OpenCard.trace` system property governs the behavior of the `Tracer`. This property specifies a list of tokens specifying packages or classes to be traced along with their associated trace level. The trace level is separated from the class or package name by a colon. The tokens containing name and trace level are separated from one another by blanks. When the `OpenCard.trace` property is not set, no tracing is performed.

The following property definition activates tracing for all classes and packages contained in the `opencard.core` package and specifically sets a higher trace level for the `CardTerminalRegistry` class.

```
OpenCard.trace = opencard.core:3 opencard.core.terminal.
CardTerminalRegistry:7
```

When an instrumented method calls one of the trace methods, the Tracer object checks if tracing is activated for the calling class. If so, it will record all trace information whose severity level is less than or equal to the value from the `OpenCard.trace` property.

With the sample property definition given above, the tracer will record all information of level ERROR or lower for the `opencard.core` package and information of level DEBUG or lower for the `opencard.core.terminal.CardTerminalRegistry` class.

8.2.4
System Access

The OpenCard Framework needs access to system resources in order to operate properly. This allows system properties to be read during framework configuration and permits device access by `CardTerminal` modules.

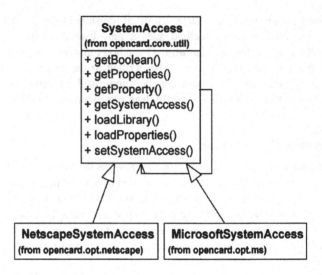

Figure 8.4:
System Access
Classes

SystemAccess
(from opencard.core.util)

+ getBoolean()
+ getProperties()
+ getProperty()
+ getSystemAccess()
+ loadLibrary()
+ loadProperties()
+ setSystemAccess()

NetscapeSystemAccess
(from opencard.opt.netscape)

MicrosoftSystemAccess
(from opencard.opt.ms)

OCF within a
browser

When an applet running within a web browser such as Netscape Navigator or Microsoft Internet Explorer uses OCF, it must somehow provide OCF with the required level of system resource access. To complicate things, each browser has a specific security mechanism for obtaining system access privileges. This means that browser specific code must be written to allow OCF access to system resources.

SystemAccess
class

The `SystemAccess` class addresses this situation by providing methods to access the most commonly used resources. The methods allow properties to be read from file, individual system properties to be retrieved, and libraries to be loaded. These methods are used by framework components as well as by plug-in components such as `CardTerminal` card reader support modules.

The methods of the default `SystemAccess` class do not obtain any special security privileges before carrying out the desired operation. This is sufficient when working with a stand-alone Java application in an environment allowing complete system access.

Microsoft policy
engine

In order to obtain privileges in a protected environment, the `SystemAccess` class must be extended for that specific environment. The opencard.opt package contains two such `SystemAccess` subclasses. The **MicrosoftSystemAccess** class uses the Internet Explorer `PolicyEngine` support and the **NetscapeSystemAccess** class uses the Navigator `PrivilegeManager` support to obtain access privileges. This mechanisms might work somewhat different for the newer browsers containing newer JVM versions.

The static **SystemAccess.setSystemAccess(...)** method allows an applet to provide a specialized version of SystemAccess for the current environment. This is best done in the applet's **init()** method. The SystemAccess object set in this manner is valid only for the current thread. This prevents concurrent threads from obtaining unauthorized access.

Netscape privilege manager

The component requiring access does not instantiate a SystemAccess object directly. Instead, it obtains a reference to the SystemAccess object valid for the current thread by calling the static **getSystemAccess()** method. If a specialized SystemAccess object has been set by the applet, it will be retrieved rather than the default object.

The following code fragment illustrates the use of the SystemAccess class by an OCF component.

```
...
SystemAccess sys = SystemAccess.getSystemAccess();
Properties props = sys.loadProperties(location);
Properties sysProps = sys.getProperties ();
...
```

See Section 11.2, "Running OCF in Browsers", for more detailed information on this subject.

8.3
The Optional Utility Classes

The **opencard.opt.util** package contains six classes that provide diverse functionality to the rest of the framework and to the application programmer. Since they are contained in the optional branch of the OpenCard tree, they might not be present in OpenCard implementations for small devices where space is at a premium.

Optional utilities

The optional utility classes can be divided into three groups. The PassThruCardService and corresponding factory provide a simple way for an application to send APDUs to any smart card. The Tag and TLV classes aid in parsing tag length value structures. Finally, the loader classes URLClassLoader and OpenCardPropertyFileLoader can load class files through the Internet and configuration data from a file, respectively.

8.3.1
The Loader Classes

The **OpenCardPropertyFileLoader** class implements the OpenCardConfigurationProvider interface from the core utility package. This class can read a file containing OpenCard configuration data and add the data to the system properties. This class can be used to load the configuration on any file-oriented platform.

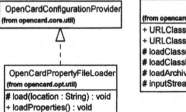

The OpenCardPropertyFileLoader looks for a configuration data file in the following four locations in order.

1. [java.home]/lib/opencard.properties
2. [user.home]/.opencard.properties
3. [user.dir]/opencard.properties
4. [user.dir]/.opencard.properties

The java.home, user.home, and user.dir directories are read from the system properties when composing the fully qualified pathnames for the property files.

If properties being added conflict with the properties read from a previous file, the properties from the subsequent file take precedence. This allows a general set of properties to be placed in a central location such as java.home above. More specific properties could be placed in a location such as user.dir above to customize OpenCard behavior for a particular use.

The property file must be in a format that can be read by the java.lang.Properties.load() method. Each line in the file contains a property key and its value. Key and value are separated by an '=' sign. Lines beginning with a pound sign '#' are treated as comments and ignored.

Table 8.2 shows the properties affecting the Framework classes. Naturally, specific CardTerminal and CardService components can define additional properties.

OpenCard.services
Specifies fully qualified class names for available CardServiceFactory modules. Multiple entries are separated by white space. Example: OpenCard.services =   com.ibm.opencard.factory.MFCCardServiceFactory
OpenCard.terminals
Specifies factory class name, friendly name, device type, and address information for each available Card-Terminal. Vertical bars separate this information. Multiple entries are separated by blanks. Example: OpenCard.terminals = com.ibm.opencard.terminal.ibm5948.IBMCardTerminalFactory | ReaderA|IBM5948-B02|1
OpenCard.trace
Specifies trace levels for OCF classes and packages. Multiple entries are separated by blanks. Example: OpenCard.trace = opencard.core:3
OpenCard.trace.eventsOnly
Boolean property set to true to suppress trace output on the System.out output stream. Example: OpenCard.trace.eventsOnly = true

The OpenCardPropertyFileLoader is used as the default configuration provider by the SmartCard class. See Section 10.1.1 for a discussion of this mechanism.

The **URLClassLoader** loads Java class files from an Internet or Intranet site. The URL of the site containing the class is provided to the constructor. Optionally, either through an additional parameter to the constructor or through use of the **loadArchive** (...) method, the URLClassLoader will read a Java archive to locate the class.

Loading classes from the Internet

The **loadClass** (...) method returns a Class object for the class name specified as an input parameter. The **loadClassData** (...) method returns a byte array containing the class data.

8.3.2
The PassThruCardService

The **PassThruCardService** shown in Figure 8.6 fulfills two functions – it provides a quick and easy way to exchange information with a smart card and it provides the simplest imaginable example for CardService programming.

PassThruCardService
(from opencard.opt.util)
+ PassThruCardService()
+ sendCommandAPDU(command : CommandAPDU) : ResponseAPDU

PassThruCardServiceFactory
(from opencard.opt.util)
+ PassThruCardServiceFactory()
+ knows(cardID : CardID) : boolean
+ cardServiceClasses(cardID : CardID) : Enumeration

An application can use this class's single method, sendComman-
dAPDU(...), to send an application protocol data unit (APDU) to the
smart card and receive an APDU from the card in reply.

Naturally, this means that the application must generate the
command APDUs and must interpret those returned by the card.
This goes somewhat against the grain of OpenCard, since the purpose of the OCF CardService layer is to shield the application
programmer from generating and interpreting APDUs. However, it
is sometimes convenient to be able to do this.

Every CardService requires a factory that can create new instances of it. Such is also the case here. The PassThruCard-
ServiceFactory instantiates the PassThruCardService.

The usual CardServiceFactory will construct a Card-
Service only for the particular smart card it was written to support. Since the PassThruCardService can be used with any smart
card, the PassThruCardServiceFactory will create an instance
for any card whatsoever.

The OpenCard Framework must be configured properly to use
the PassThruCardService. This entails setting up the system
properties for OCF. In particular, the opencard.services property must include a reference to the PassThruCardServiceFactory. In the opencard.properties file on a Windows system,
this could appear as follows:

*PassThru
configuration*

```
OpenCard.services =
   opencard.opt.util.PassThruCardServiceFactory
```

The following code fragment initializes the OpenCard Framework, obtains a PassThruCardService object, and sends a command to a card. Don't expect to understand all of the classes used
here – this is just to give you a first taste of OpenCard programming.

```
// initialize the OpenCard Framework
SmartCard.start();

// Wait for card to be inserted
CardRequest cr = new CardRequest( CardRequest.ANYCARD,
    null, PassThruCardService.class );
SmartCard sc = SmartCard.waitForCard(cr);

// make sure card is available
if (sc != null) {
  // Request a PassThruCardService.
  PassThruCardService ptcs = (PassThruCardService)
   sc.getCardService(PassThruCardService.class, true);

  // build an ISO command to read an 8 byte random number
  byte[] apdu = { (byte)0, (byte)0x84, (byte)0, (byte)0,
   (byte)8 };
  CommandAPDU command = new CommandAPDU(apdu);

  // send command and get response from card
  ResponseAPDU response = ptcs.sendCommandAPDU(command);
  ...

// Analyze response, etc.
// for example, print the APDU using response.toString()
}
```

8.3.3
The Tag and TLV Classes

The ISO 8825 standard defines rules for encoding information in a Tag Length Value (TLV) structure, where each data unit consists of a tag defining the type of data, the length of the data, and the value, or the actual data itself. These encoding rules are frequently used in the world of smart cards.

Tags and TLV structures

The variable-length tag consists of three fields. The tag class field is two bits long and specifies whether the tag is of the Universal, Application, Context-Specific, or Private class. The constructed bit indicates whether the tag is a primitive or is composed of further TLV structures. The tag code field has a variable length and identifies the data contained in the value field.

Tag field

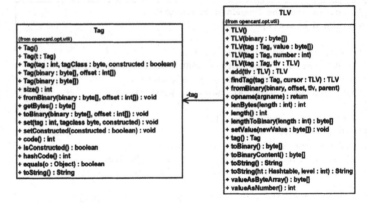

The **Tag** class supports interpretation and creation of ISO 8825 tags.

Creating and interpreting tags

To create a new tag, the application can construct either an empty Tag object, or can construct a Tag object with data for the three tag fields described above. The Tag class provides methods for filling the class, constructed bit, and tag code fields. The Tag class also provides methods for determining the tag length and for obtaining its binary representation.

To interpret binary tag information, the application constructs a Tag object with binary tag data. The Tag class provides methods for reading the three tag fields.

TLV

The **TLV** class represents an entire Tag Length Value structure. To create a new TLV structure, the application can construct either an empty TLV object, or can construct a TLV object from a Tag object and a byte array containing the value. The TLV class provides methods for setting the tag and value fields. The length field of the TLV structure is calculated automatically.

The TLV class also allows additional TLV structures to be added to an existing constructed structure.

The TLV class provides methods for determining the TLV structure length and obtaining its binary representation.

Interpreting binary TLV data

To interpret binary TLV information, the application constructs a TLV object with binary data. The TLV class provides methods for reading the tag, length, and value information. The application can use the **findTag()** method to search for a specific tag within a composed TLV structure.

The **toString()** method provides conveniently formatted output allowing the tags and values to be easily identified.

9 The Terminal Layer

One of the main issues addressed by the OpenCard Framework is device support for card readers. The mechanism provided allows support for a new card reader[1] to be easily added by implementing a `CardTerminal`.

The `CardTerminal` is a type of device driver for the card reader. It contains all required device-specific code.

The **CardTerminalFactory** is used by the OpenCard Framework to create an instance of the `CardTerminal`. The `CardTerminalFactory` must also be provided when adding support for a new card reader.

The OpenCard Framework provides a number of constructs to minimize the effort required for adding device support. These constructs consist of classes that provide functionality used directly or indirectly by the `CardTerminal`, interfaces that can be implemented by the `CardTerminal`, and exceptions to be thrown when problems occur.

Card reader device support

The interfaces and classes can be divided into core and optional components. The core components provide base functionality that is required in all OCF installations. The optional components provide specialized interfaces for extended device support.

Core and optional components

Figure 9.1 shows an overview of all OCF terminal layer components. The optional components are shown with shaded boxes. We will be covering the terminal layer components in detail in the following sections.

---

[1] In the literature, many terms are used to designate devices that interface with smart cards. Common terms are card acceptance device, card terminal, and card reader. In this chapter, we will use the term card reader for such devices.

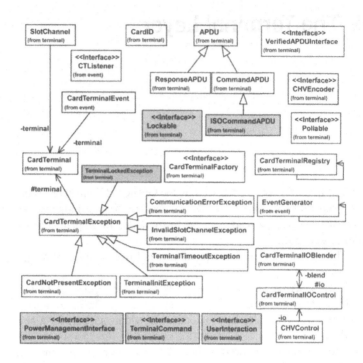

9.1
Terminal Layer Core Components

Terminal layer
core
components

This section describes the core terminal layer components. These are contained in the `opencard.core.terminal` and `open-card.core.event` packages and make up the basis for Card-Terminal programming.

We will organize the core components into groups to aid discussion. The first group is oriented around the terminal registry and event mechanism. We will then cover the device abstractions, the data transport classes, and the terminal layer exceptions. Finally we discuss the PIN and password support.

9.1.1
Terminal Registry and Event Mechanism

The `CardTerminalRegistry` is a singleton object that keeps track of all card readers known to the OpenCard Framework and provides methods that allow devices to be added and removed from the system. You can use `CardTerminalRegistry` methods to obtain the number of registered devices or references to the installed `CardTerminals`.

CardTerminal Registry

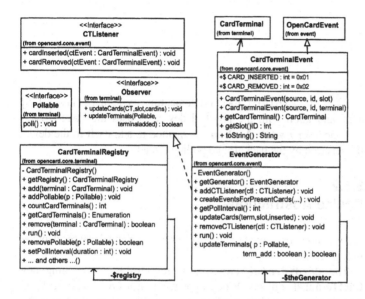

Figure 9.2: CardTerminal Events and Related Classes

The `EventGenerator` reports events to the application using the **CardTerminalEvent** class provided by the `opencard.core.event` package. The event contains references to the `CardTerminal` object and the slot where it was posted.

Card insertion and removal events

The polling mechanism provided by the `EventGenerator` can be very useful to `CardTerminal` programmers. The polling thread runs in the background and periodically calls every registered `CardTerminal` that implements the **Pollable** interface. This interface contains one method, **poll()**, that is used to check device status. When **poll()** is called, the `CardTerminal` implementation should check if a card has been inserted or removed and generate the appropriate events if the state has changed. The `CardTerminal` base class provides two methods, **cardInserted(...)** and **cardRemoved(...)**, to aid this process. Figure 9.3 illustrates proper operation of poll() when a card is inserted.

Polling mechanism

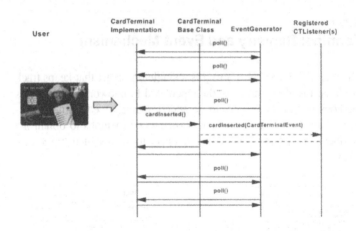

*Figure 9.3
Card Inserted
Event*

After a `CardTerminal` implementing `Pollable` has set up communication with the physical device, it uses the `CardTermi-nalRegistry` **addPollable**(...) method to add itself to the device list serviced by the background polling thread.

9.1.2
Device Abstractions

We will now turn our attention to the device-oriented classes depicted in Figure 9.4.

Factory   The **CardTerminalFactory** is responsible for creating new CardTerminal objects. When implementing a `CardTerminal`, the programmer must also implement a `CardTerminalFactory` that can instantiate it.

After creating a new `CardTerminal` instance, the `CardTermi-nalFactory` registers it with the `CardTerminalRegistry` using registry's **add**(...) method.

CardTerminal   The **CardTerminal** represents a physical card acceptance device and is the main abstraction of the terminal layer. This component contains the specialized code required to support the specific card acceptance device.

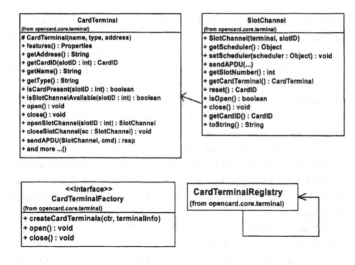

CardTerminal
(from opencard.core.terminal)
CardTerminal(name, type, address)
+ features() : Properties
+ getAddress() : String
+ getCardID(slotID : int) : CardID
+ getName() : String
+ getType() : String
+ isCardPresent(slotID : int) : boolean
+ isSlotChannelAvailable(slotID : int) : boolean
+ open() : void
+ close() : void
+ openSlotChannel(slotID : int) : SlotChannel
+ closeSlotChannel(sc : SlotChannel) : void
+ sendAPDU(SlotChannel, cmd) : resp
+ and more ...()

SlotChannel
(from opencard.core.terminal)
+ SlotChannel(terminal, slotID)
+ getScheduler() : Object
+ setScheduler(scheduler : Object) : void
+ sendAPDU(...)
+ getSlotNumber() : int
+ getCardTerminal() : CardTerminal
+ reset() : CardID
+ isOpen() : boolean
+ close() : void
+ getCardID() : CardID
+ toString() : String

Figure 9.4: The Device-Oriented Classes

<<Interface>> CardTerminalFactory
(from opencard.core.terminal)
+ createCardTerminals(ctr, terminalInfo)
+ open() : void
+ close() : void

CardTerminalRegistry
(from opencard.core.terminal)

The application can obtain information about the device using CardTerminal methods. The CardTerminal returns this information in the form of Java properties. The standard properties provided by a CardTerminal are:

- Name: Identifier of this CardTerminal
- Type: The device type
- Address: Information about communication with the device
- Slots: Number of slots provided by this CardTerminal

A physical card reader can have one or more slots. Each physical slot can accept one smart card. An OCF CardTerminal implementation can support one or more slots. The application can obtain the number of supported slots from the CardTerminal, which is useful when testing for card presence at a particular location.

When a smart card is inserted into a slot, the CardTerminal automatically powers up the card and retrieves its **CardID** (the OpenCard packaging for the ATR). The application can obtain the CardID from the CardTerminal for a specified slot. Before calling this method the caller should make sure that a card is present, otherwise null may be returned.

CardID

The CardTerminal **openSlotChannel** (...) method creates a unique **SlotChannel** object for communication with an inserted smart card. The CardTerminal makes sure that there is exactly one SlotChannel for each card. Once one thread has obtained a SlotChannel, no other thread can obtain a SlotChannel for the

SlotChannel

same slot until the first thread releases it. A SlotChannel can only be obtained when a card is present in the specified slot. The SlotChannel is invalidated when the card is removed.

SlotChannel and session concept

In a sense, the SlotChannel is a session object that is valid for communication with exactly one smart card. This session concept was introduced to prevent a card from being accessed using a stale driver stack, and also to prevent unauthorized access to the card from separate application threads.

The SlotChannel and related CardTerminal methods are mainly for use by the OCF CardService layer. However, the OCF terminal layer can also be used separately from the CardService layer. The application would directly use the SlotChannel in this situation.

SlotChannel methods

The **sendAPDU**() method of the SlotChannel provides the actual mechanism for communicating with the smart card. This synchronous method allows a Command APDU to be sent to the smart card and blocks until a Response APDU has been received. A soft reset can also be carried out using a SlotChannel method. Additional methods provide the slot number and a reference to the CardTerminal object associated with the SlotChannel. The SlotChannel is opened when it is created and can be closed explicitly to terminate communication with the card.

9.1.2.1
Data Transport Classes

CardID methods

As mentioned previously, the CardID class provides packaging for the ATR response from the card. Methods allow either the entire ATR or only the historical bytes to be extracted as a byte array. The ability to extract only the historical bytes is useful since determining the start of the historical bytes in the ATR requires considerable bit level work. Also, a comparison method is provided that allows two ATR responses to be compared with one another and a method is provided that returns a reference to the slot containing the smart card.

The APDU classes package the data passed to and from the card. The **APDU** base class provides a reusable buffer that can be initialized with a byte array of fixed length. APDU class methods allow data to be added to the buffer and allow the length of data within the buffer to be set.

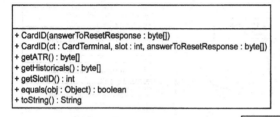

+ CardID(answerToResetResponse : byte[])
+ CardID(ct : CardTerminal, slot : int, answerToResetResponse : byte[])
+ getATR() : byte[]
+ getHistoricals() : byte[]
+ getSlotID() : int
+ equals(obj : Object) : boolean
+ toString() : String

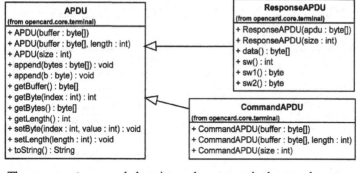

APDU
(from opencard.core.terminal)
+ APDU(buffer : byte[])
+ APDU(buffer : byte[], length : int)
+ APDU(size : int)
+ append(bytes : byte[]) : void
+ append(b : byte) : void
+ getBuffer() : byte[]
+ getByte(index : int) : int
+ getBytes() : byte[]
+ getLength() : int
+ setByte(index : int, value : int) : void
+ setLength(length : int) : void
+ toString() : String

ResponseAPDU
(from opencard.core.terminal)
+ ResponseAPDU(apdu : byte[])
+ ResponseAPDU(size : int)
+ data() : byte[]
+ sw() : int
+ sw1() : byte
+ sw2() : byte

CommandAPDU
(from opencard.core.terminal)
+ CommandAPDU(buffer : byte[])
+ CommandAPDU(buffer : byte[], length : int)
+ CommandAPDU(size : int)

The **CommandAPDU** subclass is used to transmit data to the smart card. Typically a reusable CommandAPDU object is created at the beginning of a series of transactions with the smart card. To prepare for data transmission to the card, the length is set to zero and data is then appended to the buffer. Appending data to the buffer has the side effect of setting the length properly. After the response data has been processed and data for the next command generated, the CommandAPDU object length is again set to zero and data is once more appended. Reusing the CommandAPDU object in this manner rather than creating a new object for each command improves performance considerably.

Response-APDU

The **ResponseAPDU** subclass is used to return information from the card. ResponseAPDU provides methods for extracting the APDU status bytes and data fields.

Response-APDU

9.1.3
The Terminal Layer Exceptions

Let's have a look at the terminal layer exception structure. The base class, **CardTerminalException**, extends the OCF base exception class, **opencard.core.OpenCardException**. The remaining terminal layer exceptions extend CardTerminalException.

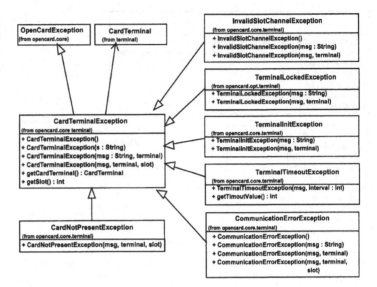

Each `CardTerminalException` contains references to the responsible slot and the `CardTerminal` object. The application can use these references to identify the device reporting the problem. The following table describes when the exceptions are to be used.

CardNotPresentException
Thrown when an attempt is made to communicate with the card, but the card is no longer present in the slot.
CommunicationErrorException
Thrown to indicate that an error has occurred when communicating with the card acceptance device.
InvalidSlotChannelException
Thrown if an invalidated SlotChannel is reused.
TerminalInitException
Thrown when a CardTerminal cannot be initialized.
TerminalTimeoutException
Thrown when the card acceptance device does not respond within the expected length of time.
TerminalLockedException
Thrown when the card terminal has already been locked.

9.1.4
PIN / Password Support

The OpenCard Framework terminal layer provides support for obtaining a PIN or password from the user and passing it to the smart card. The rationale behind the implementation of this support requires some explaining.

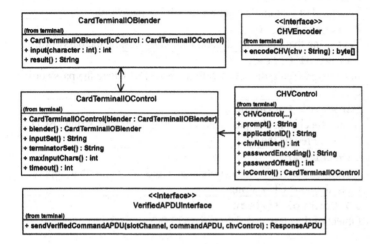

Looking at the OpenCard Framework globally, we see that the `CardService` layer is responsible for generating the APDUs that are sent to the card. When card holder verification (CHV) is required, the PIN or password must be added to the APDU.

PIN support rationale

The OpenCard Framework is designed to support a wide range of card acceptance devices. Some of these devices provide only a slot into which a smart card can be inserted, while others provide extended functionality.

The most common form of extended functionality consists of a simple display with PIN pad. When a device of this type is used, the intention is to use the display to prompt and the PIN pad to obtain the PIN from the user. Among devices with a PIN pad and display, there are considerable differences in how they must be programmed.

Card reader with PIN pad

Some devices merely allow keystrokes to be retrieved and messages to be displayed. For these devices, code on the host side must obtain the PIN keystroke by keystroke and insert the resulting PIN into the APDU. Other devices are capable of processing a partial APDU received from the host. The device can independently obtain the PIN from the user, insert it at the proper location in the APDU, and pass the completed APDU to the smart card.

The PIN / Password Support interfaces and classes allow the CardTerminal programmer to develop support for this type of functionality. These classes are shown in Figure 9.7. We should note that the classes and interfaces described in this section are only needed to support a card acceptance device that has PIN pad and display functionality.

Table 9.2:
CHVControl
Characteristics

Prompt String
Text used to prompt the user for his PIN or password.
Application ID
Text string that identifies the application requesting the password.
Password Offset
Integer specifying the offset within the APDU where the password is to be placed.
Password Encoding
String specifying the password encoding (character string, BCD, etc.) required by the card.
CHV Number
Identifies the CHV to be obtained. Used for cards that support more than one CHV string.
IO Control Object
Object of the class `CardTerminalIOControl`.

The **CHVControl** is a container class for CHV characteristics. These characteristics are listed in the Table 9.2. It is not required that all fields are used in all cases.

When a password is required, the `CardService` typically creates a `CHVControl` object and passes it to the `CardChannel` using the **sendVerifiedAPDU()** method (see Section 10.1.1, "The Card Access Classes").

The **CardTerminalIOControl** is a container class for parameters relating to the card acceptance device PIN pad and display. These parameters are listed in the following table. Again, not all parameters are required.

Table 9.3:
IO Control
Parameters

Maximum number of input characters
Maximum number of input characters expected.
Character Set
List of the allowed characters. This list may be used to enable or disable specific keys on the PIN pad.
Terminator Set
Set of codes that will terminate user input. This list may be used to enable cancel or correction keys, for example.

Timeout Value
Maximum time to wait for user input.
IO Blender Object
An object of the class `CardTerminalIOBlender`.

The `CardTerminalIOBlender` is an abstract class that can be implemented to provide special handling such as data formatting if required by the card. The `CardService` would generally provide an implementation of the `CardTerminalIOBlender` class if necessary.

The **CHVEncoder** interface contains constant definitions for common PIN or password encoding schemes. This interface also defines a method that can be used to provide special encoding.

CHVEncoder

The `CardTerminal` can implement the **VerifiedAPDUInterface** if the card reader is capable of obtaining a PIN from the user, inserting it into an APDU, and passing it to the card. If the `CardTerminal` implements this interface, the OpenCard Framework will automatically use the card reader PIN pad.

9.2
Terminal Layer Optional Components

The optional components relating to the terminal layer are contained in two packages. The **opencard.opt.terminal** package contains direct extensions to the core package, while the **opencard.opt.terminal.protocol** package contains specialized classes used for handling the protocol between the host and the card reader.

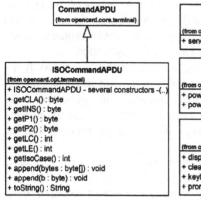

Figure 9.8:
Terminal Layer
Optional
Components

These components may be useful in special cases, but the programmer should be aware that the optional components might not be available in all OpenCard implementations.

When OpenCard is installed on a device with limited resources such as a Personal Digital Assistant (PDA) device or hand-held phone, the optional components may not be available. This will usually be of no consequence for the CardTerminal writer, since such devices will generally not support the use of arbitrary card readers.

9.2.1
The opencard.opt.terminal Package

Terminal layer optional components

The opencard.opt.terminal package contains classes that directly extend the functionality of the terminal layer core components. Figure 9.8 shows the optional OpenCard terminal layer components. The optional components provide two new classes and four new interfaces to the CardTerminal programmer.

ISO command support

The **ISOCommandAPDU** class adds extended support for APDUs that conform to the ISO 7816 standard. Constants describe the seven APDU cases defined by the standard. Additional methods are provided that can be used to extract the APDU case according to the 7816 standard, the class byte, the instruction byte, the parameter bytes P1 and P2, and the expected response length.

Power management

The **PowerManagementInterface** provides functions to explicitly power-up and power-down an inserted smart card. When a card is inserted into a slot, the CardTerminal must always automatically power it up. The methods provided by the PowerManagementInterface can be used in addition to the automatic card power-up function.

Terminal command

The **TerminalCommand** interface provides a type of 'transparent' interface to the card acceptance device. An arbitrary device command contained in a byte array is transmitted to the card acceptance device. The response returned is passed back to the application.

User interaction

The **UserInteraction** interface adds methods for directly accessing display and PIN pad capability of the card acceptance device. These methods allow text display and allow the application to directly obtain input from the keyboard. Another method, **promptUser(...)**, displays a text string and returns keyboard input with one simple call.

Terminal locking

In addition to the above interfaces, OCF 1.2 introduced the feature of locking either entire CardTerminal objects or individual slots within a terminal. This feature is introduced in the Lockable interface without breaking any existing code.

The locking mechanism is based on the following requirements:

Application requirement	OCF behavior
No lock required	The behavior of OCF 1.1.1 is unchanged
Lock on CardTerminal or slot is required	Only the owner of the lock is able to use the terminal or lock. The service layer also respects this behavior. A SmartCard object may only be created for the owner of the lock

To lock an entire CardTerminal, the method lock() can be used. This method also locks all slots and, if available, the PIN pad and display of the terminal. This method can only be called successfully when the card terminal has no slot channels open and no other thread has locked a slot. If the terminal is already locked, the methods will generate a TerminalLockedException.

The lock() method will try to lock the entire card terminal including all slots, the PIN pad, the display and will return a reference to the new slot owner. If only one slot is to be locked, use the lockSlot(...) method.

If a lock has been acquired, the lock owner can use either unlock() or unlockSlot(...) to release the ownership of the lock. If a multithreaded application needs access to a locked terminal/slot from multiple threads, the SmartCard object can be passed from the thread that has locked the terminal/slot to the other threads. The SlotChannel, which is allocated for this communication, plays the role of a gate object at the card terminal layer.

The **AbstractLockableTerminal** class is a convenience class to avoid that each card terminal implementer has to deal with the complexity of the locking functions and the security implications of such an implementation. To handle most of the the locking specific processing, subclass AbstractLockableTerminal and implement the methods **internalLock()**, **internalLockSlot(slotID)**, **internalUnLock()**, **internalUnLockSlot(slotID)** and **lockableOpenSlotChannel(slotID)**.

Abstract lockable Terminal class

9.2.2
The opencard.opt.terminal.protocol Package

This package aids the CardTerminal developer by providing support for the common protocols used between host and card reader devices. They do not represent an external interface used by applications.

Figure 9.9 shows these classes. The current implementation provides support for a limited T=1 protocol variant commonly used to communicate with card readers. *These classes do not provide support for T=1 communication between card reader and smart card!*

Also, this is not a complete implementation of the T=1 protocol. Neither chaining nor CRC calculation is supported.

T1Block class   The **T1Block** class represents data blocks to be exchanged with the terminal. T1Block defines a number of constants relating to the T=1 protocol. Methods are provided for querying the error detection code (EDC) algorithm type, calculating the EDC for the block, and checking the EDC contained in the block. Also, accessors are provided for many fields within the T=1 block such as block type, destination address, and data field.

Figure 9.9
T1 Protocol
Classes

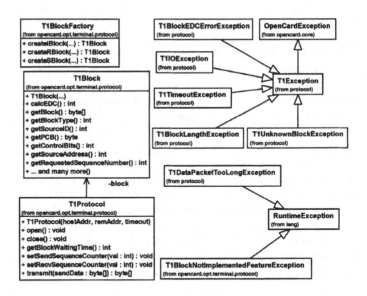

T1Protocol class   The **T1Protocol** abstract class handles the actual communication with the card. The single abstract method, **exchangeData()**, sends a block of data to the card and receives a block from the card. Since exchanging data with the card is dependent on the underlying communication mechanism used, this method must be implemented separately for each CardTerminal implementation. The **exchangeData()** method is protected since it is meant to be used by the T1Protocol class internally.

The T1Protocol base class constructor requires a default source address, remote address, and timeout value. The derived class that implements the **exchangeData()** method may require other parameters that relate to communication with the card.

After the CardTerminal implementation creates a T1Protocol object, it should call the **open()** method. The **open()** method synchronizes communication with the card by issuing the appropriate S-block requests.

The CardTerminal implementation can use one of the **transmit()** methods to communicate with the card. The simplest **transmit()** method accepts a byte array of data to be sent to the reader and returns a byte array containing data received from the reader. The remaining **transmit()** methods allow the default host address and remote address to be overridden.

Using T1 protocol support

The T1Protocol class also provides accessors and modifiers for many data fields representing the protocol internal state. Examples of these fields include block waiting time, send sequence count, and receive sequence count.

The opencard.opt.terminal.protocol package provides exceptions for many protocol error conditions that may occur. These are explained in the table below.

T1BlockEDCErrorException
Thrown when an error is detected in the checksum.
T1BlockLengthException
Thrown when a difference is detected between calculated and received block length.
T1BlockNotImplementedFeatureException
As mentioned above, this implementation of the T1 protocol is not complete. This exception is thrown if an attempt is made to use an unsupported feature.
T1DataPacketTooLongException
Thrown when the info field of an I-block is greater than 254 bytes.
T1Exception
Base exception for all T1 exceptions.
T1IOException
Thrown if a communication error occurs.
T1TimeoutException
Thrown when a send or receive timeout occurs in the T1 protocol.
T1UnknownBlockException
Thrown if a T1 block of unknown type is processed.

Table 9.4:
T1 Protocol
Support
Exceptions

9.3
Tracing in the Terminal Layer

The OpenCard terminal layer classes are instrumented with trace calls. Typically, each method will issue a debug level trace on entrance or when something interesting, such as card insertion or removal, happens.

Terminal layer traces
The terminal layer classes will issue critical level traces when run-time exceptions occur.

Tracing can be activated either for a single class or for an entire package. This is done by setting the **OpenCard.trace** system property accordingly.

To activate debug tracing for the CardTerminal class, set the OpenCard.trace property as follows:

Activating trace output

```
OpenCard.trace = opencard.core.terminal.CardTerminal:7
```

The '7' following the colon specifies the debug trace level. Note that this setting activates tracing only for the base class, not for the CardTerminal implementation. To activate tracing for the Card-Terminal implementation, specify the fully qualified path name of the implementation class or its package in the OpenCard.trace system property.

To activate debug tracing for the entire core terminal package, set the OpenCard.trace property as follows:

```
OpenCard.trace = opencard.core.terminal:7
```

We recommend that you include ample trace statements in your CardTerminal implementation as a debugging aid.

A complete discussion of the OpenCard trace facility is found in Section 8.2.3.

9.4
Communicating with the Card Reader

The CardTerminal implementation acts as a device driver for the card reader, so communicating with the physical device is one of its essential functions. There are two basic possibilities for communication with the device.

1. You can use the Java Communications API, also known as the javax.comm interface, to create a pure Java solution. This is the preferred mechanism, since it allows you to achieve a high degree of platform independence.

Communication possibilities

2. If you are working with a device that is not supported by the standard serial and parallel ports, or if the Java Communications API is not available on the platform of your choice, you can write a driver using the Java Native Interface. This will require 'C' as well as Java programming, and will also be highly platform-specific.

At this point, you might be asking yourself about the PC/SC interface. The Personal Computer / Smart Card interface was developed by an industry consortium to provide smart card access primarily for the Windows platform.

OCF PC/SC support

The OpenCard Framework reference implementation provides PC/SC CardTerminal drivers. When running on a Windows platform, all installed PC/SC card acceptance devices can be accessed through OpenCard if the OpenCard PC/SC CardTerminal is configured.

9.4.1
The Java Communications API

The Java Communications API provides stream-oriented serial and parallel device support and is available on many platforms. Since many card acceptance devices are serially attached, the Java Communications API is quite useful to the CardTerminal programmer.

Java Communications API

The Java Communications API provides classes that allow serial port access. These classes provide the capability to access and change the serial port parameters such as baud rate, number of stop bits, and parity to be used during communication. They also provide methods to obtain an output stream for sending data to the serial port and an input stream for receiving data from the port.

The CardTerminal implementation can also register itself as an event listener in order to be notified when data becomes available or when the serial port control line state changes.

For more information, please see the JavaSoft documentation [JNI98].

Using the Java Native Interface

Java Native
Interface

The Java Native Interface (JNI) provides a means of accessing operating system native binaries from a Java Application. A Java native class consists of the actual Java class that can be used by a Java application along with a portion, typically written in 'C', that runs in the native operating system environment.

Since the native portion is operating system dependent, such code is much less portable than code written to the Java Communication Interface. If your application is to run on multiple platforms, you will have to port the native portion of your code to each platform individually.

However, if you are writing a CardTerminal for a device that is not serially attached, the JNI provides a good alternative.

Please see the JavaSoft documentation [JCM98] for more information about the Java Native Interface.

9.5
The Implementation

Figure 9.10:
CardTerminal
Implementation

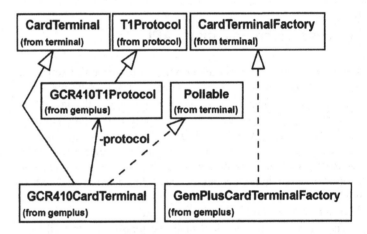

Now armed with in-depth knowledge of the OpenCard Framework terminal layer, we will discuss the implementation of a CardTerminal. We will limit ourselves to a basic implementation that provides support for a simple card acceptance device having a single slot and having no additional hardware such as a PIN pad or display.

The CardTerminal programmer must provide two classes in order to implement OpenCard support for a card acceptance device. He must extend the CardTerminal abstract class, implementing all of the abstract methods, and must write a `CardTerminalFactory` capable of creating instances of the `CardTerminal` derived class.

Figure 9.10 shows the classes we will be using for the implementation. The `CardTerminal` implementation extends the `CardTerminal` abstract class, and the `CardTerminalFactory` implementation implements the `CardTerminalFactory` interface.

This section uses a `CardTerminal` implementation for the GemPlus GCR410 card acceptance device as an example. The source code fragments shown in the following sections are taken from that code. The complete source code can be found at http://www.opencard.org/SCJavaBook/.

GCR 410 reader

The GCR 410 reader uses the T=1 protocol for communication with the host. The example code uses the T=1 protocol support classes from the `opencard.opt.terminal.protocol` package.

9.5.1
Using the T=1 Protocol Support

Since `T1Protocol` is an abstract class, the `CardTerminal` programmer must extend it and implement the **exchangeData()** method. This customizes the T=1 protocol support to use the communication mechanism selected for this `CardTerminal` implementation – in this case, the Java Communications API.

The `GCR410T1Protocol` class extends `T1Protocol`. This implementation assumes that the `CardTerminal` implementation initializes communication through the port. The `CardTerminal` provides an output stream to send commands to and an input stream to receive responses from the card acceptance device. The class declaration and constructor for this class is shown below.

```
public class GCR410T1Protocol extends T1Protocol {

GCR410T1Protocol(int hostID, int remoteID, int timeout,
                 InputStream in, OutputStream out) {
  super(hostID, remoteID, timeout);
  this.in = in;
  this.out = out;
}
}
...
```

Extending T1Protocol

The input and output streams passed as parameters to the constructor are saved for use by the **exchangeData()** method. The default host ID, remote ID and timeout needed by the protocol are passed to the `T1Protocol` base class.

The **exchangeData()** method, shown in the following code fragment, sends a T=1 protocol block to the smart card and waits for a T=1 protocol block in reply. The data to be sent is transmitted to the card using the output stream. The response bytes are read byte for byte from the input stream. The code checks if the block waiting time has been exceeded after each byte is read. If it has, then a timeout exception is thrown.

After the entire block has been received, the routine creates a T1Block object to pass to the caller. The T1Block constructor will verify that the data is in the proper format according to the protocol.

This routine will catch any IOException thrown by the input stream and throw a T1IOException on its behalf. This is done for convenience of the code calling **exchangeData()**.

```
protected T1Block exchangeData(T1Block sendBlock)throws …
list of exceptions … {
    …
    try {
        // send block to reader
        out.write(sendBlock.getBlock());

        // calculate the timeout
        stopTime = System.currentTimeMillis() +
                                    getBlockWaitingTime();

        // receive each response character in turn
        do {
            receiveChar = in.read();
            if (receiveChar != -1) {
                … add new character to buffer …
            }

            if (System.currentTimeMillis() > stopTime)
                throw new T1TimeoutException(…);

        } while (… block not yet received …);

        // make a new T1 block with the data received.
        receiveBlock = new T1Block(receiveBuf,T1Block.EDC_LDR);

    // remap IOException to T1IOException
    } catch(IOException e) {
        throw new T1IOException(…);
    }

    return receiveBlock;
} // exchangeData
```

9.5.2
Implementing the CardTerminal

Figure 9.11:
CardTerminal
Implementation
Methods

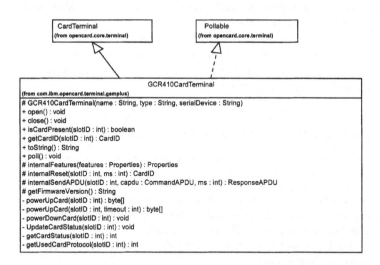

The programmer must implement a number of abstract methods defined by the `CardTerminal` base class in order to create a `Card-Terminal` implementation. These methods are shown in Figure 9.11 and described in the table below. Figure 9.11 also shows a few private methods not required for the implementation that are nevertheless interesting and are discussed below.

Table 9.5:
CardTerminal
Implementation
Methods

`<Constructor>` The constructor is protected since the `CardTerminal` is meant to be instantiated by a `CardTerminalFactory`.
`getCardID()` Returns the ATR packaged in a `CardID` object for a specified slot.
`isCardPresent()` Returns 'True' if card is present in specified slot.
`open()` Generally used to set up communication with card acceptance device.
`close()` Terminates communication and releases resources.
`internalFeatures();` Enhances the properties object provided as an input parameter with card reader specific features. Used by the `CardTerminal` base class.

InternalReset()
Performs a warm reset on the card in the specified slot. Used by the CardTerminal base class.
internalSendAPDU()
Sends a command to the card and receives a response. Used by the CardTerminal base class.

This example also implements the Pollable interface as an aid in generating card inserted and card removed events. This adds one method to the implementation:

Table 9.6
The Poll Method

Public void poll()
The implementation must check the device status and generate appropriate events.

We will now cover the example implementation in more detail. Since going through the code line-by-line would be exhausting, we explain the concepts behind the method implementations and illustrate the relevant points with code fragments.

The file GCR410CardTerminal.java contains the complete example implementation.

9.5.2.1
Initialization and Termination

To start off, the new CardTerminal class must be declared. This provides the abstract method definitions we must implement.

Class
declaration

```
public class GCR410CardTerminal extends CardTerminal
                                implements Pollable {
...
}
```

Constructor   The **GCR410CardTerminal** constructor creates a new instance of the CardTerminal. The name parameter is just a human-friendly identifier for the device supported by this instance of the CardTerminal. The type parameter specifies the device type and the serialDevice parameter specifies the communications medium through which the device is accessed – in this case, it is the serial port identifier.

In addition to passing information to the constructor of the base class, it must also define the number of slots supported by the device – in this case, one.

```
protected GCR410CardTerminal( String name, String type,
                              String serialDevice)
                         throws CardTerminalException {
   super(name, type, serialDevice);
   addSlots(1);
}
```

The **open()** method initializes the CardTerminal. After this *open()* method has been called, the CardTerminal must be in a state that allows communication with the card acceptance device.

The **open()** method of the example implementation first sets up communication using the Java Communication API. After obtaining access to the serial port, it sets the communication parameters appropriately for communication with the GCR 410 device.

This example also shows the use of the tracer when implementing a CardTerminal. It is generally a good idea to insert plenty of trace statements into your code at critical locations.

The **ctracer** object is a static instance of the Tracer class. The *Tracer* **ctracer.info()** method provides an informational trace, while the **ctracer.debug()** method traces debugging information. The first parameter of each trace call should specify the method name ("open") and the second provides arbitrary string information to be traced.

```
ctracer.info("open", "open terminal: " + getName());

// open serial port, application name is terminalname
ctracer.debug("open", "opening serial port " + getAddress()
portId = CommPortIdentifier.getPortIdentifier(getAddress());
serPort = (SerialPort)portId.open(getName(), PORT_TIMEOUT);

// configure port parameters
ctracer.debug("open", "set port to " + PORT_BAUDRATE
                                + " baud with 8N1");
serPort.setSerialPortParams(PORT_BAUDRATE,
                            SerialPort.DATABITS_8,
                            SerialPort.STOPBITS_1,
                            SerialPort.PARITY_NONE);
serPort.setFlowControlMode(SerialPort.FLOWCONTROL_NONE);
serPort.enableReceiveThreshold(1);
serPort.enableReceiveTimeout(PORT_TIMEOUT);
```

Serial port setup

After setting up the serial port for communication, the **open()** method has to obtain the data stream objects used for actual communication with the device.

```
// setup streams
serOut = serPort.getOutputStream();
serIn = serPort.getInputStream();
```

Next, the method creates a new GCR410T1Protocol object to handle the T=1 protocol used to communicate with the GCR 410 device. References to the input and output stream objects are provided to the constructor.

```
protocol = new GCR410T1Protocol(HOST_ID, TERMINAL_ID,
                                TERMINAL_TIMEOUT,
                                serIn, serOut);
protocol.open();
```

The final major task for the **open()** method is adding the Card-Terminal object to the CardTerminalRegistry polling list. After this is done, the **poll()** method will be called periodically by the CardTerminalRegistry polling thread.

```
// add this terminal to polling-list
ctracer.debug("open", "add terminal to polling-list");
CardTerminalRegistry.getRegistry().addPollable(this);
```

The CardTerminal implementation should release all resources and terminate communication with the acceptance device terminated when the **close()** method is called. Our example implementation closes the T=1 protocol handler, the input and output streams, and finally the serial port itself.

```
// close protocol
ctracer.debug("close", "close communication protocol");
protocol.close();

// close the streams
ctracer.debug("close", "close input and output streams");
serIn.close();
serOut.close();

// close the serial port
ctracer.debug("close", "close serial port");
serPort.close();
```

As a final point, we should mention the **internalFeatures()** method. This method allows the CardTerminal implementation to add details about any special features the card acceptance device might have. Since our example device is very simple, we do not have to override the **internalFeatures()** method.

9.5.2.2
Some Private Helper Methods

This section describes a few helper methods contained in our example implementation (See Figure 9.10 above). These methods are not required by the CardTerminal base class or the Pollable interface, but they provide frequently required functionality.

The **UpdateCardStatus()** method sends a command to the GCR 410 that returns information about the inserted card. Depending on the input parameter, this function is used in two ways. If the input parameter is 0, **UpdateCardStatus()** checks if a card is inserted in the slot. If it is 1, the method will obtain information about the inserted card – most importantly, it will retrieve the communication protocol (T=0 or T=1) being used between the GCR 410 and the inserted card.

Checking card status

The **getCardStatus()** method merely retrieves the status information collected by the **UpdateCardStatus()** method.

The **getUsedCardProtocol()** method evaluates the card status information and returns a 1 if the protocol between card reader and card is T=1 and returns 0 if the protocol is T=0.

The **powerUpCard()** method sends a command to the GCR 410 to power up the card. It uses the T=1 protocol support set up by the **open()** method to communicate with the device:

Power-up card

```
...
byte[] sendData = new byte[] { (byte)0x6E, (byte)0x00,
                               (byte)0x00, (byte)0x00};
...
try {
    rcvData=protocol.transmit(HOST_ID,TERMINAL_ID,sendData);
} catch (T1Exception t1e) {
    throw new CardTerminalException(t1e.toString());
}
```

Send power-up command

The **powerUpCard()** method maps all exceptions to CardTerminalException. It then updates the card status and pieces together the ATR string from the information returned by the reader:

```
UpdateCardStatus(slotID);
...
tmpATR[lenATR++]=rcvData[4]; // TS 3B=direct, 3F indirect
tmpATR[lenATR++]=rcvData[5]; // T0

// copy TA-TD according to the T0-Byte
```

Getting ATR

```
if ((tmpATR[1]&0x10)==0x10) tmpATR[lenATR++] = rcvData[6];
if ((tmpATR[1]&0x20)==0x20) tmpATR[lenATR++] = rcvData[7];
if ((tmpATR[1]&0x40)==0x40) tmpATR[lenATR++] = rcvData[8];
if ((tmpATR[1]&0x80)==0x80) tmpATR[lenATR++] = rcvData[9];

// complete ATR with rest of data (historicals etc...)
System.arraycopy(rcvData, 10, tmpATR, lenATR,
                     rcvData.length-10);

// calc whole length of ATR
lenATR = lenATR + rcvData.length - 10;

// copy tmpATR into ATR
ATR = new byte[lenATR];
System.arraycopy(tmpATR, 0, ATR, 0, lenATR);
```

To finish up, **powerUpCard()** stores the extracted ATR string in the cachedATR field:

Cache ATR

```
cachedATR = ATR;

return ATR;
} // powerUpCard
```

The ATR is cached so that the **getCardID()** method can be used any time a card is inserted. The cachedATR field also acts as a flag indicating that the card has been powered up. When the card is removed from the slot, this field is cleared.

9.5.2.3
First Contact with the Card

Now that we have covered the helper methods, we can turn to detecting a card insertion or removal.

Detecting card insertion

The **isCardPresent()** method returns true if a card is present and returns false otherwise. It checks for card presence by examining the status byte retrieved by the **GetCardStatus()** methods:

```
public boolean isCardPresent(int slotID) throws
                              CardTerminalException {
  return ((getCardStatus(slotID) & STATE_CARD_INSERTED)
          == STATE_CARD_INSERTED);
}
```

Poll() method

You will remember that the **poll()** method is called periodically. The **poll()** method must check if a card is present and generate the card insertion and removal events as appropriate. The method must also contain logic that produces events only if there has been a state change.

Our **poll()** method contains such logic. It first retrieves the current card status and tests it to determine if a card is present. The **cardInserted()** and **cardRemoved()** methods from the CardTerminal base class generate the events:

Poll method logic

```
UpdateCardStatus(0);
  if (!cardInserted) {
    if (isCardPresent(0)) {
      cardInserted = true;
      cardInserted(0);
    }
  } else {
    if (!isCardPresent(0)) {
      cardInserted = false;
      cachedATR = null;
      cardRemoved(0);
    }
  }
}
```

The **internalReset()** method also makes contact with the card. This method sends a command to the card acceptance device causing it to perform a warm reset on the card in the specified slot.

Reset the card

9.5.2.4
Data Exchange

The final set of methods to be implemented get data from or exchange data with the card.

The **getCardID()** method retrieves the ATR for an inserted card. First, the method verifies that a card is present. If no card is present, the cached ATR string is set to null, and null is returned to the caller.

Get Card ID

When the method is called for the first time, the example implementation powers up the card and receives the ATR. The ATR string is cached, as discussed previously.

When called subsequently, the method simply returns the ATR string packaged in a CardID object.

```
public CardID getCardID(int slotID) throws
                CardTerminalException {

  CardID cardID = null;
  byte[] cardStatus;

  // check if card is inserted
  if ((getCardStatus(slotID) & STATE_CARD_INSERTED)
```

```
            == STATE_CARD_INSERTED) {

    // check if card is powered (==> cachedATR != null)
    if (cachedATR == null) {
      cardID = new CardID(getSlot(slotID),
                                powerUpCard(slotID));
    } else {
      cardID = new CardID(getSlot(slotID), cachedATR);
    }

  } else {
    // no card inserted - invalidate cached ATR
    cachedATR = null;
  }
  return cardID;
} // getCardID
```

Sending the APDU

The **internalSendAPDU()** method transmits a block of data to the card and waits for a response. The response data block is packaged in a ResponseAPDU object and returned to the caller.

The GCR 410 reader requires a different exchange command depending on the transmission protocol being used between reader and card and depending also on the length of the data block. This necessitates some data manipulation to get the entire block of data to be sent into a single buffer.

```
// check the card protocol and setup the right command
if (getUsedCardProtocol(slotID) == 1)
  sendCmd[0] = (byte)0x15;     // T1 used...
else                          // T0 used...
  sendCmd[0] = (byte)((sendAPDU.length<=5) ? 0x13 : 0x14);

System.arraycopy(sendAPDU, 0, sendCmd, 1, sendAPDU.length);
```

Please note that the T=0 implementation requires additional processing depending on the different cases specified in the ISO 7816-3 specification (see Section 2.2.2, "T=0 and T=1").

The method transmits the command to the reader, which will in turn pass it to the card. The first byte returned by the reader is a status byte. Data following the status byte is the response from the card.

```
tmpReceiveBuf = protocol.transmit(HOST_ID, TERMINAL_ID,
                                          sendCmd);

if (tmpReceiveBuf == null)
 throw new CardTerminalException("no response from reader");

// remove status code when copying receive buffer
```

```
receiveBuf = new byte[tmpReceiveBuf.length - 1];

System.arraycopy(tmpReceiveBuf, 1, receiveBuf, 0,
                    receiveBuf.length);

if (receiveBuf != null)
  if (receiveBuf.length > 0)
    rAPDU = new ResponseAPDU(receiveBuf);
  else
    throw new CardTerminalException("no response from
                                    smartcard");
```

9.5.3
Implementing the CardTerminalFactory

Implementing a **CardTerminalFactory** is a straightforward task. The CardTerminalFactory interface from the open-card.core.terminal package defines the required methods.

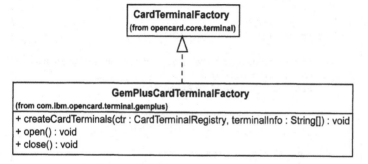

Figure 9.12:
CardTerminalFactory
Implementation

The **open()** and **close()** methods are used to initialize and shutdown the CardTerminalFactory. The factory can perform any needed setup and cleanup actions in these methods. The **create-CardTerminals()** method accepts a reference to the CardTerminalRegistry and an initialization string as parameters. Typically the CardTerminalFactory will parse the initialization string to verify that all needed information has been provided. Information from the initialization string is passed to the CardTerminal constructor to create the new CardTerminal instance.

The file GemPlusCardTerminalFactory.java contains the complete example implementation.

In our example implementation, the `open()` and `close()` methods are not needed, so they are implemented as empty functions.

The `createCardTerminals()` method parses the initialization
strings to make sure that the proper number of parameters has been
passed. The example factory implementation requires three parameters – name, device type, and communications port. The method
checks the device type parameter to make sure that a GCR410 Card-
Terminal has been requested. After the parameters have been
checked, the method creates an instance of the CardTerminal and
registers it with the CardTerminalRegistry.

```
public void createCardTerminals(CardTerminalRegistry ctr,
                                String[] terminalInfo)
          throws CardTerminalException,
               TerminalInitException {

    // check for minimal parameter requirements
    if (terminalInfo.length < 2)
        throw new TerminalInitException(
"at least 2 parameters necessary to identify the terminal");

    // is it a GCR410?
    if (terminalInfo[1].equals("GCR410")) {

        // GCR410 needs one parameter for the serial port name
        if (terminalInfo.length != 3)
            throw new TerminalInitException(
                       "createCardTerminals: "
                    + "Factory needs needs 3 parameters
                      for GCR410-terminal");

        // creates the terminal instance
        // and registers to the CardTerminalRegistry
        ctr.add(new
            GCR410CardTerminal(terminalInfo[TERMINAL_NAME_ENTRY],
                        terminalInfo[TERMINAL_TYPE_ENTRY],
                   terminalInfo[TERMINAL_ADDRESS_ENTRY]));
    } else
        throw new TerminalInitException("Type unknown: "
                      + terminalInfo[TERMINAL_NAME_ENTRY]);

}
```

10 The Service Layer

The OpenCard Framework service layer shields the application programmer from smart card details. This layer abstracts the smart card and on-card applications. Figure 10.1 shows the general structure of this layer.

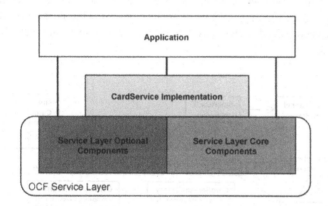

Figure 10.1:
OCF Service
Layer Structure

The OpenCard Framework provides the tools needed for card access. These tools are divided into core and optional components. The CardService implementation uses these components to offer a high-level interface to the application. The application uses the CardService implementation as well as the OCF components to communicate with the smart card.

Defining
CardService
interfaces

The CardService implementation provides a high-level interface to the application. It takes care of all APDU-level details when communicating with the card to implement the functionality defined by the interface.

Standard interfaces are available (see section 10.3, "Standard CardService Interfaces"); however, the application programmer is free to write his own CardService to encapsulate smart card specific details. This can be useful if the application is to support multiple smart cards of different types.

Standard
interface

For example, an application could be written to support a student card scheme using a 7816-4 file system oriented card. The application programmer could write a `CardService` having a method called `getStudentName(...)` that would retrieve the student name from a card file. When a Java Card is introduced later in the project, the programmer would not have to change the main portion of the application. Instead, he could implement a new `CardService` implementing a `getStudentName(...)` method that retrieves the student name from an applet on the Java Card.

Service layer core components

The service layer core components contained in the **opencard.core.service** package provide the basic tools needed by the application to activate a particular `CardService` to perform the required smart card operation. It also provides tools needed by the `CardService` itself to communicate with the smart card.

These components also synchronize smart card access when running in a multi-threaded environment. Applications using different smart cards run in parallel while applications using the same card will be synchronized so that only one application at a time can access the card.

Figure 10.2:
Service Layer
Class Diagram

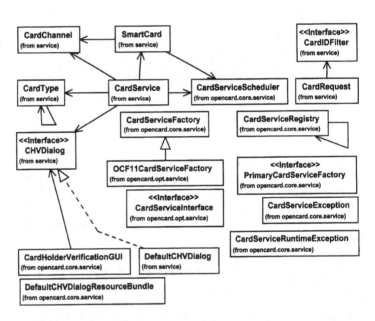

The service layer core also contains components for automatic CHV handling. If the `CardService` determines that a CHV is required, core components will check the capabilities of the CardTerminal whose slot contains the card. CHV handling will be delegated to the `CardTerminal` if it has the necessary capability.

CHV handling

The service layer optional components contained in the **open-card.opt.service** package extend the core functionality with additional interface and exception definitions.

This section provides a detailed description of the service layer core and optional components and how `CardService` implementations use them. Figure 10.2 shows a class diagram for the service layer. For clarity, only the base exceptions are shown.

10.1
The CardService Layer Core Components

The core components form the basis of the `CardService` layer. We must understand these components well in order to write our own `CardService` or to write applications that use a `CardService`. These components can be divided into five groups as shown in Figure 10.3.

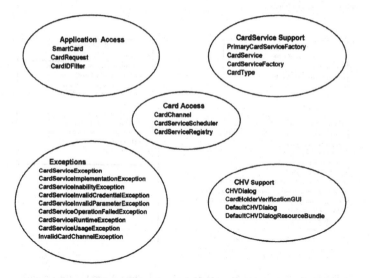

Figure 10.3:
CardService
Layer Core
Components

The application can use the **Application Access** classes to wait for card insertion and obtain a particular `CardService` for the inserted card.

Service layer
classes

The **Card Access** classes provide the base functionality for synchronizing access to the card. They are used by a `CardService` implementation or by other framework classes.

The **CardService Module Support** classes form the foundation used to create new CardService modules. These skeleton classes analyze the card type when a new card is inserted and handle any special initialization needed by the card.

The application can use the **CHV Support** classes to customize the dialog that obtains the CHV from the user.

Finally, the core components include **Exceptions** that are thrown when error conditions arise.

10.1.1
The Application Access Classes

SmartCard class   The classes making up this group are shown in Figure 10.4. An application generally uses the `SmartCard` class first when using the OpenCard Framework. We will first cover the `SmartCard` class static methods for framework initialization and shutdown, then the instance methods that are used when a `SmartCard` object has been obtained for an inserted smart card, and finally the ways to obtain a `SmartCard` object.

Figure 10.4:
The Application
Access Classes

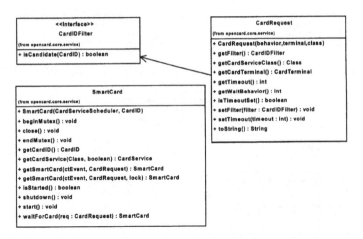

Start()   The two static methods, **start()** and **shutdown()** are provided for bringing up and terminating the framework, respectively. When `start()` is called, it first examines the system properties to determine how the framework configuration will be performed.

Configuration   The **OpenCard.loaderClassName** property specifies the name
loading   of a class that implements the `OpenCardConfigurationProvider` interface, described in Section 8.2.2, "The Configuration Provider". If this property is not present, then the default configuration provider,

OpenCardPropertyFileLoader, is used. The default provider reads OpenCard configuration information from a file, as described in Section 8.3.1, "The Loader Classes." A special-purpose configuration provider written for a specific installation can naturally obtain the configuration information from any appropriate source.

After determining the proper configuration provider to use, the **SmartCard.start()** method loads the provider class, instantiates it, and calls its **loadProperties()** method. The configuration provider loads the configuration data into the system properties during this method. Continuing on, the **start()** method configures the CardTerminalRegistry, covered in Section 9.1.1, "Terminal Registry and Event Mechanism", and the CardServiceRegistry, which we will come to shortly.

The **start()** method gets a reference to the global CardTerminalRegistry instance and looks for the **OpenCard.terminals** property string. This string contains a list of CardTerminalFactory names with configuration data such as reader name and serial port address. It parses this string, creates new factory instances, and uses the factories to create new instances of all configured CardTerminal objects.

Configuring the terminals

Configuration of the CardServiceRegistry is done in much the same way. The **start()** method gets a reference to the CardServiceRegistry object, then reads and parses the **OpenCard.services** property string to obtain a list of CardServiceFactory class names. It loads the corresponding classes and registers them with the CardServiceRegistry object.

Configuring the services

The **SmartCard.shutdown()** method works conversely. The CardTerminal and CardServiceFactory objects are removed from the registries and destroyed.

Shutdown OCF

A SmartCard object represents an inserted smart card. When the smart card is removed from the slot, the corresponding SmartCard object becomes invalid.

We should note that there could be more than one SmartCard object in the system for a given physical smart card. In a multi-application system, each application using the card will have its own SmartCard object.

Multiple SmartCard objects

There are five SmartCard instance methods of interest to the application.

The **getCardID()** method retrieves the CardID object associated with the smart card. Since a SmartCard object represents exactly one session with one inserted card, this method will always return the same CardID object.

Get CardID

*Access
CardService*

The application uses the **getCardService**(...) method to retrieve a reference to the CardService that implements the desired interface.

In the following example, the application wants to prepare a digital signature using the inserted card. This is done using methods from the SignatureCardService, which is an interface defined in the opencard.opt.signature package. The application calls **getCardService**(...) to gain access:

*Getting a
CardService*

```
signatureService = (SignatureCardService)
    card.getCardService(SignatureCardService.class, true);
```

The application passes the SignatureCardService class to the **getCardService**(...) method, which uses the CardServiceRegistry to obtain the correct implementation of the interface for the inserted card.

*Close the
SmartCard*

When the application has finished using the inserted smart card, it calls the **close**() method. The SmartCard object will close the current session with the physical card and release all associated resources.

*Exclusive
access*

The **beginMutex**() and **endMutex**() methods are bracket functions that allow the application exclusive access to the card across a sequence of CardService calls. If an application uses the **beginMutex**() method, it must be sure to call the **endMutex**() method eventually. If it doesn't, other applications wishing to access the card will be blocked.

*Getting a
SmartCard*

How do we obtain a SmartCard object? This is done with help of SmartCard class methods. There are two basic ways to go about this: the application can either wait for a CardTerminalEvent indicating that a card has been inserted and use the event to obtain a SmartCard object, or use the synchronous **SmartCard.waitForCard**(...) method to wait for card insertion and obtain a SmartCard object all in one step.

*Waiting for
events*

If the application is event-driven, waiting for events might be the best alternative. To do this, the application must register itself as a CTListener with the EventGenerator. The EventGenerator will notify the application when cards are inserted or removed. The application can pass the CardTerminalEvent object to the static **SmartCard.getSmartCard**(...) method to obtain a SmartCard object.

*Waiting
synchronously*

If the application is structured such that a synchronous method would be more advantageous, the application can describe the characteristics of the desired smart card and pass them to the static **waitForCard**(...) method.

The application creates a `CardRequest` object to describe the card characteristics. The `CardRequest` class is a container for card description information. If the application wants to wait for a card insertion at a particular card reader, that reader can be specified. Wait characteristics, a `CardService` class, and a `CardIDFilter` can also be specified.

Specifying card properties

The `CardRequest` class provides methods for setting and querying the card characteristics. `CardRequest` has a constructor that contains the most commonly used card request attributes. Additional attributes can be set using `setXXX` methods. The `CardRequest` class provides constants for the wait characteristics. As default behavior, a card already present in a reader when **SmartCard.waitForCard(...)** is called will be detected. If the application wants to ignore cards already present and wait for a new card insertion, the wait characteristics must be set to **NEWCARD.** The constants used for wait characteristic selection are shown in the table below.

`CardRequest.NEWCARD`	Wait for a new card insertion. Cards already present will not be detected.
`CardRequest.ANYCARD`	Creates a `SmartCard` object even for cards already present at the time of the call.

Table 10.1: CardRequest Constants

If the application provides a `CardService` class, the **waitForCard(...)** method will wait until a card is inserted for which the `CardService` is available. After **waitForCard(...)** completes successfully, the **SmartCard.getCardService(...)** method can be used to obtain an appropriate `CardService` instance.

When a card is inserted, the **waitForCard(...)** method will check if it possesses the specified characteristics. If so, it will create a `SmartCard` object and return it to the application. If the request cannot be satisfied, `null` will be returned.

The **CardIDFilter** interface can be implemented by the application if it is necessary to wait for a card with a certain ATR. The `CardIDFilter` implementation will receive the `CardID` object containing the ATR in the **isCandidate(...)** method. The `CardIDFilter` implementation must analyze the `CardID` and return `true` if the inserted card can be processed and `false` otherwise.

CardIDFilter

The application can specify any subset of card characteristics in a `CardRequest` object. All must be fulfilled for a `SmartCard` object to be created. The following code fragment shows a typical simple application of `CardRequest` in the **waitForCard(...)** method.

```
SmartCard.start();        // initialize the OpenCard Framework

// Create a new CardRequest and set to wait for any card
CardRequest cr = new CardRequest(CardRequest.ANYCARD, null,
                                  null);
SmartCard sm = SmartCard.waitForCard(cr);
if (sm != null)
   System.out.println("got a SmartCard!\n");
else
   System.out.println("No SmartCard object!\n");

SmartCard.shutdown();   // shutdown the framework.
```

This code will wait for any type of card to be inserted into any reader. It will also detect cards already present. If no card is inserted after a certain timeout period, **waitForCard(...)** will return a null reference.

10.1.2
The Card Access Classes

The card access classes shown in Figure 10.5 are primarily of interest to CardService programmers. The CardServiceRegistry keeps track of the installed CardServiceFactory objects. It is responsible for using the factories to create CardService instances. The CardService instances use the CardServiceScheduler and CardChannel objects to access the card.

Since the **CardServiceRegistry** is the central repository for information about available CardServices, it is important that only one such object exists in the system. The CardServiceRegistry uses the singleton design pattern to implement this. Framework objects can obtain a reference to the single CardServiceRegistry object by using the **getRegistry()** method.

Public Card-
ServiceRegistry
methods

You will recall that the **SmartCard.start()** method configures the CardServiceRegistry by instantiating CardServiceFactory objects and adding them to the registry list. This is done by using the registry's **add(...)** method. CardServiceFactory objects can be deleted from the registry using the **remove (...)** method. The application can get an enumeration of installed CardServiceFactory objects by calling the **getCardServiceFactories()** method.

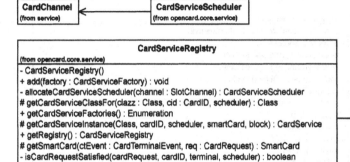

These are actually the only available public methods. Generally these methods are not used by the application, since the configuration of the CardServiceRegistry is done via system properties. However, if necessary, the application can use these methods to update the configuration. When an applet is downloaded by a web browser, for example, registration of any factories downloaded with the applet could be done directly.

Other framework classes, primarily the SmartCard class, call protected CardServiceRegistry methods to get SmartCard and CardService objects. The OpenCard Framework was structured in this manner to reduce complexity for the application programmer. The SmartCard class is a front-end that makes functionality from a number of OCF classes available to the application programmer.

Protected registry methods

When a smart card is inserted, OCF uses the protected Card-ServiceRegistry **getSmartCard(...)** method internally to instantiate a SmartCard object. This method sets up the communication stack and ties the new SmartCard object to the CardServiceScheduler for the inserted card.

The CardServiceRegistry maintains a list of all configured CardServiceFactory objects. The SmartCard object calls the registry's **getCardServiceInstance(...)** method specifying the required CardService class. The CardServiceRegistry attempts to create the required CardService instance from each CardServiceFactory in turn. When the appropriate factory is found, the CardService is instantiated and returned to the Smart-Card object.

```
┌─────────────────────────────────────────────────────────────────────┐
│                            CardChannel                                │
├─────────────────────────────────────────────────────────────────────┤
│ (from opencard.core.service)                                          │
├─────────────────────────────────────────────────────────────────────┤
│ # CardChannel(slotchannel : SlotChannel)                              │
│ + isOpen() : boolean                                                  │
│ - assertCardChannelOpen() : void                                      │
│ + getCardTerminal() : CardTerminal                                    │
│ + setState(state : Object) : void                                     │
│ + getState() : Object                                                 │
│ + sendCommandAPDU(cmdAPDU : CommandAPDU) : ResponseAPDU               │
│ + open() : void                                                       │
│ + close() : void                                                      │
│ # closeFinal() : void                                                 │
│ + finalize() : void                                                   │
│ + toString() : String                                                 │
└─────────────────────────────────────────────────────────────────────┘
                                    △
                                    │
┌─────────────────────────────────────────────────────────────────────┐
│                        CardServiceScheduler                           │
├─────────────────────────────────────────────────────────────────────┤
│ (from opencard.core.service)                                          │
├─────────────────────────────────────────────────────────────────────┤
│ + CardServiceScheduler(slotchannel : SlotChannel)                     │
│ + getSlotChannel() : SlotChannel                                      │
│ + allocateCardChannel(applicant : Object, block : boolean) : CardChannel│
│ + releaseCardChannel(channel : CardChannel) : void                    │
│ + reset(ch : CardChannel, block : boolean) : CardID                   │
│ + cardInserted(ctEvent : CardTerminalEvent) : void                    │
│ + cardRemoved(ctEvent : CardTerminalEvent) : void                     │
│ + toString() : String                                                 │
│ + ... and more()                                                      │
└─────────────────────────────────────────────────────────────────────┘
```

The **CardServiceScheduler** (Figure 10.6) coordinates access to the smart card. There is always exactly one CardServiceScheduler for each inserted physical smart card in the system. This is guaranteed by tying the CardServiceScheduler instance to the SlotChannel object for the card. You will recall from the discussion in section 9.1.2, "Device Abstractions", that the SlotChannel represents the unique communication channel with an inserted smart card. Since the SlotChannel is invalidated when the card is removed, the CardServiceScheduler is also only valid for a single inserted card.

The CardServiceScheduler coordinates access to the smart card by controlling the allocation of CardChannel objects. The CardService implementation uses a CardChannel object to communicate with the smart card.

CardChannel   The **CardChannel** represents a logical communication channel to the card. The ISO 7816 specification provides for cards supporting multiple logical channels, but so far use of this mechanism is not used. If smart cards supporting multiple logical channels become available, OCF could easily be expanded to administrate multiple

CardChannel objects per smart card. For now, however, only one CardChannel object can be allocated per smart card.

The **CardServiceScheduler** allocates the CardChannel object to CardServices sequentially. If a CardService attempts to allocate a CardChannel when all channels are already in use, the attempt will either block until a CardChannel becomes available or fail. The CardServiceScheduler provides methods to allocate and release CardChannel objects. When allocating a CardChannel, the caller can specify whether or not to wait if a CardChannel is not immediately available. If the caller does not wish to wait, the **allocateCardChannel**(...) call will return null if no CardChannel is available.

CardService-
Scheduler

The CardChannel class provides methods for exchanging data with the smart card. The **sendCommandAPDU**(...) method sends an APDU to the card, waits for the response, and returns the response APDU to the caller.

The **SendVerifiedAPDU**(...) method exchanges data with the card, but also obtains a password or PIN from the user before doing so. The password is inserted into the APDU at the appropriate location, either through the user dialog provided as a call parameter, or through the card reader. The CardChannel checks if the CardTerminal implements the VerifiedAPDUInterface. If so, the APDU will be sent to the card reader, which will obtain the password from the user, complete the APDU, and send it to the card. If the CardTerminal is not capable of password handling, the CHVDialog provided with the **sendVerifiedAPDU**(...) call will be used to obtain the password.

CHV support

The CardServiceScheduler has two more interesting methods. Calling the **reset**(...) method causes a warm reset to be carried out on the card. This method can be useful, for example, when the Card-Service implementation wishes to reset the card security state. The **reset**(...) method requires a blocking flag as parameter and returns a CardID object. If the blocking flag is set to true, the method will wait until the card has been reset and will return the new CardID object for the card. If the blocking flag is false, the **reset**(...) method will immediately return a null object if the channel is currently in use. The **getSlotChannel**() method will return the SlotChannel object associated with the CardServiceScheduler. The active slot and the CardTerminal object can be obtained from the SlotChannel.

More scheduler
methods

To round off the discussion of the CardChannel, we will mention two methods that help CardService implementations share information about the card state. It is important to realize that Card-Services for a particular smart card are often related. By building

Card state

upon and using the functionality provided by already existing Card-Services, the CardService programmer can save time and code. When building a set of related CardServices, it is important to have a mechanism that allows information concerning the state of the card – the last file selected, for example - to be passed from Card-Service to CardService.

The **setState** (...) and **getState** (...) methods allow an arbitrary object to be stored and retrieved from a CardChannel object. Related CardServices can define a common object representing the card state and store the state object with the CardChannel.

10.1.3
The CardService Support Classes

The CardService support classes provide the basic framework needed to write a CardService module. These classes are shown in Figure 10.7.

10.1.3.1
The CardService

So far, we have dealt with the CardService as though it were a single entity. Now we need to distinguish between the CardSer-vice base class, which is provided as part of the opencard. core.service package, and the CardService subclass that provides the desired functionality. We will use the terms **Card Service base class** to refer to the base class and **Card Service module**, or simply **CardService,** to refer to the CardService subclass.

CardService
reuse

As we stated at the beginning of this section, a CardService provides a high-level interface to the application. In addition, the CardService layer is designed to allow a CardService to build upon the functionality provided by other CardService modules. For example, a CardService for digital signatures might use a file system CardService to select the key file directory. This aids code reuse and allows logical structuring of the CardService modules written for a particular card.

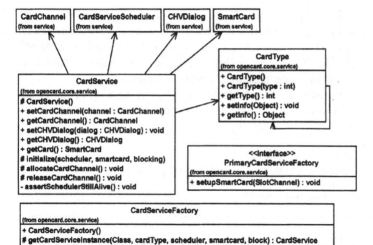

Every CardService module must extend the abstract **Card-** | *Extending the*
Service base class. This class provides methods for use by the ap- | *base class*
plication as well as methods to be used by the CardService mod-
ule. We will begin by discussing the methods intended for use by the
CardService implementation.

As discussed in the preceding section, the CardService allocates
a CardChannel to communicate with the smart card. This allows the
CardService module exclusive access to the card.

When one CardService module calls another, how does the | *Sharing the*
called CardService module obtain a CardChannel? The Card- | *CardChannel*
Service base class achieves this by providing its own methods for
CardChannel handling. In particular, the **setCardChannel**(...)
method allows an already allocated CardChannel object to be
passed in from an external source. This is a public method, so it could
theoretically be used by the application, but it is actually meant for
use by other CardService modules.

The protected **allocateCardChannel()** method is used by the | *CardService*
CardService module itself. It makes sure that a CardChannel is | *methods*
available for communication with the card. If a CardChannel has
been provided via **setCardChannel**(...), then **allocateCard-**
Channel(...) does nothing. Otherwise, it uses the CardServiceScheduler to allocate a new CardChannel object.

After the CardService implementation has called **allocate-**
CardChannel(), it uses the **getCardChannel()** method to retrieve the CardChannel object.

When the `CardService` implementation finishes using the `CardChannel` object, it calls the **releaseCardChannel()** method. This releases the `CardChannel` only if it had been allocated using the `CardServiceScheduler`. A `CardChannel` passed in through **setCardChannel(...)** will be ignored.

The following code fragment taken from a `CardService` module shows how the `CardChannel` is allocated, used, and released.

Allocate a CardChannel

```
try {
    allocateCardChannel();
    response = getCardChannel().sendCommandAPDU(command);
} finally {
    releaseCardChannel();
}
```

The `CardService` module does not concern itself with the source of the `CardChannel` – this is taken care of by the `CardService` base class.

Instantiate a CardService

`CardService` modules are instantiated by the `CardService-Factory` (which we shall cover shortly) in a two-step process. First an instance is created using the standard constructor and then the module is initialized. This two-step process allows `CardService` modules to be constructed without use of the Java Reflection API, which might not be available on embedded systems.

When requested to create a new instance of a `CardService` module, the `CardServiceFactory` will first choose the appropriate `CardService` module class from its list of available classes. The `CardServiceFactory` will then use the **newInstance()** method of the standard Java class `Class` to create a new object instance. The execution of this method causes the default constructor of the `Card-Service` module to be called. For this reason, every `CardService` module must provide a default constructor that, as a minimum, simply calls **super()**.

CardService initialization

After it has created a new instance, the `CardServiceFactory` will call the `CardService` module's **initialize(...)** method, passing it three parameters – the associated `CardServiceScheduler` and `SmartCard` objects, and a blocking flag indicating whether the application wishes to wait for a `CardChannel` if one is not immediately available.

The `CardService` base class handles the blocking flag and provides a method for getting the associated `SmartCard` object. However, no method is provided for obtaining the `CardServiceScheduler` object. Sometimes the `CardService` module will need to access the scheduler – for example, when customized `CardChannel` objects are used. In this case, the `CardService` module must im-

plement its own **initialize**(...) method, overriding that of the
CardService base class. The CardService module can save a reference to the CardServiceScheduler object from within its **initialize**(...) method.

If the CardService module provides its own **initialize**(...)
method, it must be sure to call **super.initialize**(...) to properly
initialize the CardService base class.

The final CardService base class method of interest to the
CardService module is **getCHVDialog**(), which retrieves the
current CHVDialog object stored by the CardService base class.
The CHVDialog object is needed when the CardService module
uses the CardChannel **sendVerifiedAPDU**(...) method.

CHV support

The remaining CardService base class methods are primarily
for use by the application.

The application calls the **setCHVDialog**(...) method to customize the dialog used to obtain the card holder verification string from
the user.

The **getCard**() method provides the application with a reference
to the SmartCard object associated with the CardService. This is
primarily useful when the application needs the SmartCard bracket
functions **beginMutex**() and **endMutex**() to execute several
CardService module methods without interruption.

*Exclusive
access*

10.1.3.2
The CardServiceFactory

As explained previously, the CardServiceRegistry holds references to all configured CardServiceFactory objects in the system. When creating a new CardService module instance, the
CardServiceRegistry goes through its CardServiceFactory
list attempting to create the instance until it is successful.

We will now focus on the CardServiceFactory itself. The
CardServiceFactory creates CardService module objects. The
CardServiceFactory base class contained in opencard.
core.service is an abstract class that must be extended by the implementation in order to produce specific CardService module objects. If you will, the CardServiceFactory module extends the
CardServiceFactory base class. The CardServiceFactory
module is used to create instances of CardService modules.

*CardService
Factory*

The methods provided by the CardServiceFactory base
classes are protected and are not meant for application use.

The CardServiceRegistry calls the factory's **getCard-
Type**(...) method passing it a CardID and CardServiceScheduler object. The CardServiceFactory analyzes the CardID to
determine whether it recognizes the card. If necessary, the Card-

ServiceFactory can communicate with the card using the Card-ServiceScheduler to make further determinations.

The **getCardType**(...) method must return null if the card is not recognized. If the card is recognized, it returns a valid CardType object.

The **CardType** object is simply a container for information resulting from the analysis of the card. This object is passed to other CardServiceFactory methods when attempting to create a new CardService module instance, for example. Proper use of the CardType object can make it easy to write a CardServiceFactory module that supports a number of different smart cards (cards of a particular family, for example) and CardService modules.

Only the CardServiceFactory module that created it evaluates the data it contains, so in effect the CardServiceFactory module writer determines its meaning.

A CardType constructor can accept a numeric value that could, for example, be used to identify a specific type of card. Additionally, the **setInfo**(...) and **getInfo**(...) methods can be used to store and retrieve an arbitrary object with the CardType object.

The next CardServiceFactory method used by the CardServiceRegistry is **getClasses**(...). This method accepts a CardType object as parameter and returns a list of all the CardService classes supported.

To instantiate a new CardService object, the CardServiceRegistry will call the **getCardServiceInstance**(...) method. This method is passed all parameters required for instantiating and initializing the CardService.

Both **getCardType**(...) and **getClasses**(...) are abstract methods of the CardServiceFactory base class. To create a CardServiceFactory to support your CardService classes, you must extend the CardService base class and implement these two methods.

The following code fragment shows the basic framework for a CardServiceFactory implementation.

```
public class TestCardServiceFactory
        extends CardServiceFactory
{

  // constructor
  public TestCardServiceFactory() {}

  protected CardType getCardType(CardID cid,
                    CardServiceScheduler scheduler) {

    ... analyze the card, like the ATR or with additional
        commands executed via the CardServiceScheduler ...

    return cardType;
  }

  // return all CardServices supporting cards of this
  // type
  protected Enumeration getClasses(CardType type) {

    ... create enumeration based on CardType ...

    return enumerateClasses(...);
  }

} // class TestCardServiceFactory
```

The **PrimaryCardServiceFactory** is an optional interface that may be implemented by a CardServiceFactory. For a particular smart card, only one CardServiceFactory may implement this interface.

Primary factory

The PrimaryCardServiceFactory contains one method, **setupSmartCard**(...), which is called by the CardServiceRegistry when the CardServiceScheduler is first set up for the card. It will always be called before any CardService gains access to the card. This method can be used to carry out any necessary initialization before the card is accessed.

10.1.4
The CHV Support Classes

The CHV support classes, shown in Figure 10.8, help OCF to obtain a card holder verification string from the user. As you recall from section 10.1.2, "The Card Access Classes", the CardChannel provides the **sendVerifiedAPDU**(...) method, which is used by the CardService when a CHV value must be sent to the card.

CHV support

CardChannel

The `CardChannel` is responsible for obtaining the CHV value either from the `CardTerminal` if it possesses the necessary capabilities, or through the `CHVDialog` class. This section discusses the `CHVDialog` and related classes.

CHVDialog

The `CHVDialog` is actually an interface having only one method – **getCHV (...)**. Since a smart card may have more than one CHV value used for different purposes, this method accepts a numeric parameter specifying the CHV needed.

Figure 10.8
CHV Support
Classes

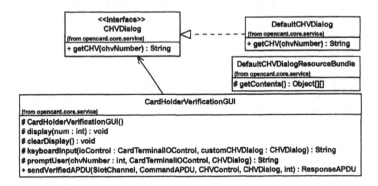

Application
CHVDialog

A default `CHVDialog` is provided by the OpenCard Framework, but the application can provide its own `CHVDialog` by implementing the interface and passing the class to the **setCHVDialog (...)** method of the `CardService`.

CardChannel
CHV
mechanism

The `CardChannel` uses the **CardHolderVerificationGUI** class to obtain the CHV from the user. `CardHolderVerificationGUI` is a final class that has no user interface itself, but contains the code that examines the capabilities of the `CardTerminal` and decides whether the `CardTerminal` or the `CHVDialog` should be used to obtain the CHV. The methods of `CardHolderVerificationGUI` are not meant for use by the application.

Default CHV
dialog

The **DefaultCHVDialog** class contains a Java AWT-based dialog box as an inner class that is used when the `CardTerminal` is not capable of CHV handling and when the application has not provided its own `CHVDialog`. When the `CardHolderVerificationGUI` calls **getCHV (...)**, `DefaultCHVDialog` displays the dialog box to prompt the user for a CHV string. The string entered by the user is returned.

Resource
bundle

The `DefaultCHVDialog` reads the text strings for display from the **DefaultCHVDialogResourceBundle** to enable national language support.

One drawback of the above mentioned card holder verification approach is that an application has no control about which card holder verifications are performed at what time. For example, it is generally not possible to check whether the user has already been prompted for a password. Also, it is not possible to simply enforce card holder verification at application startup, or to reset the card holder verification when the application is done with the card. There may be applications that require more control of the Card Holder Verification as is currently provided. These applications should be given a way to perform card holder verification explicitly. Also, applications should be able to undo a successful card holder verification.

By defining a card service for this purpose, applications can take control of the card holder verification. Applications that do not need this control may still rely on the transparent mechanism, as long as the CardService to be used supports it. The transparent mechanism for card holder verification may still be useful. However, its use is restricted by the definition of the interface opencard.core.service.CHVDialog, which returns a string holding the password or PIN. The card channel that evaluates this string can only apply a default conversion and paste the resulting byte array into a prepared Command APDU. This is appropriate only for alphanumeric passwords in the locale of the Java environment in which the OpenCard Framework is running. It also assumes that the password has to be presented in plain format, not with secure messaging.

CHVCard-Service

Performing card holder verification is a complex task with multiple dependencies. Requesting the password from the card holder depends on the hardware that is available. For example, a screen dialog may be popped up, or an attached card reader's display and PIN pad can be used. The command or commands to verify the password depend on the card OS. Length, encoding, padding, and the range of valid characters depend on the application and on the card layout. When specifying a CardService for card holder verification, it has to be decided which of these dependencies shall be handled by the Card-Service, and which will have to be dealt with by the applications. There is no one, perfect solution to this problem.

Specifying a CardService at this level of abstraction does not rule out the specification of other CardServices, performing the same task at a higher level of abstraction. There may still be CardServices for card holder verification that do convert a string presented by an application to an encoding appropriate for the card.

The CHVCardService class obviously needs a method that performs card holder verification with the smart card. Typical file system based smart cards, like the German GeldKarte, support different passwords for sub-trees of the file system, and also multiple passwords within the same sub-tree. On Java Cards, each applet may specify it's own set of passwords, too. Parameters to the verification method have to indicate the sub-tree or applet as well as the password within that sub-tree. To specify the sub-tree on a file system card or the applet on a Java Card, the tag interface `opencard.opt.security.SecurityDomain` can be used. It is implemented by class `opencard.opt.iso.fs.CardFilePath`, and may in the future be implemented by classes that identify security domains in other cards.

To specify the password within a security domain, a simple integer should be sufficient. The GeldKarte, already mentioned above as an example, supports passwords 0 and 1, IBM's MFC smart cards passwords 1 and 2, Gemplus' GPK cards passwords 0 to 7. Although all these are file system based cards, it seems likely that an integer allows to distinguish the passwords on other cards, too.

The third argument to `verifyPassword(...)` method is the password itself. It should be passed as a byte array, giving the application full control of the encoding of the password. To use a protected PIN path, in which the application does not get to know the password at all, null can be passed instead. In this case, it is the service's responsibility to query the password, to encode it, and to prepare an appropriate APDU to send to the smart card. If the terminal supports it, this responsibility may be delegated to it. The return value for performing card holder verification is a boolean that indicates whether the password was correct or not. Since the return value is generated by the `CardService`, it can only be trusted if the `CardService` is trusted.

Passing the password as a byte array leaves the question of the length of the byte array. File system based, ISO 7816-4 compliant smart cards have a password length of 8 byte. However, considering Java Card and the flexibility of applets, other password lengths may also occur. To allow the application to prepare a byte array of appropriate length, the `getPasswordLength(...)` method can be used to query the required length. For ISO cards, this method can simply be implemented to return a constant 8, causing minimal overhead.

Other properties of the password, for example the encoding and padding rules, can be rather complex and may depend on application data that is not accessible to the `CardService`.

10.1.5
The CardService Exceptions

Figure 10.9 shows the rich exception structure provided by the `CardService` layer. These exceptions can be thrown by OCF classes or by `CardService` implementations.

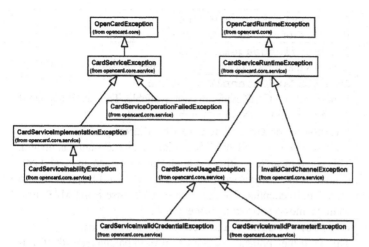

The checked exceptions (those exceptions that must be explicitly declared in a `throws` clause) stemming from **CardServiceException** should be caught and handled by the application. These are described in Table 10.2.

CardServiceException
Base class for all CardService checked exceptions.
CardServiceImplementationException
Indicates a possible problem with the `CardService`, for example a bug or mismatch between `CardService` and smart card.
CardServiceOperationFailedException
Indicates that the `CardService` attempted an operation that could not be carried out by the card, such as deleting a DF that still contains files.
CardServiceInabilityException
Thrown when the CardService detects that it cannot carry out the required operation. This could come up when using secure messaging, which may be disabled due to US export restrictions.

Exceptions stemming from **CardServiceRuntimeException** generally indicate an error in the application, such as a `null` reference passed as a required parameter. These are explained in Table 10.3.

Table 10.3: CardService Runtime Exceptions

CardServiceRuntimeException Base class for all CardService runtime exceptions.
CardServiceUsageException Indicates that the application has used the CardService incorrectly.
InvalidCardChannelException Indicates that a CardChannel is not available. This could happen if the card is removed before it can be accessed.
CardServiceInvalidCredentialException Thrown when the credential used with secure messaging is invalid. This could mean that either the application supplied an invalid credential to the CardService, or that the smart card responded with an invalid credential. The latter case could arise if the MAC protecting a message is wrong, for example.
CardServiceInvalidParameterException Thrown if the application passes an invalid parameter to the CardService.

10.2 The CardService Optional Components

The `opencard.opt.service` package extends the `CardService` layer core functionality by providing additional classes and exceptions. We will begin by explaining the optional classes, which are shown in Figure 10.10.

CardService-Interface

The **`CardServiceInterface`** is provided merely as a convenience to the `CardService` programmer. The two methods defined are those from the `CardService` base class that are frequently used by application programmers.

Figure 10.10: CardService Optional Classes

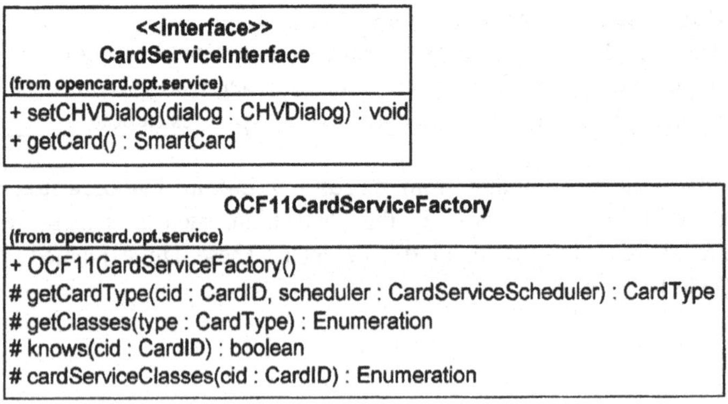

<<Interface>>
CardServiceInterface
(from opencard.opt.service)
+ setCHVDialog(dialog : CHVDialog) : void
+ getCard() : SmartCard
OCF11CardServiceFactory
(from opencard.opt.service)
+ OCF11CardServiceFactory()
# getCardType(cid : CardID, scheduler : CardServiceScheduler) : CardType
# getClasses(type : CardType) : Enumeration
# knows(cid : CardID) : boolean
# cardServiceClasses(cid : CardID) : Enumeration

When the `CardService` programmer defines a new interface by extending `CardServiceInterface`, these two frequently used methods will be available to the application programmer without downcasting to the `CardService` base class.

The **OCF11CardServiceFactory** retains the function of the OCF Version 1.1 `CardServiceFactory`. It is provided for compatibility purposes.

Compatibility with OCF 1.1

Figure 10.11 shows the exception hierarchy after addition of the `opencard.opt.service` exceptions. The optional package adds one new runtime exception and six new checked exceptions. Table 10.4 explains how they are used.

CardServiceMissingCredentialsException   The `CardService` is responsible for satisfying the access conditions required for card access. It does this by using the security credentials provided by the application. If the application does not provide the required credentials, this runtime exception is thrown.
CardServiceUnexpectedResponseException   Thrown when the `CardService` receives an unexpected response from the card.
CardServiceInvalidCommandException   Thrown when the smart card indicates it cannot interpret the command sent by the `CardService`.
CardServiceMissingAuthorizationException   Thrown when the `CardService` cannot fulfill the access conditions required by the card. Indicates a limitation or bug in the `CardService` implementation.
CardServiceObjectNotAvailableException   The requested object cannot be located on the smart card.
CardServiceInsufficientMemoryException   Thrown when the smart card runs out of EEPROM space. This could happen when a new Java Card applet is being loaded onto the card, for example.
CardServiceResourceNotFoundException   Thrown when the `CardService` cannot find the necessary resources.

Table 10.4: Optional CardService Exceptions

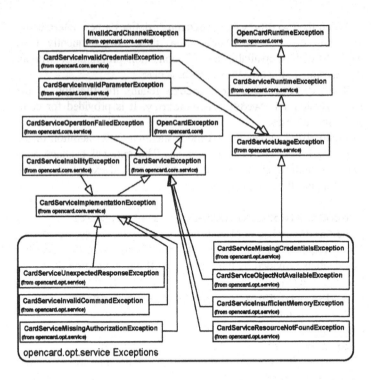

opencard.opt.service Exceptions

10.3
Standard CardService Interfaces

Standard
interfaces

The OpenCard Consortium Technical Committee is responsible for, among other things, definition of standard `CardService` interfaces. Once these interfaces have been defined, they are made available in the OCF reference implementation. Card manufacturers and on-card application providers are encouraged to implement these interfaces for their cards. Off-card application providers are encouraged to base applications on them.

Application
advantages

When an off-card application is based on a standard `Card-Service` interface, support for a new smart card can be added simply by implementing the interface for the new card. The OCF factory mechanism will select and instantiate the appropriate `CardService` implementation for the inserted card.

Card provider
advantages

When the card manufacturer or on-card application provider implements standard `CardService` interfaces, the cards can automatically be used in existing OCF applications.

The OpenCard Consortium welcomes proposals for new standard interfaces. Contact the consortium through the OpenCard homepage on http://www.opencard.org/ for more information on the standardization process.

The OCF reference implementation provides standard interfaces, or better interface groups. For some of these standard interfaces we will describe the details in the following sections. The ISO File System `CardService` provides access to ISO file system-oriented cards, the Signature `CardService` digital signature generation and key handling, and the Application Management `CardService` describing and managing on-card applications.

Current standard interfaces

10.3.1
The ISO File System CardService

Although called an interface, this standard package contains a set of classes and interfaces that encapsulate file access for ISO file system cards. Figure 10.12 shows the `opencard.opt.iso.fs` package containing these classes.

This package extends `opencard.opt.service` to obtain the standard methods required by all `CardService` modules. It also extends the `opencard.opt.security` package to make it possible to implement secure messaging.

Extending OpenCard packages

The file I/O capability defined by the ISO file system package is modeled after the stream I/O classes from the `java.io` package.

The ISO file system package contains three interfaces that must be implemented in order to provide support for a specific smart card. These are the `FileAccessCardService`, the `FileSystemCard-Service`, and the `CardFileInfo` interfaces. Figure 10.35 shows the main abstractions provided by this package in more detail.

ISO file system interfaces

The **FileAccessCardService** provides methods for accessing transparent as well as structured files on the smart card as defined by the ISO 7816 specification. Methods include **read(...)**, **readRe-cord(...)**, **write(...)**, and **appendRecord(...)**. These methods are primarily intended for use by `CardFile` and associated classes.

File access

The **FileSystemCardService** defines extensions to the ISO 7816 functionality. The application can use methods from this interface to create, delete, invalidate, and rehabilitate files.

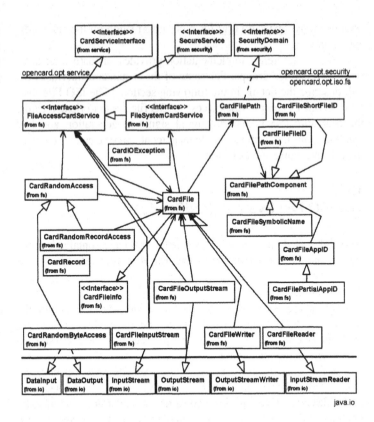

CardFileInfo

The **CardFileInfo** interface provides information about the structure of a file. It provides methods that allow the application to determine whether the file is a directory, or whether it is a cyclic file, etc. This information is typically contained in the file header, which is returned by the select command. Since the file header is card operating system specific, the CardFileInfo interface must be implemented separately for each supported card.

CardFile

The **CardFile** class is the main abstraction of this package, representing a file or directory on the card. The CardFile uses the implementation interfaces to select, read, and write files on the smart card. It uses CardFilePath and its subclasses to specify paths on the card.

Each CardFile object represents exactly one file on the card. The file is selected when the object is constructed. If only a File-AccessCardService instance is provided, the root directory is automatically selected. It is also possible to construct a CardFile object using an absolute path specification or using path information relative to an existing `CardFile` object.

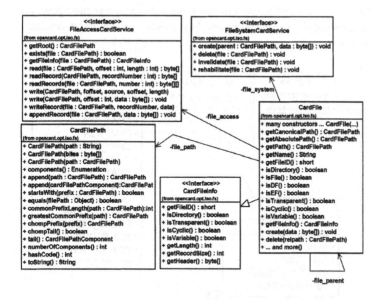

Figure 10.13:
Main ISO FS
Classes

The `CardFilePath` object and its subclasses encapsulate the various means of addressing files on a smart card. Files can be addressed through the following mechanisms:

CardFilePath

- File ID paths: the path is specified by a sequence of two-byte file identifiers as defined in ISO 7816-4.

- Short File ID: the path is specified by a one-byte file identifier (EF's only).

- Application ID: 5-16 bytes for selecting applications as defined by ISO 7816-4/5

- Symbolic paths: a sequence of symbolic names

The `CardFilePath` class also provides numerous methods for manipulating and extracting portions of paths.

10.3.2
The Signature CardService

This group of interfaces defines methods for digital signature generation, signature verification, and key handling. The interfaces are
contained in the opencard.opt.signature package.

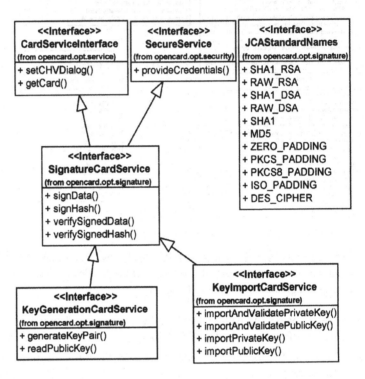

Figure 10.14:
Signature
CardService

Interface split   This package provides three interfaces that together provide the
signature capability. The interface was split into three parts to reflect
the view that the complete functionality will often not be needed.
During personalization, the KeyGenerationCardService and
KeyImportCardService functionality will be required. After deployment, the capability provided by the SignatureCardService
will be required. Also, not all smart cards provide key generation capability. The CardService provider can implement a subset of
these interfaces depending on the capabilities of the smart card being
used.

Signature
generation   The **SignatureCardService** extends the CardServiceInterface from the opencard.opt.service package and the Se-
cureService interface from the opencard.opt.security package.

Methods allow for signature generation and verification for either a hash generated by the application or on raw data. If the operation is carried out on raw data, the hash is generated on the card and signed or verified.

The `KeyGenerationCardService` supports key pair generation on the card. The `generateKeyPair`(...) method causes a key pair to be generated on the card. The `readPublicKey`(...) method allows the resulting public key to be retrieved. The private key remains on the smart card.

Key generation

The KeyImportCardService allows public and private keys to be imported onto the smart card.

10.3.3
The Application Management CardService

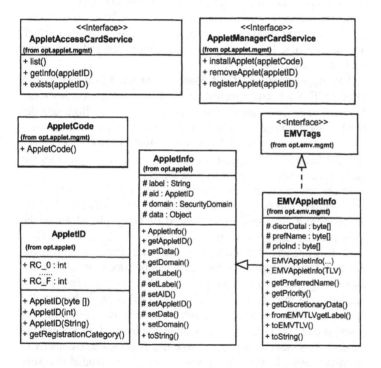

Figure 10.15: Application Management

The base classes for describing and managing on-card applications, or better, applets are contained in the package open-card.opt.applet and opencard.opt.applet.mgmt. The term "applet" as we use it in this documentation can be either a program, which is executed on the card itself (like a typical Java Card applet), or it can be an application specific set of files and directory structures (as we will find on ISO compliant file system oriented cards). In both cases an `AppletID` is used to identify the applet in a world wide unique way. There are standards which define how each smart card should hold a directory of `AppletIDs`, allowing any card-external application to decide, if it supports a particular card or not. Card-resident applets are described by meta-information encapsulated in `AppletInfo` objects. This meta-information includes the user-friendly label, the `AppletID` and the `SecurityDomain` to which the applet belongs.

You can obtain the `AppletInfos` from your `SmartCard` object using the `AppletAccessCardService`'s **list()** method. `AppletID` is a subclass of `ID` and has been formerly named as `ApplicationID`. In OCF 1.1.1, the `AppletInfo` has been named as `ApplicationTemplateclass`. The `ID` class can be used as superclass for any other kind of identification (such as a GUID).

In the package `opencard.opt.applet` a base class `CardService` named `BasicAppletCardService` is introduced, which implements logic for selecting the applets on a card and for keeping track of the selection.

The Application and Card Management Card Services known from OCF 1.1.1 are renamed in OCF 1.2 to `AppletAccessCardService` and `AppletManagerCardService`. Both are defined in the package `opencard.opt.applet.mgmt`. The `AppletAccessCardService` includes the methods **list()**, **exists()** and **getInfo()**. The `AppletManagerCardService` provides the methods to install, register or remove applets.

Implementations of these `CardServices` will be placed in specific domain sub-packages like `opencard.opt.javacard.mgmt` or `opencard.opt.emv.mgmt` instead of being placed all in the same package `opencard.opt.mgmt`, as it was the case with OCF 1.1.1. It is intended that the `AppletInfo` class can be extended and that new features/types of information can be added for specific domains (e.g. `JavaCardAppletInfo`). The abstract class named `AppletCode` models the actual code of a card applet to be installed in the card. It can be constructed either by specifying a file name that is supposed to contain the code, or giving all bytes of the code in parameter. This class is the generic type that is passed as parameter to an install method. As in the previous case, it is intended that subclasses can be defined, with new features and/or different ways of reading a file to get the actual applet code.

11 The OCF Security Concepts

Security is a central issue with smart cards. Security protocols protect access to data on the smart card through secure messaging. Additionally, they allow the off-card application to use cryptographic algorithms and keys stored on the smart card for digitally signing data and signature verification. Implementing a smart card security concept requires dealing with environmental and legal constraints as well as with smart card specifics.

Security

Secure messaging protects communication between the application and the smart card. A message authentication code (MAC) can be used to detect changes in the transmitted data, and encryption can be used to ensure privacy.

Secure messaging

This is an area where the standardization process has not progressed as much as the application programmer would perhaps wish. Each different card type tends to implement its own mix of algorithms and to use them in its own way. Cards can differ in which APDU bytes are used to calculate the MAC code, and in the padding bytes used when encrypting the data, for example.

Lack of standards

On a 7816-4 file system-oriented card, the card type determines the available secure messaging mechanisms. However, with freely programmable cards such as the Java Card, secure messaging can also differ from application to application.

The CardService, as a card or application specific component, could deal with some of these differences, but the application environment must also be taken into account. The off-card application and the environment in which it runs will determine how access to the cryptographic algorithms and keys needed for secure messaging can be obtained. Often the keys will not be directly available to the application, but will instead be stored in a security access module, or SAM. Some cards may require the use of a key derived from an unprotected card characteristic such as the card serial number. A SAM could also be used to hold the special algorithm and master key used

Security access module

to generate the derived key for communication with the inserted smart card. Programming such environment dependencies into the `CardService` would reduce its general usefulness.

Internal and External authentication

ISO 7816-4 specifies two commands for authentication. EXTERNAL AUTHENTICATE is used to satisfy access conditions that may be imposed by the smartcard, it therefore authenticates the external world to the card. INTERNAL AUTHENTICATE is the reverse operation; it authenticates the card to the external world (see also Section 4.2.1 and 4.2.2).

In both cases, authentication is based on the knowledge of a secret. This can be either a secret key, using a symmetric cryptographic algorithm, or a private key in the case of an asymmetric algorithm. The authenticating party (challenger) has to know either the same secret key or the matching public key. The party to be authenticated receives a random challenge, encrypts it with the secret and sends the result back to the challenger. The challenger uses the same key (in the case of a symmetric algorithm) or the matching public key (in the case of an asymmetric algorithm) to verify that the secret is know to it's partner.

For external authentication, the smartcard needs information about the key (secret or public) to be used to verify the outside world's knowledge of the secret. For internal authentication, the smartcard needs information about the secret for which to prove the knowledge. In OCF 1.1 `CardService` interfaces, only the `CardServices` in `opencard.opt.signature` explicitly reference keys, using interfaces defined in `opencard.opt.security`. The `CardServices` in `opencard.opt.signature` deal with asymmetric cryptography, and the key referencing interfaces cover only public and private keys. OCF 1.2 introduced a new interface `SecretKeyRef`. To allow the definition of a single interface for authentication, regardless of the symmetry of the underlying cryptographic algorithm, a common base interface for all three kinds of keys has to be introduced, resulting in the following inheritance tree:

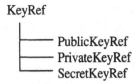

KeyRef

    ├────── PublicKeyRef
    ├────── PrivateKeyRef
    └────── SecretKeyRef

Credentials

The OpenCard Framework uses **Credential** objects to encapsulate such environment dependencies on cryptographic keys and algorithms. The application creates credentials appropriate for the environment in which it runs and passes them to the CardService, which uses them to protect the data exchanged with the card.

A single smart card can contain several keys that are used under various circumstances. The CardService must also have a mechanism for selecting the appropriate key on the card when using secure messaging to access a file or application. This mechanism must be general enough to accommodate the selection mechanisms available on different cards.

OCF introduces **KeyRef** and **KeyFile** classes to specify the on-card key. These are useful when signing data, internal and external authentication as well as when using secure messaging.

KeyRef, KeyFile

In addition to the technical challenges, we must also deal with the export restrictions on cryptographic code imposed by some countries, notably the United States. Freely exportable code is restricted in the cryptographic algorithms that may be used, and in the manner in which cryptography in employed.

Export restrictions

In the following sections we will see how the OpenCard Framework security concept deals with these issues.

11.1
OpenCard Security Overview

Before getting onto the class description, we will cover the basic ideas behind the OpenCard security concept.

Since the CardService is the OpenCard component that deals with card and card application specifics, it must also implement the appropriate security mechanisms. The application using the CardService is written to run in a particular environment. In particular, the application must be able to obtain access to the cryptographic algorithms needed for secure messaging. The environment can provide these algorithms either directly in software or through use of a SAM. The application also has access, directly or indirectly, to the required keys.

The exportable version of the OpenCard Framework does not implement any cryptographic algorithms; this is to avoid conflict with U.S. export control regulations. Since the CardService, and not the framework itself, implements data security mechanisms, the CardService provider must observe the appropriate export rules.

Exportable OCF version

The application must provide the CardService with the algorithms and keys. This is done through use of **credentials**, which are objects encapsulating key information and the corresponding algorithms. The credential implements an interface that allows the cryp-

Credentials

tographic algorithm to be executed using the encapsulated key information.

The mechanism used to execute the algorithm is up to the credential implementation. In its simplest form, the credential will implement the algorithm directly in software and will hold the key information in a data field. If a SAM is used, the credential will access the SAM to execute the cryptographic algorithm. In some cases, the SAM will be available on a remote machine rather than locally. In this case, the credential will contain the necessary code to communicate with the remote SAM.

The idea of a credential is central to the OpenCard security concept. The classes and interfaces provided in the opencard.opt.security package define the mechanism through which the application can create credentials and pass them to the CardService. These classes are shown in Figure 11.1 along with the Java Security classes from the java.security.interfaces and java.security.rity packages that the OCF classes build upon.

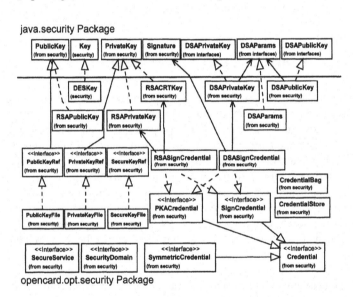

Java security classes

For the most part, the Java security interfaces used by OCF are containers for cryptographic key information. The **Key** class provides simple methods describing the key information it contains. **PrivateKey** and **PublicKey** each extend Key merely to provide type safety when dealing with public key algorithms. The interfaces **DSAPrivateKey**, **DSAPublicKey**, and **DSAParams** provide accessors for DSA key parameters as well as type safety when using the DSA algorithm. The `Signature` class from the Java security package is used to compute digital signatures.

11.2
OpenCard Security Classes

To begin with, we should note that the OpenCard Framework distribution conforms to U.S. export restrictions. Extreme care was taken to structure OCF so that cryptographic code must be provided by the application or by the specific `CardService` implementation.

The OpenCard developers divided the actual framework code consisting of the `opencard.core` and `opencard.opt` packages into a freely exportable deliverable and an export-restricted deliverable package. The freely exportable OCF package contains no code that can be used for data encryption. The export-restricted deliverable package contains exactly one class[1] – `RSASignCredential` from the `opencard.opt.security` package. Since this class directly implements the RSA public key algorithm for arbitrary data with an arbitrary key length, it cannot be freely exported from North America.

Figure 11.2 shows the OpenCard security classes separated into categories according to their use. The **Cryptographic Key Classes** define wrappers for cryptographic key material. The **Smart Card Key Classes** provide a means for specifying which key on the smart card is to be used for a secure messaging operation. The **Card-Service Interface Classes** influence the `CardService` interface directly. The **Credentials** provide interfaces to cryptographic algorithms and data definitions.

We will cover each of these categories in detail in the following sections.

---

[1] The actual export-restricted deliverable package contains one OCF class and additional classes used by the reference implementation and demonstration code.

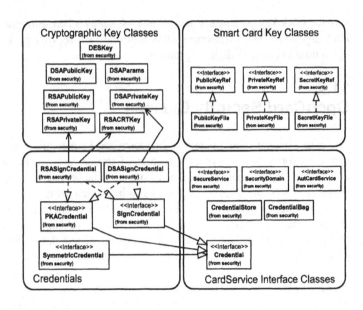

11.2.1
Cryptographic Key Classes

Key classes Figure 11.3 shows the cryptographic key classes with their methods. The classes whose methods are not displayed belong to the java.security and java.security.interface packages. Relationships among the java.security classes are not displayed.

In general, these classes can store key information. All key classes implement the base class methods inherited from java.security.key. The **getAlgorithm()** method retrieves the name of the algorithm with which this key is to be used. The **getEncoded()** method retrieves the key in a standard format. The final common method, **getFormat()**, returns the name of the format returned by **getEncoded()**. Additional methods allow access to the key material appropriately for the involved algorithm.

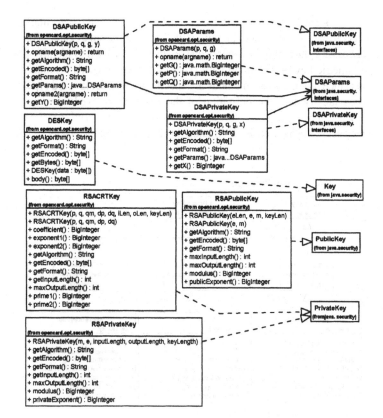

Figure 11.3:
Cryptographic
Key Classes

11.2.2
The Smart Card Key Classes

Different types of smart cards store keys in different ways. File system oriented cards generally store keys in files, while a Java Card stores key information in objects.

Smart card keys

When performing a cryptographic operation such as signing with the card, the key to be used must be specified. The different ways keys are stored on a card are reflected in the methods for key selection. Some cards require the key to be specified using a file path, while others require a key index or number.

The smart card key classes shown in Figure 11.4 provide a general mechanism for key identification and also a specific implementation for cards that require a key to be identified by file path.

The `PublicKeyRef` and `PrivateKeyRef` tag interfaces mark classes that can be used to identify a PKA key on the smart card. The `SecureKeyRef` interface marks classes that can be used to identify a symmetric key on the smart card. These interfaces provide no methods since the necessary methods are specific to a particular card type. They are used in the definition of the `SignatureCardService`, `KeyImportCardService`, and `KeyGenerationCardService` interfaces (see Section 10.3, "Standard `CardService` Interfaces").

Figure 11.4:
Smart Card Key
Classes

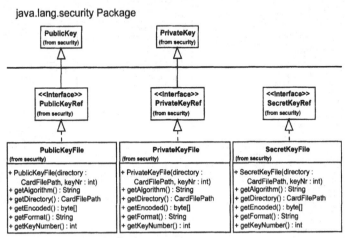

opencard.opt.security Package

Key files

The `PublicKeyFile, PrivateKeyFile`, and `SecretKeyFile` classes implement the corresponding key reference interfaces specifically for ISO file system oriented cards. They contain a `CardFilePath` object that points to the proper directory on the card and a key number to be used within that path.

Signing data

The digital signature `CardService` implementations provided in the `com.ibm.opencard.signature` package of the reference implementation use these classes. For example, in order to sign data using the `MFCSignatureService`, the application must create a `PublicKeyFile` object that points to the desired key on the smart card. This object is passed to the `signData(...)` method along with the data to be signed. The `MFCSignatureService` uses information from the `PublicKeyFile` object to select the key before passing the data to the card.

11.2.3
CardService Interface Classes

The classes discussed in this section are primarily used for secure messaging. Their goal is to allow the application to communicate with smart cards implementing diverse types of secure messaging. The classes discussed in this section are shown in Figure 11.5.

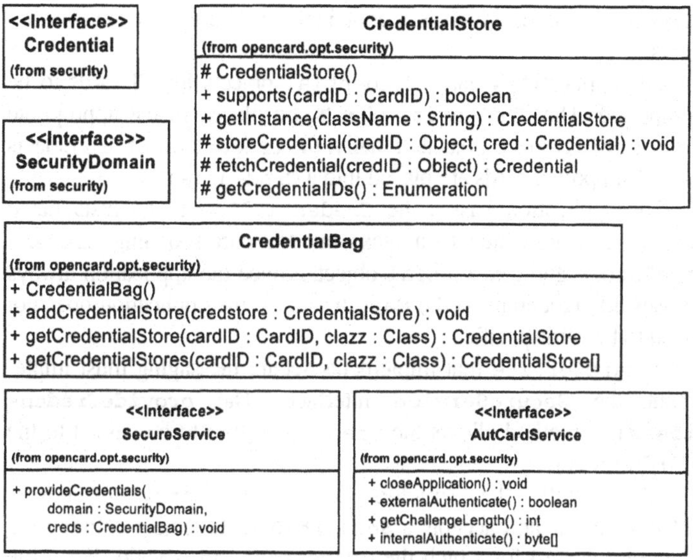

Figure 11.5: CardService Interface Classes

```
┌─────────────────┐   ┌──────────────────────────────────────────────────────┐
│   <<Interface>> │   │                    CredentialStore                     │
│    Credential   │   │               (from opencard.opt.security)             │
│  (from security)│   ├──────────────────────────────────────────────────────┤
└─────────────────┘   │ # CredentialStore()                                    │
                      │ + supports(cardID : CardID) : boolean                  │
┌─────────────────┐   │ + getInstance(className : String) : CredentialStore    │
│   <<Interface>> │   │ # storeCredential(credID : Object, cred : Credential) : void │
│  SecurityDomain │   │ # fetchCredential(credID : Object) : Credential        │
│  (from security)│   │ # getCredentialIDs() : Enumeration                     │
└─────────────────┘   └──────────────────────────────────────────────────────┘
```

```
┌────────────────────────────────────────────────────────────────────────┐
│                              CredentialBag                               │
│                     (from opencard.opt.security)                         │
├────────────────────────────────────────────────────────────────────────┤
│ + CredentialBag()                                                        │
│ + addCredentialStore(credstore : CredentialStore) : void                 │
│ + getCredentialStore(cardID : CardID, clazz : Class) : CredentialStore   │
│ + getCredentialStores(cardID : CardID, clazz : Class) : CredentialStore[]│
└────────────────────────────────────────────────────────────────────────┘
```

```
┌──────────────────────────────┐  ┌──────────────────────────────┐
│        <<Interface>>         │  │        <<Interface>>         │
│        SecureService         │  │        AutCardService        │
│   (from opencard.opt.security)│  │  (from opencard.opt.security)│
├──────────────────────────────┤  ├──────────────────────────────┤
│ + provideCredentials(        │  │ + closeApplication() : void  │
│     domain : SecurityDomain, │  │ + externalAuthenticate() : boolean │
│     creds : CredentialBag) : void │ + getChallengeLength() : int │
│                              │  │ + internalAuthenticate() : byte[] │
└──────────────────────────────┘  └──────────────────────────────┘
```

As discussed previously, the credential encapsulates a crypto-graphic algorithm along with key data. Since the methods needed by the credential are highly dependent on the algorithm used, the `Cre-dential` interface provided by OCF is just a tag interface.

Credential, algorithms, keys

This interface is extended for some common algorithms by other classes in this package, which we will discuss shortly. If needed, other `CardService` implementations can extend `Credential` for algorithms not yet supported by the standard OpenCard package.

`Credentials` whose algorithms are implemented completely in software can be provided along with the `CardService`. To use these, the application must instantiate the `Credential` by providing the required key material.

If the application environment calls for the keys and algorithms to be stored in a SAM, the application will have to implement a `Cre-dential` for the card or cards in use.

CredentialStore	Credentials for a specific smart card type are collected in a **CredentialStore** object. CredentialStore is an abstract class that must be implemented to support a particular type of card. The CardService provider generally implements the CredentialStore since it must match the CardService.
CredentialStore methods	The **fetchCredential**(...) and **storeCredential**(...) methods access the credentials with the help of an identifier whose type is defined appropriately for the smart card.
CredentialBag	Support for different types of smart cards is provided through the CredentialBag, which is a container for CredentialStore objects.
Setting up credentials	The application creates Credential objects for all cards to be supported. The Credential objects are placed in the appropriate CredentialStore objects. Finally, the CredentialStore objects for all supported cards are placed into a CredentialBag.

The application passes the CredentialBag to an instantiated CardService, which then picks out the corresponding CredentialStore and Credential objects. Since the application always passes all credentials to the CardService, the application does not need to be card specific. |
| *Secure CardService* | A CardService that implements secure messaging must implement the **SecureService** interface. The **provideCredentials**(...) method allows the CredentialBag to be passed to the CardService. |
| *Security domain* | Along with the CredentialBag, the **provideCredentials**(...) method accepts a **SecurityDomain** object defining the area on the card for which the CredentialBag is valid. For a file system oriented card, the SecurityDomain interface is implemented by the opencard.opt.iso.fs.CardFilePath class, which designates a specific dedicated file on the smart card.

The following code fragments illustrate how the application uses the credential mechanism.

First the application creates credentials for the cards to be supported and sets up the CredentialStore and CredentialBag objects. This can be done during initialization if the user operation is clear from the beginning. |

```
rootKeyDomain = new CardFilePath(":3f00");
rootKeyBag    = new CredentialBag();
MFCCredentialStore store = new MFCCredentialStore();

store.storeCredential(0,
        new DESSecureCredential("0x6b258f15d07c43ea"));
store.storeCredential(1,
        new DESSecureCredential("0x31323437383b3d3e"));
store.storeCredential(5,
        new DESSecureCredential("0x70737576797a7c7f"));

rootKeyBag.addCredentialStore(store);
```

Filling the
CredentialBag

This fragment sets up a key bag for the root security domain. The
MFCCredentialStore class extends the CredentialStore abstract class for the IBM MFC smart cards. It can be found in the
com.ibm.opencard.access package in the OCF reference implementation.

The **DESSecureCredential** class implements the DES algorithm in software. For this reason it is in the export restricted OCF
package. The UML diagram shown in Figure 11.6 gives an idea of
the functionality provided by a typical credential.

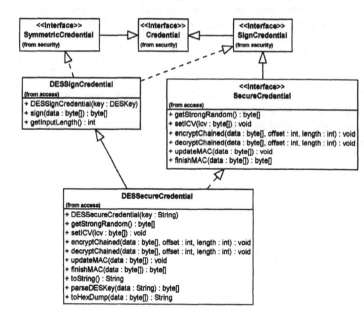

Figure 11.6:
The DESSecure
Credential

Each DESSecureCredential is constructed by providing a key
in string format. The DES key is parsed and stored by the credential.
When cryptographic methods are called by the CardService to

implement secure messaging, the key provided to the constructor is used.

The previous code fragment sets up the credentials for only a single card. To support additional cards, CredentialStore objects of the appropriate type must be instantiated and filled with Credential objects. The application then adds the CredentialStore objects for the additional cards to the existing CredentialBag.

After setting up the CredentialBag, the next code fragment waits for a card to be inserted, obtains a CardService, passes the CredentialBag to the CardService, and then reads some data.

After obtaining a FileAccessCardService, the application calls **provideCredentials**(...) to pass the credentials and key domain to it. The application then goes on to read some data from the card. If secure messaging is required, the CardService will protect the APDU packets appropriately. From the application point of view, this happens transparently.

Using credentials

```
...
SmartCard sc = SmartCard.waitForCard (cr);
if (sc != null) {
  FileAccessCardService fs = (FileAccessCardService)
       sc.getCardService (FileAccessCardService.class, true);
  fs.provideCredentials(rootKeyDomain, rootKeyBag);
  CardFilePath file = new CardFilePath(":3f00:b010:bb04");
  byte[] data = fs.read(file, 0, 20);
...
```

Card independent programming

From this example we also see that the application contains no code specific to a particular CardService. The application will work with any card as long as a FileAccessCardService and corresponding credentials are available.

11.2.4
Credentials

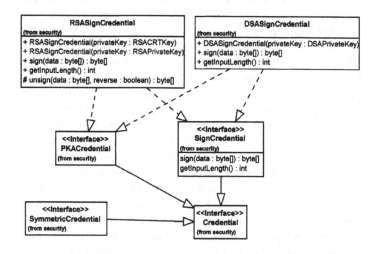

These classes extend the `Credential` interface for specific purposes.

SymmetricCredential is a tag interface that designates credentials using a symmetric key algorithm. Similarly, **PKACredential** tags credentials based on a public key algorithm.

Defined credentials

The **SignCredential** interface adds two methods needed to sign data. This type of credential always signs a single block of data whose length is dependent on the algorithm and key length used. The caller is responsible for data padding, if needed. This interface will usually be extended by `CardService` specific classes to provide a more general interface like those shown in Figure 11.6.

The **getInputLength**(...) method returns the required length of the input block. The **sign**(...) method calculates the digital signature of a single data block.

The **DSASignCredential** is a generally exportable signature credential based on the DSA algorithm. It is exportable since it uses the `java.security.Signature` class to calculate the signature rather than implementing the algorithm directly in code.

The `RSASignCredential` class directly implements the RSA algorithm. For this reason, it is not part of the freely exportable distribution.

A `CardService` that supports internal/external authentication must implement the **AutCardService** interface. The **externalAuthenticate**(...) method performs an external authentication against the smartcard, the **internalAuthenticate**(...) method re-

AutCardService

quests an internal authentication from the smartcard. To get the length of the challenge for internal authentication, the method `getChallengeLength`(...) can be used. The terminal or host application can then prepare a random challenge of the given length. The encrypted challenge has to be checked, either in software or by using a Secure Access Module (SAM) or backend host system. The result of the internal authentication is a boolean value that specifies whether the card is in possession of the secret in question or not. Using a credential here is not appropriate, since the interpretation of the smartcard's response cannot be the responsibility of the CardService. Internal authentication is performed to verify that the smartcard can be trusted. When passing a credential, the application would have to query from the credential whether the internal authentication was successful, for which a credential has no method. Instead, the `internalAuthenticate`(...) method is a lower level interface, where the random challenge is passed in as a byte array, and the encrypted response is returned as another byte array.

The `closeApplication`(...) method resets the achieved external authentications on the smartcard. Typically, other permanent access conditions that have been satisfied will also be reset. If the card does not allow to reset access conditions for a specific application, it is expected that all access conditions for all on-card applications are reset. The name of this method implies that an application on the smartcard is first selected and then opened by performing external authentication, giving access to the application data. By resetting the external authentication, the on-card application therefore gets closed.

External authentication can be required to satisfy access conditions that are imposed by the card. The operation expected to be performed when invoking this method is to reset the state in the smartcard so that these access conditions are no longer satisfied. This avoids that another terminal or host application accesses the smartcard's data without proving its authorization first.

11.3
Running OCF in Browsers

OCF in a browser

One especially interesting application of the OpenCard Framework is access to smart cards from Java applets running in a web browser. In this section, we explain how OCF adapts to the security models used by different browsers and how signed applets can use the OpenCard Framework.

In Section 11.3.1, we give an overview of browser security models and point out their impact on the framework. In Section 11.3.2, we describe how invocation of privileged methods is handled in the OpenCard Framework without introducing browser dependencies in the framework's core. Finally, in Section 11.3.3, we discuss the security implications.

11.3.1
Browser Security Models

The OpenCard Framework encapsulates access to smart card readers and therefore needs to access system resources not accessible from the Java sandbox. Communication with the card reader requires hardware access and configuration of the framework requires access to the system properties. For example, when using the Java Communication API or the OCF PC/SC support to access the card reader, a shared library must be loaded.

System and shared library access

The JDK 1.1 already provided an extension to the sandbox that allowed Java classes contained in a signed JAR-file to access all system resources. However, the security model was very primitive: unsigned applets were limited to the Java sandbox while signed applets were allowed unlimited system access.

JDK 1.1 security model

Users soon realized that a security model with finer granularity was needed, but before Sun responded to that need with the improved Java 2 security model, Microsoft and Netscape had introduced their own security models (see [NET01], [MIC01]). These models are based on signed archives that must be created with proprietary packing and signing tools.

In contrast to the JDK 1.1 security policy, signed applets cannot access system resources by default. An applet that needs to perform a privileged action must explicitly request the required privilege from the web browser's `PrivilegeManager` before actually performing the action. This introduces a dependency of the applet's code on browser-specific privilege manager classes.

Browser security models

The task was to make the OpenCard Framework work together with the predominant browsers on the market without introducing a direct dependency on browser-specific behavior – and doing this without weakening security.

OCF concept is browser independent

11.3.2
Invocation of Privileged Methods

SystemAccess

In the OpenCard Framework, all access to protected system resources is performed via the `SystemAccess` class. This class provides instance methods to access protected system resources (See Section 8.2.4, "System Access", for detailed discussion).

All OpenCard code that needs to perform privileged actions (getting a system property, for example) calls the appropriate `SystemAccess` method rather than accessing the system directly:

```
SystemAccess sys = SystemAccess.getSystemAccess();
String services = sys.getProperty("opencard.services");
```

The OpenCard Framework obtains the current `SystemAccess` object and uses it to access the system.

Installing
browser-specific
object

The default `SystemAccess` class accesses the system directly. When running within a browser, the applet must set the current `SystemAccess` object within its **init()** method appropriately for the browser platform. This is done using the static **setSystemAccess(...)** method:

```
SystemAccess sys =
             opencard.opt.netscape.NetscapeSystemAccess();
SystemAccess.setSystemAccess(sys);
```

Figure 11.8 illustrates how a signed applet installs the required `SystemAccess` object.

Browser
support in OCF

OCF provides specific `SystemAccess` subclasses for the pre-dominant web browsers. The applet detects the browser environ-ment and installs the appropriate support. The applet can install `opencard.opt.netscape.NetscapeSystemAccess` when run-ning under Netscape Navigator and `opencard.opt.ms.MicrosoftSystemAccess` when running under MS Internet Explorer. The methods in these classes obtain the needed privileges before actually making a call to a privileged method as shown in the following example.

Netscape
SystemAccess
method

```
public String getProperty(String key) {
   Netscape.security.PrivilegeManager.
        enablePrivilege("UniversalPropertyRead");
   return System.getProperty(key);
}
```

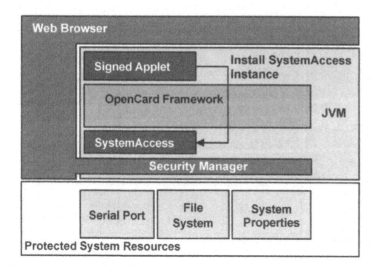

Figure 11.8:
OCF System
Resource
Access

11.3.3
Security Implications

The mechanism described in the previous section allows the Open-Card Framework to access protected system resources via a common interface, even on different browsers.

To assure that a SystemAccess instance can not be misused by other applets [NET97], the scope of each SystemAccess instance is limited to the thread that installed the specific subclass. In other words, each thread has its own SystemAccess instance.

If an applet uses OCF, it must be packaged with the appropriate, browser-specific subclass of SystemAccess and must install an instance of this class in each thread that uses OCF.

This approach guarantees that no applet that is not properly signed, but that is running in the same Java Virtual Machine as a signed applet, can make use of the system resources obtained by that signed applet. The situation is depicted in Figure 11.9.

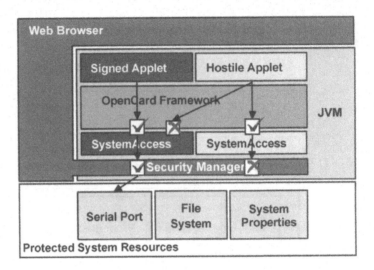

The signed applet has installed a SystemAccess instance for use by the OpenCard Framework. The SystemAccess class always checks the calling thread. Only the thread that installed the SystemAccess instance is allowed to perform system actions.

Since the SystemAccess instance is installed by the signed applet, there is no possibility for hostile applets to access the resources that the SystemAccess class makes available.

A hostile applet may install its own SystemAccess instance, but then the security manager of the browser will not grant any privileges to that SystemAccess instance, because it does not belong to a trusted principal.

Part III
Smart Card Application
Development Using OCF

"Don't condescend to unskilled labor,
try it for half a day first."

Brooks Atkinson

12 Using OCF

In this chapter, we develop two smart card sample applications. We start small with a simple application that reads the cardholder's name from a smart card. Then we work on a more advanced sample program.

Before we get started with the first sample program, we need to address installing and configuring OCF.

12.1
Preparing Your System

Prior to developing an application that accesses a smart card through OCF, you need to take care of a few prerequisites:

1. First you need to have Sun's JDK (Java Developer's Kit) installed – preferably version 1.1.6 or later. Sun provides the JDK on http://java.sun.com/products/jdk/. Alternatively, you can get the JDK with one of the commercially available integrated development environments for Java.

2. Download OCF from http://www.opencard.org/ (the web site of the OpenCard Consortium) and install it. Before you can start working with OCF, you need to bring the executable class files into the Java class path. If you are using native code together with OCF, like the bridge from OCF to PC/SC on Windows, you need to put this executable code into the path for native binary code.

3. Obtain a smart card reader with support for the OpenCard Framework. The OpenCard Consortium maintains a list of supported readers on http://www.opencard.org/.

4. Take the smart card provided in this book.

12.2
Configuring OCF on Your System

You must specify to OCF which smart card reader(s) and CardServices you want to use on your system. The OpenCard Framework reference implementation obtains its configuration information via the Java system properties. Java system properties are a platform-independent mechanism to make information about the operating system and the system configuration available to Java programs. The Java run-time environment defines a set of default properties that are always part of the system properties. Applications can extend this set of properties by loading additional properties and merging them with the system properties. This is how the OCF configuration parameters are added to the system properties.

The default that is established in the OCF reference implementation is to retrieve the OCF configuration properties from a file with the name opencard.properties. Next, we explain where to place that file and what entries to add to it.

12.2.1
Setting the OCF Configuration Properties

As we have explained in Chapter 9.1 "Terminal Layer Core Components", the CardTerminalRegistry singleton keeps track of the configured CardTerminal objects and the CardServiceRegistry keeps track of all CardServiceFactory classes that are able to instantiate a CardService. When the framework starts up, these registries are initialized based on the OCF configuration properties. The OpenCard.terminals property defines how the CardTerminalRegistry is initialized, the OpenCard.services property defines how the CardServiceRegistry is initialized.

The syntax of the property string for either property is as follows:

```
<record-0> <record-1> ... <record-n>
```

where records are separated by a white-space and each record consists of a class name and optional string parameters separated by a "|", i.e.

```
class-name|<parameter-1>| ... |<parameter-N>
```

To initially retrieve the property strings, OCF calls the method loadProperties() of an OpenCardConfigurationProvider.

The default for this provider is `OpenCardPropertyFileLoader`, which expects the properties in property files. It looks in the following places for the property files (in the given order):

1. `[java.home]/lib/opencard.properties`
2. `[user.home]/.opencard.properties`
3. `[user.dir]/opencard.properties`
4. `[user.dir]/.opencard.properties`

where [xxx.yyy] are the respective path variables as defined in the default system properties. It loads the properties from each file, in turn merging them with the system properties. If the properties file being read contains a property name that has already been defined in the properties set, the new definition will be ignored by default.

It is possible to override a property that is already defined in the properties set. You can do this by defining the property name anew and adding an additional property to your property file with the name `name.override` that has the value `true`.

A typical opencard.properties file is:

```
# Configure the CardService Registry:
# Use the service factory for the IBM MultiFunction Cards
OpenCard.services =\
  com.ibm.opencard.factory.MFCCardServiceFactory

# Configure the CardTerminal Registry:
OpenCard.terminals =\
com.gemplus.opencard.terminal.\
GemplusCardTerminalFactory|mygcr|GCR410|COM1

# Configure Tracing.  Detailed for all samples only:
OpenCard.trace = opencard:1 com.ibm:1 samples:7
```

Example opencard. properties

You can determine the locations where OCF will look for the opencard.properties file using the following short application:

```
import java.util.Properties;
public class queryPropertiesLocation {
  public static void main( String[] argv )   {
    Properties props = System.getProperties();
    System.out.println(
      "Looking for OpenCard Properties file in:\n\t" +
        props.getProperty("java.home") +
      "\\lib\\opencard.properties\n\t" +
        props.getProperty("user.home") +

      "\\.opencard.properties\n\t" +
        props.getProperty("user.dir") +
      "\\opencard.properties\n\t" +
        props.getProperty("user.dir") +
      "\\.opencard.properties\n");
  }
}
```

12.3
The First Simple Application

After you have set up your system with both hardware and software, you are now ready to develop the first simple smart card application. Let us develop a little program that reads the information on the cardholder from the smart card provided with this book (for a description of this card's layout see Appendix A "The Card"). This data is stored in the file EF_CARD_HOLDER_DATA, which has the file ID 0xC009. The operations to read or update this file are protected with the password "password".

We start our file ReadFile.java with some import statements, a class definition, and a main (...):

```
import opencard.core.service.SmartCard;
import opencard.core.service.CardRequest;
import opencard.opt.iso.fs.FileAccessCardService;
import opencard.opt.iso.fs.CardFile;

public class ReadFile {
    public static void main(String[] args) {
        System.out.println("reading file from smart card..
");
        // We will add the application code here.
        System.exit(0);
    }
}
```

Our reasons for using the classes `SmartCard`, `CardRequest`, `CardFile`, and the interface `FileAccessCardService` will become apparent shortly.

12.3.1
Starting OCF and Shutting it Down Again

A block of code that you will find in every program using OCF are the calls to start the framework before using it and to close down the framework when it is no longer used. The designers of OCF decided to make you start the framework explicitly instead of having it started implicitly during the first usage. The explicit starting was chosen, because during framework startup all configuration work and initialization of attached card terminals must be done. This could add unexpected delays when done implicitly during an access. In addition, errors might occur during the initialization phase. We need to provide exception-handling code for the framework startup as well as for the shutdown.

We need to make sure that the `SmartCard.shutdown()` command is executed no matter what, even if the program ends with an exception. The application must always release all system resources allocated by OCF. Therefore we place the `SmartCard.shutdown()` call into the `finally` block.

```
try {
    SmartCard.start();

    // Now OCF can be used

} catch (Exception e) {
    e.printStackTrace();

} finally { // even in case of an error..
    try{
        SmartCard.shutdown();
    } catch (Exception e) {
    e.printStackTrace();
    }
}
```

At first glance, it may seem strange that shutting down OCF could raise another exception. However, the shutdown may cause dynamic link libraries to be unloaded. You should not ignore errors in such operations because they would hint at serious problems in the operating system.

12.3.2
Obtaining a SmartCard Object via waitForCard(...)

After we took care of starting and closing the framework, we can now use OCF to interact with the smart card. We make our program wait until the user inserts her card. For waiting, we use Smart-Card.waitForCard(CardRequest), which blocks until a card is inserted that matches the given CardRequest.

```
// Wait for a smart card with a FileAccessCardService
CardRequest cr = new
            CardRequest(CardRequest.ANYCARD, null,

FileAccessCardService.class);
SmartCard sc = SmartCard.waitForCard(cr);

if (sc == null) {
  // A smart card was inserted that does not match
  // Handle how it would be appropriate in your app
}
else {
  // Here we need to add code to work with the card

  // We are done with this smart card.
  sc.close();
}
```

The arguments to the CardRequest constructor specify that we are interested only in cards for which a FileAccessCardService can be instantiated. If a card of the expected type is inserted, wait-ForCard(CardRequest) returns a SmartCard object that we will use in our application to refer to that card. This type of request accepts either an already inserted card in the reader or a newly inserted one. By using null as the card terminal parameter, we signal that all possible readers will be suitable for this CardRequest.

waitForCard(CardRequest) blocks the current thread until a card is inserted into the reader. A more elegant way of waiting for a card to be inserted uses CardTerminalEvents. This alternative requires only slightly more programming effort.

We will demonstrate the alternative in the next sample program. In this first simple example here we will wait synchronously for the card to be inserted.

After we have worked with the card and do not need to access it any longer, we call the close() method to indicate that the card is no longer needed in this application.

12.3.3
Obtaining a CardService Object

Now we have taken care of getting a SmartCard object to work with. Next, we need to create the required CardService. Then we specify which file we want to access and finally we read the data:

```
FileAccessCardService facs = (FileAccessCardService)
        sc.getCardService(FileAccessCardService.class, true);


CardFile file = new CardFile(facs, ":c009");


byte[] data = facs.read(file.getPath(),
                           0, file.getLength());
System.out.println(new String(data));
```

The second parameter to the getCardService(...) invocation specifies whether to wait blocking for the CardService until the channel to the card is available (true), or to get an exception if the channel is busy (false). We pass true to indicate that we want to wait until the channel to the card is available.

Files and directories on a card are represented by CardFile objects. These objects offer several methods to obtain information about files or directories.

For the constructor of the file that we want to read, we specify the file access card service and the absolute path. Thus, we create an instance of CardFile that now represents the elementary file containing the cardholder information. When we had created the card's data layout, we had allocated the file directly in the root directory of the smart card and given it the identifier 0xc009. This determines the path that we need to specify now for instantiating the CardFile object.

For the actual read operation we use an absolute path specification that we obtain from the CardFile object using its method get-

Path(). The first argument to the read() method is this absolute path, the second the offset within the file, where the read operation should start and the third argument specifies the number of bytes to read. With this single method invocation, the full content of the file is read and returned as a byte array. The byte array is converted into a string and printed to the screen.

This is all it takes to read a file from a file system smart card for which the corresponding FileAccessCardService exists. You may also note that even though the access to the file 0xc009 is protected using a card holder verification, the sample code contains no extra code to handle the verification step. This operation is provided directly through the FileAccessCardService.

You might want to download the complete source code for our simple example from http://www.opencard.org/SCJavaBook/. You find this sample in the package samples.readfile.

12.3.4
Using this Sample Program with Other Cards

If you want to use another smart card instead of the card that is provided in this book, you need to make sure that a FileAccessCard-Service is available for this card. The smart card should have a file with the ID 0xC009 and the access conditions for that file should be set to ALWAYS or CHV for read and write access.

Usually, the manufacturers of smart cards support the creation of new card layouts with appropriate tools. Of course, you might want to modify the program to read other existing files instead of the file with the ID 0xC009.

12.4
Smart Card Access of a Digital Signature Application

In Section 13.1 "Internet Stock Brokerage", we present a demo application that allows buying stock over the Internet and having the order digitally signed by the personal signature smart card. In this section, we show how the smart card related part of the brokerage applet can be implemented using the OpenCard Framework.

The client side of this demo application executes as an applet in a web browser. The applet should not make any assumptions on when the signature card is inserted. The user may have inserted the signature card before the applet was started or she may not insert it until being prompted to do so. In addition, if the applet is used for several orders, the card may be removed between submission of individual orders.

We can elegantly handle the different cases of card insertion and removal by encapsulating the signature card's functions in a separate object that is always aware of the presence or absence of the signature card. This object can indicate to the applet when it has to prompt for a signature card. As type of this object, we define a class named SignatureCard. We provide this class with methods for reacting on card insertion and card removal events, and for checking whether a suitable card is present. Further, we add methods for getting and setting the information about the cardholder, for generating digital signatures, and for releasing all allocated resources.

Since we want to take advantage of the event mechanism provided by the OpenCard Framework, we have the class SignatureCard implement the interface CTListener:

```
public class SignatureCard implements CTListener
{
    ...
```

12.4.1
Attributes

The attribute card is a reference to a SmartCard object, which is the application's representation of an inserted smart card.

For the services that we are expecting from the smart card, we need references to the appropriate OCF CardServices. For the services of reading and writing data, we maintain in fileService a reference to a FileAccessCardService. For generating digital signatures, we maintain in signatureService a reference to a SignatureCardService. We set the references card, fileService, and signatureService when a smart card is inserted and reset them to null when the smart card is removed.

It is possible that our SignatureCard objects are used in situations with more than one card terminal slot. To react appropriately on card removal events, we need to test if the event came from the slot that contained our signature card. We keep a reference to this slot in the attribute slot.

We create the attribute earlierException to temporarily store exceptions that may be caught in the cardInserted method to be re-thrown or analyzed in one of the access methods.

We let the attribute iTracer refer to a Tracer object that we
want to use for OpenCard-style tracing.

```
// All attributes of SignatureCard:
private SmartCard card = null;
private FileAccessCardService fileService = null;
private SignatureCardService signatureService = null;
private int slot = 0;
private Exception earlierException = null;
private Tracer iTracer
                = new Tracer(this,
SignatureCard.class);
```

12.4.2
Constructor

In the constructor, we start OCF by calling the static start()
method of the class SmartCard. Then we add the object being created as a listener for CardTerminalEvents by calling the method
addCTListener(...) of the EventGenerator singleton. This singleton monitors all registered card terminals and sends card insertion or
card removal events to its listeners. You can always obtain the
EventGenerator singleton by calling the static method EventGen-
erator.getGenerator().

Once the SignatureCard object is registered as a CTListener,
the EventGenerator singleton will call the registered object's
cardInserted() or cardRemoved() method whenever a card is
inserted or removed respectively. To find out about any cards, which
were inserted in a reader before the object was registered as a
CTListener, we use createEventsForPresentCards() to create card insertion events for cards which are already present:

```
SignatureCard() throws SignatureCardException  {
   try {
     SmartCard.start();
     EventGenerator.getGenerator()
                         .addCTListener(this);
     EventGenerator.getGenerator()
                     .createEventsForPresentCards(this);
     ...
```

In the rest of the constructor, which we do not show here, we merely
deal with tracing and exception handling.

12.4.3
cardInserted()

The OpenCard Framework calls the method `cardInserted()`
whenever any smart card is inserted in a card terminal. We are only
interested in cards for which at least a `FileAccessCardService`
can be instantiated. Therefore, we create a card request, specifying
`FileAccessCardService.class` as the desired interface and try
to get a smart card object using the event obtained in the parameter
event.

If the `getSmartCard(...)` was successful, we call the method `al-
locateServices()` (see below) to create the file access and signa-
ture services required by the other methods. As the method `cardIn-
serted(...)` is a listener method that is called by the framework, it
may neither perform any long running operation nor throw an exception. Therefore, we store any exception that might occur and keep it
for later processing by one of the methods `sign(...)`, `getCard-
HolderData()`, or `setCardHolderData(...)`.

In addition to the functional code, we insert two tracer invocations
with different levels and purposes into `cardInserted()`. We use
the method `Tracer.info(String, String)` to inform that the
function `cardInserted()` was entered. With the call to
`Tracer.critical(String, Throwable)` we record information
about the exception at the place where it was caught.

```
public void cardInserted(CardTerminalEvent ctEvent) {
    iTracer.info("cardInserted",
                "Got a CARD_INSERTED event.");
    try {
      CardRequest cr = new CardRequest(
                          CardRequest.ANYCARD, null,
                          FileAccessCardService.class);
      card = SmartCard.getSmartCard(ctEvent, cr );
      if (card != null)
        allocateServices( card, ctEvent.getSlotID() );
    }
    catch (OpenCardException e) {
        iTracer.critical("cardInserted", e);
        earlierException = e;
    }
    catch (ClassNotFoundException e) {
        iTracer.critical("cardInserted", e);
        earlierException = e;
    }
}
```

In all methods of class SignatureCard we do not leave the handling of OpenCard exceptions to the caller of the method because we want to encapsulate all OCF dependencies in that class. In addition, in the method cardInserted() we must deal with exceptions in a special way, because in this method we must immediately return to the caller. Therefore, we merely store an exception that occurred in the instance variable earlierException to later handle it in one of the other methods.

12.4.4
allocateServices(SmartCard, int)

The private method allocateServices(...) allocates a file access service and a signature service for a smart card represented by a given smart card object. First, we get a file access service by calling the getCardService(...) method of the smart card object specified by the parameter card. Then we use the same mechanism for obtaining a signature service.

If we were successful in getting the first service, we set the attribute slot with the reference passed in as a parameter. This enables us to react appropriately on card removal events.

```
private void allocateServices(SmartCard card, int slotID)
        throws ClassNotFoundException,
               CardServiceException {
  fileService = (FileAccessCardService)
                 card.getCardService(
                      FileAccessCardService.class, true);
  // If we get here, remember the slot for card removal
  slot = slotID;

  SBCHVDialog dialog = new SBCHVDialog();
  fileService.setCHVDialog(dialog);

  try {
    signatureService = (SignatureCardService)
                       card.getCardService(
                       SignatureCardService.class, true);
    signatureService.setCHVDialog(dialog);
  }          // Special handling of failure to allocate
             // a signature service:
  catch (ClassNotFoundException e)  {
     iTracer.critical("allocateServices", e);
  }
}
```

We provide both card services with a cardholder verification dialog, using the method setCHVDialog(...). We set this dialog because the card is set up with the cardholder data file as well as the private key file for generating signatures protected by a password. The dialog must implement the interface CHVDialog. This interface declares the method getCHV(int), which is called by the service whenever a cardholder verification is required for accessing a certain function of the smart card.

allocateServices(...) is private and only called from other methods of the class SignatureCard. Therefore, we do not need to handle all exceptions within the method. The only exception that we want to handle is the ClassNotFoundException that might occur from trying to allocate a signature service. This exception is expected for a card without digital signature capability, as the card provided in this book. With such a card, our program will still be able to read and write the cardholder information.

12.4.5
cardRemoved()

OCF calls the method cardRemoved() whenever a card is removed from a card terminal. We use it to reset the references to the smart card object and the services to indicate that no card is present anymore. Note that we do not assume that only one card reader with one slot is connected to the system. We only reset the references to the card services, the card, and the slot if the card was removed from the slot we are using with our signature card:

```
public synchronized void cardRemoved(
                            CardTerminalEvent ctEvent)
{
    iTracer.info("cardRemoved",
                "Got a CARD_REMOVED event.");
    if (ctEvent.getSlotID() == slot)  {
      iTracer.info("cardRemoved",
                "The removed card was ours.");
      card = null;
      Slot = 0;
      fileService = null;
      signatureService  = null;
    }
}
```

12.4.6
signatureCardPresent()

The method `signatureCardPresent()` checks for the presence of a signature card. This is the case if a card is present for which a file service and a signature service were instantiated.

```
public boolean signatureCardPresent()
{
  return fileSystemCardPresent()
         && (signatureService != null);
}
```

There are similar methods `fileSystemCardPresent()` and `cardPresent()`, which are obvious enough to be omitted here.

12.4.7
getCardHolderData()

The method `getCardHolderData()` reads data about the card-holder from the smart card, i.e. her name and e-mail address, and returns this data in a byte array.

First, we check whether an exception has been thrown by a preceding invocation of the method `cardInserted()`, and re-throw the exception if that is the case. This is done in the private method `propagateAnEarlierException()` (see Section 12.4.8).

```
public byte[] getCardHolderData()
                throws SignatureCardException,
                    IOException, FileNotFoundException
{
  try {
    propagateAnEarlierException();

    ...
```

Then we check whether a suitable smart card is present by calling the method `signatureCardPresent()`. If no such card is present, we return `null`. If a suitable card is present, we create a card file object for the file holding the cardholder data. This file has the file identifier `0xC009`.

Next, we create a card file input stream and use it to create a data input stream. OCF lets us operate with these streams like with standard Java I/O streams. We create a byte array with the size of the cardholder data file. We determine that size by calling the method getLength() of the file object representing the cardholder data file. We read the data from the file into the new byte array and close the file. Finally, we return the byte array with the cardholder data.

```
// If no card is present, indicate to the application
// that it must prompt for card
if (!fileSystemCardPresent())
  return null;

// The file holding cardholder name and e-Mail address:
CardFile file = new CardFile(fileService, ":C009");

// Create a CardFileInputStream for file
DataInputStream dis = new DataInputStream(
                         new CardFileInputStream(file));

// Read in the owner's name
byte[] cardHolderData = new byte[file.getLength()];
iTracer.info("getCardHolderData", "Reading data");
dis.read(cardHolderData);

// Explicitly close the InputStream to yield the card
// to other applications
dis.close();
return cardHolderData;
}
catch ( …
```

We do not leave any exceptions from OCF for handling by the caller, because we do not want the source code of the caller to be dependent on OCF. Instead, we catch any OpenCardException, log it using the tracer object, and throw a new exception of the type SignatureCardException that we define ourselves (see Section 12.4.12).

```
catch (OpenCardException e) {
      iTracer.critical("getCardHolderData", e);
      throw new SignatureCardException(
            "Exception from getting cardholder data", e);
}
```

12.4.8
propagateAnEarlierException()

The private method propagateAnEarlierException() checks whether there was an earlier exception that was not handled, because it occurred in a method that had to return immediately. If this is not the case, propagateAnEarlierException() has no effect.

If the attribute earlierException contains an earlier exception, we wrap it into a new SignatureCardException object which we then throw. We reset the attribute containing the earlier exception because the exception is handled now.

```
private void propagateAnEarlierException()
                    throws SignatureCardException
{
    if (earlierException == null)  return;

    SignatureCardException signCardExcp
        = new SignatureCardException("Exception of "
            + earlierException.getClass().toString()
            + " from earlier method execution:",
            earlierException);
    earlierException = null;
    throw signCardExcp;
}
```

12.4.9
setCardHolderData(String)

The method setCardHolderData(String cardHolderData) writes the given cardholder data to the smart card.

In the first part, which we do not show here, we perform the same steps as in getCardHolderData(). Again, we try to obtain a card file object that we refer to as file.

Once we have the card file object, we use standard Java I/O stream mechanisms again, this time for writing to the card. We create a CardFileOutputStream and then, using this stream, a DataOutputStream that we call dos, to which we then write.

```
...
DataOutputStream dos = new DataOutputStream(
                        new CardFileOutputStream(file));
if (cardHolderData == null) {
  cardHolderData = " ";
}
byte[] temp = new byte[file.getLength()];
byte[] chd = cardHolderData.getBytes();
System.arraycopy(chd, 0, temp, 0, chd.length);
dos.write(temp, 0, temp.length);
dos.close();
} catch   ...
```

12.4.10
sign(int, byte[])

The method sign(...) lets the smart card generate a digital signature
for given data using a given key and returns it as a byte array.

After the same error handling and checking code that you have
seen before, we create a private-key file object for the private key
with the key number given by the parameter keyNumber. Then we
let the card generate the signature by calling signData(...) of the
signatureService instance, in this example using the RSA algorithm in combination with SHA-1 and Zero-Padding. If this is successful, we return the obtained signature as a byte array, otherwise
we return null:

```
byte[] sign(int keyNumber, byte[] data)
        throws SignatureCardException, InvalidKeyException
 {
    byte[]   signature = null;
    try {
      ...
      // specify the key used for signing
      PrivateKeyFile kf = new PrivateKeyFile(
                    new CardFilePath(":C110"), keyNumber);

      // Let the card generate a signature
      signature = signatureService.signData(
                    kf, JCAStandardNames.SHA1_RSA,
                    JCAStandardNames.ZERO_PADDING, data);
    }
    catch ...
```

Note that the sign(...) method will not work with the card provided in this book, because this card is not capable of performing public key cryptography.

12.4.11
close()

The method close() cleans up the SignatureCard object, i.e. calls the static method shutdown() to shut down the OpenCard Framework and to free access to all attached card terminals.

```
void close () throws SignatureCardException
{
    iTracer.debug("close", "Stopping OpenCard ...");
    try {
        SmartCard.shutdown ();
    }
    catch (OpenCardException e) {
        iTracer.critical("close", e);
        throw new SignatureCardException(
            "Exception from closing OCF", e);
    }
}
```

12.4.12
Class SignatureCardException

Our class SignatureCard uses SignatureCardException objects to communicate all exceptions from the smart card access through OCF to the caller.

Strategies of exception handling are a topic in its own right. A good and exhaustive strategy might be to create an own exception type for the most likely failures, like no smart card reader was found, no card was found, a PIN was not accepted by the card, or the card was not of the expected type. The application can then handle these failures with good user guidance. Errors, which obviously are caused by program defects, like for example null-pointer exceptions, are not caught and bring the program to a halt at the place where they surfaced.

For this example we have tried to not let the straight functional code become buried in exhaustive error handling. We have used the single exception type SignatureCardException for all failures that are no program defects. To allow the caller to find out more about the failure, we pass the primary exception as an attribute of the `SignatureCardException`. The attribute can be obtained with the method `getPrimaryException()`.

We also add the primary exception's message text to the text passed in when creating the new `SignatureCardException` object. Thus, the message text that is returned or displayed by the functions `getMessage()` or `printStackTrace()` contains the primary exception's text in addition to the new text.

Here is the complete source code for this class with commentary lines removed:

```java
public class SignatureCardException extends Exception {

  private Exception primaryException;

  public SignatureCardException(String message)
  {
  super(message);
      primaryException = null;
  }

  public SignatureCardException(String message,
                                Exception exception)
  {
  super(message + '\n' + exception.getMessage());
      primaryException = exception;
  }

  public Exception getPrimaryException()
  {
      return primaryException;
  }
}
```

12.4.13
The Complete Sample Source Code

Now we have examined the smart card access part of the Internet Stockbroker demo application.

The next steps you might want to take are downloading the complete sample code from http://www.opencard.org/SCJavaBook/, compiling it, and running it with the card provided in this book and with the simple test stub `Test.java`. You will find all files for this sample in `samples.stockbroker`. We recommend that you try different trace settings in `opencard.properties` to follow the control flow.

After you understand the concepts and mechanics of this sample, you might want to review the original complete Internet Stockbroker demo that is part of the OCF reference implementation. You will not be able to execute this demo with the card provided in this book. However, the demo source code will help you to understand how the class `SignatureCard` that we developed in this section fits into the overall application context.

13 OCF and e-business

Today, a lot of companies and businesses are transforming into e-businesses to improve their internal efficiency, to improve the link to their suppliers, and to reach new markets via the Internet. The rising number of e-business transactions and increasing transaction values make security a top priority. As a result, integration of secure tokens like smart cards into e-business applications becomes more and more important (see Chapter 3).

In this chapter, we give two examples of using smart cards to secure e-business applications. In Section 13.1, we describe an Internet stock brokerage scenario, where the smart card is used to digitally sign stock orders. In Section 13.2, we present a scenario, where smart cards are used to pay via the Internet.

13.1
Internet Stock Brokerage

In this section, we present an example that shows how smart cards can be used for securing stock brokerage over the Internet. We start by discussing the topics of data integrity and non-repudiation, which are very important in this scenario. Further, we describe a 3-tier architecture the stockbroker may choose for the implementation of his brokerage solution. We conclude this chapter by showing how the smart card related part of the client software might be implemented using the OpenCard Framework.

13.1.1
Security Considerations

In an Internet stock brokerage application, apart from the usual Internet security issues, especially data integrity and non-repudiation are important to the broker. Data integrity means that orders sent from the customer to the broker cannot be changed without detection. Non-repudiation means that once the broker received an order, he can be sure that the customer cannot later deny that he gave the order.

Data integrity can be assured by using digital signatures: Each order is signed before it is sent to the broker, so that any change would be detected. Non-repudiation is harder to achieve. If all customers have unique key pairs, the broker can prove the owner of the key pair that has been used to sign a particular order. However, the customer could claim that somehow somebody obtained his key pair and was thus able to abuse it for fraud.

Legal non-repudiation can only be achieved if it is infeasible to obtain a customer's private key. This can only be guaranteed, if the private key is stored in a secure token, which it never leaves. Modern smart cards that support public-key cryptography are the ideal tokens for this purpose. They are low-cost, can generate and securely store several key pairs and they can generate digital signatures using the stored private keys. Usually, signature generation is only possible after the cardholder proved his identity to the card by providing a personal identification number (PIN). As private keys are generated, stored, and used on card only, they are not accessible for an attacker. The only way to fake a signature is to steal a smart card as well as the PIN for that card.

13.1.2
Secure Stock Brokerage Architecture

In this section, we sketch a possible architecture for a brokerage application. It employs the classical three-tier model involving clients, application servers, and database servers. Figure 13.1 shows the system structure.

At Tier-3, we have the database server, usually a mainframe with a high performance database holding all relevant data like user account information, analyst reports, stock portfolios, user profiles etc., a transaction system for clearing orders, and a certificate server that stores the certificates of authorized customers. At Tier-2, we have the application server that makes selected data contained in the database server available to customers. We assume that a web server with a servlet engine is used as application server. At Tier-1, we have the personal computers, workstations, network computers, screen phones or set-top boxes of the customers with a web browser. Finally, we have a smart card capable of generating key-pairs on card, storing data, private keys, and certificates, and generating digital signatures.

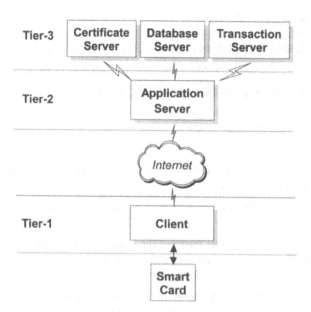

13.1.3
Protocols

Given the architecture described above, all application functionality is located on the application server in HTML-Pages, applets and servlets. In this scenario, ordering shares works as shown in Figure 13.2.

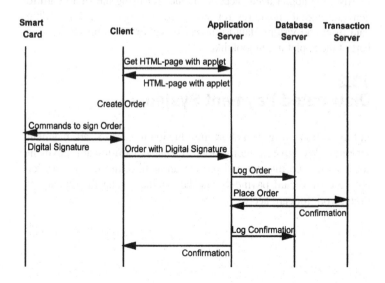

Figure 13.2
Simplified
Representation
of the Purchase
Process

1. The customer navigates to the broker's homepage. Along with HTML-content, an applet for conducting stock orders is downloaded from the web server and displayed in his browser.

2. Using this applet, the customer creates an order and submits it.

3. The applet requests the customer's smart card.

4. The customer inserts the card and enters the PIN for activating the card's signature function.

5. The signature is generated (see Chapter 3).

6. The applet connects to the server and sends the signed order to the brokerage servlet.

7. The brokerage servlet receives the signed stock order and archives it.

8. The brokerage servlet retrieves the customer's certificate from a certificate directory and uses it to verify integrity of the received data and the identity of the sender.

9. If the validation of the signature is successful, the servlet accesses the transaction system on Tier-3 to conduct the order.

10. The servlet sends a confirmation back to the applet on the customer's computer, indicating that the order was successfully placed.

11. The applet receives the confirmation and informs the customer.

In this scenario, the applet needs to display a user interface that allows to create orders and to provide a submit button for sending the order.

Also, the applet needs access routines for using the smart card to generate digital signatures for stock orders and maybe for reading data from and writing data to the card. Section 12.4 shows how this part of the applet might look like.

13.2
Distributed Payment Systems

In this section, we give a short introduction to card-to-card payment schemes. We give a motivation to enable card-to-card payment schemes for the Internet and present an architecture that allows for secure card-to-card payments via the Internet, using the OpenCard Framework for card access.

13.2.1
Card-to-Card Payment Schemes

What we call card-to-card payment schemes in this book are payment schemes involving purse cards and merchant cards. A payment is conducted during a communication, where the cards mutually authenticate and a certain amount is transferred from the purse card to the merchant card.

The most important scheme in terms of issued cards is the Geld-Karte scheme that was established by a consortium of German banks. In 1998, there were already about 50,000,000 cards issued in Germany in a nation wide mass rollout and pilots are starting in other European countries (see Chapter 3 for more information). Other card-to-card payment schemes are VisaCash and Mondex (see Chapter 3). These schemes are not yet used in nation wide rollouts, but there are several pilots around the world.

What all these schemes have in common is that the payment protocol includes the following elements:

1. Authentication of the purse card to the merchant card.

2. Authentication of the merchant card to the purse card.

3. Transfer of a certain amount from the purse card to the merchant card.

4. A mechanism for ensuring integrity of payment messages.

5. A commit mechanism for the payment.

6. A logging mechanism.

To avoid communication overhead, several of the above elements are usually combined; e.g. authentication may be performed implicitly by including challenges and appropriate MACs in payment messages. Figure 13.3 shows how a payment is conducted in a payment terminal according to the GeldKarte scheme. Note that both the figure and the explanation below only cover the part of the protocol that is conducted in a successful payment. More information on the error handling mechanisms can be found in [ZKA99].

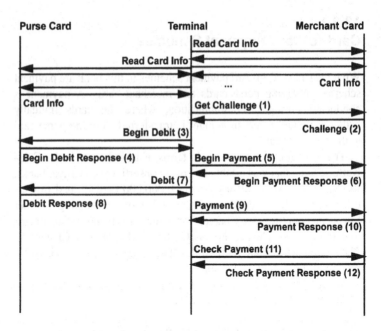

Figure 13.3:
A Payment
According to the
GeldKarte
Payment
Scheme

When the terminal is switched on, it reads certain data from the merchant card. This data is needed whenever a payment shall be conducted. The merchant enters the amount to be paid on the counter to initiate the payment. The payment terminal displays the amount and asks the customer to insert his card. The customer inserts her purse card and the terminal reads the current amount and some other information like the card identification number. If the information read from the purse card is consistent and the amount of money stored on the purse card is greater than the amount to be paid, the terminal conducts the card-to-card payment protocol:

1. The terminal sends a command to the merchant card to obtain a random challenge to be used.

2. The merchant card generates a random number and sends it back as the random challenge.

3. The terminal sends the challenge and the key-generating key ID to the purse card with a begin-debit command.

4. The purse card sends back a begin-debit response that amongst other data contains the merchant card's random challenge and is signed by a message authentication code (MAC).

5. The terminal sends the relevant parts of the begin-debit response to the merchant card with a begin-payment command. As it contains the merchant card's challenge and is signed by a MAC, this

message is a non-replayable message, authenticating the purse card to the merchant card.

6. The merchant card checks the begin-debit message and sends back a begin-payment response which contains the amount to be obtained from the purse card and which is also signed by a MAC.

7. The terminal displays the amount to be debited from the purse card and waits for the customer to press a confirmation button. If the customer confirms the payment, the terminal sends the relevant part of the begin-payment response to the purse card with a debit command.

8. The purse card decreases its amount by the debit value if the MAC of the debit-command is correct and sends back a response singed by a MAC, which proves that the value has been subtracted from its amount.

9. The terminal sends the relevant parts of the debit response to the merchant card with a payment command.

10. The merchant card checks the MAC in the message and adds the value that has been subtracted from the purse card to its own amount if the MAC is correct.

11. The terminal sends a check payment command to the merchant card to assure that the value has been transferred properly.

12. The merchant card checks whether the payment was successful and returns a check-payment response that has to be logged by the terminal for later clearing.

Finally, the terminal prompts the customer to remove her card if the response is positive, indicating that the payment has been completed successfully.

13.2.2
Card-to-Card Payments via Internet

Today, a large number of companies already offer their goods or services in the Internet and some of these companies also allow customers to purchase goods or information via the Internet. In most cases, the customer's credit card has to be used to pay. This has some drawbacks. Using a credit card is quite expensive for the merchant, because credit card companies charge to the merchant significant percentages of the paid amount, depending on the business segment of the merchant and the value of the purchased goods. Also, credit cards do not allow for anonymous payments. Credit card companies exactly know when and where a customer buys something with his credit card.

Using a prepaid and anonymous electronic purse scheme overcomes these problems. Customers can load a certain amount on their purse cards and spend it anonymously. The charges for payments from a prepaid purse are much smaller than charges for credit card transactions, typically about 1 % or less. As purses are prepaid, the payment is a simple debit operation, which requires no online checking. A certain amount is moved from the purse card to the merchant card for each payment. Thus, a large number of payments can be accumulated by the merchant card and can be cleared in one burst. This feature of card-to-card payment schemes is especially useful in the Internet environment, because it allows merchants to offer cheap goods or information via the Internet, e.g. a record company could sell individual music titles and a newspaper could sell individual articles with additional background.

In the rest of this section, we describe a Distributed Acceptance Terminal for payments via the Internet using the GeldKarte.

13.2.2.1
Protocol

When a customer wants to buy goods offered on a web site, he puts his purse card into the reader connected to his PC, his Network Computer or a self-service terminal. On the merchant's side, a merchant card or a secure token simulating several merchant cards is required. The payment via the Internet basically works as follows:

1. The customer navigates to the merchant's web site using a browser like Netscape Navigator or Internet Explorer, selects goods and presses some "BUY" button.

2. An applet is loaded from the merchant's site. This applet is able to conduct the GeldKarte payment protocol and to access the inserted card using the OpenCard Framework. Alternatively, this applet could also be present on the customer's machine already, e.g. if a bank decides to distribute it on CD.

3. On the merchant's server, there is a servlet that can conduct the merchant's part of the payment protocol and can access present merchant cards via OpenCard Framework.

4. The customer is asked by the applet to enter his card, if it is not already inserted.

5. The payment protocol is conducted between the customer applet and merchant servlet. Before the amount on the card is actually re-

duced, the applet pops up a requester that asks the customer to confirm the payment. No PIN is required to perform the payment.

6. The goods are delivered.

To be able to conduct the payment protocol via the Internet, we need a distributed version of the terminal software described in Section 13.2.1. One part of the payment protocol must be conducted on the customer's client machine while the other part must be conducted on the merchant's server or the payment server of a service provider respectively. As communication via the Internet can be very time-consuming in times of high network load, the distributed payment system must be designed to minimize the number of messages sent via the net. The picture below shows how the GeldKarte payment protocol can be conducted in a distributed payment system with only three request/response pairs exchanged via the net.

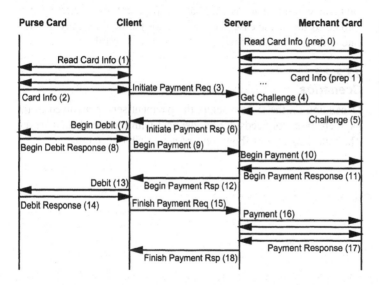

Figure 13.4:
The Message
Trace of a
GeldKarte
Payment via
Internet

As Figure 13.4 shows, there is no direct relation of messages exchanged with cards and messages exchanged via the Internet. Some parts of the protocol can be conducted with the local smart card and do not require communication with the peer on the other side of the network connection.

When the merchant part of the distributed payment system is started, it needs to initialize by reading information from the smart card, which will be required in later payments. Having done this, it waits for payments to be initiated by the client.

Before initiating a payment, the customer's part of the distributed payment system initializes, reading information from the purse card. With initiation of the payment by the client, usage of the network connection starts.

A random number must be obtained from the merchant card, which results in the first communication with the server. Having obtained the challenge, the client provides it to the purse card with the begin-debit command. Parts of the response must be sent to the merchant card with the begin-payment command.

Getting these parts to the server results in a second communication step. With the response sent back by the server, the client receives data that must be provided to the purse card with the debit command.

The relevant parts of the debit response must be sent to the server to complete the payment, resulting in the final communication step. The server provides this data to the merchant card with a payment command to credit the amount to that card, followed by a check payment command to assure that the payment was correctly performed. If this is the case, the server sends the final response to indicate to the client that the payment has been successful.

13.2.2.2
Scenarios

Depending on the system setup, the payment server involved in the payment protocol needs not be identical with the merchant's server. The following figures show some of the possible scenarios.

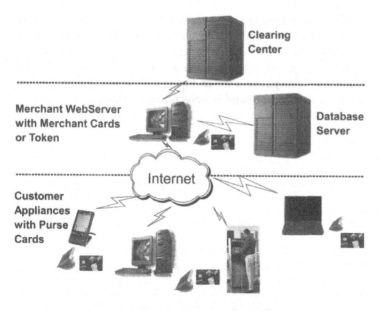

In the scenario shown in Figure 13.5, the merchant himself runs the server on which payments are accepted. Another option for a merchant would be to outsource payment acceptance, as in the scenario shown in Figure 13.6, where a service provider who operates a payment server accepts payments on behalf of the merchant.

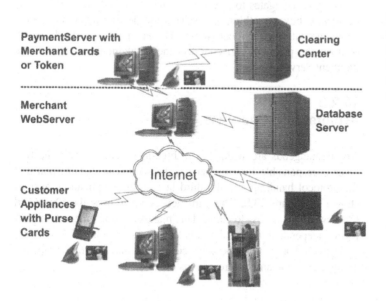

Figure 13.6:
A Service
Provider Accepts
Payments on
Behalf of a
Merchant

To allow for scenarios like the latter, the payment protocol needs to be independent from the trading protocol. The trading protocol would be conducted between the customer's computer and the merchant's server, but in between, the payment protocol would be conducted with the payment server. Figure 13.7 shows how the payment protocol may be embedded in a purchase transaction.

Figure 13.7:
The Payment
Protocol
Embedded in a
Trading
Protocol

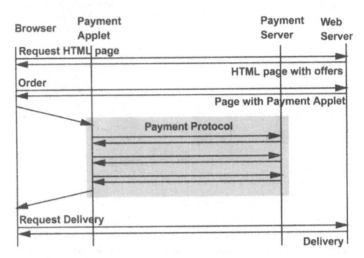

The user navigates to a web page that contains offers. When she decides to buy something, she selects the desired items and gets a new page with the Payment Applet. The Payment Applet asks her to confirm the payment and conducts the payment protocol with the Payment Server.

13.2.3
Architecture Overview

An advantageous architecture is a three-layer stack, where the first layer is responsible for card access, the second layer is responsible for protocol handling and the third layer is the application layer as shown in Figure 13.8. The card access layer uses the OpenCard Framework for access to cards. This makes the implementation platform independent and makes readers exchangeable. The software will run on workstations, personal computers, and network computers on the client side and different kinds of servers.

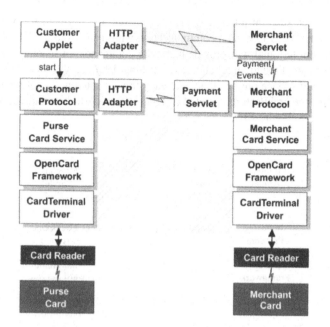

Figure 13.8:
Architecture of a
Web-based
Distributed
Payment System

The basic steps for conducting a payment are as follows: The Customer Applet invokes the Customer Protocol Module. It communicates with the local purse card via the Purse Card Service and with the Merchant Protocol Module at the server via the HTTP Adapter. The HTTP Adapter allows for communication with the servlet via HTTP requests. The Merchant Protocol Module receives requests from the Customer Protocol Module on the client through the Payment Servlet and handles these requests using the Merchant Card Service for access to the local merchant card. When the payment is completed or failed, the Merchant Protocol Module notifies the Merchant Server who may take the appropriate action - either deliver goods or report an error.

Figure 13.8 assumes that the used card readers are rather primitive and that the entire communication with cards both on the client as well as on the server side is conducted by OpenCard services. These services provide high level interfaces with methods for reading card information, beginning debit, and finishing debit. In some payment schemes, more intelligent card terminals may be used. For GeldKarte payments via the Internet involving personal computers, secure Internet Customer Terminals with RSA capability, a display and, a PIN-pad are required by the central credit council of German banks, the ZKA.

When such an intelligent terminal is used, the payment software does not need to handle communication with the card itself. The intelligent terminal will provide particular commands for reading card information, beginning debit, and finishing debit, i.e. the function of the card service on the client is already implemented in the terminal. Thus, the architecture depicted in Figure 13.8 has to be modified as shown in Figure 13.9.

Figure 13.9:
Architecture for a
Web-based
Distributed
Payment
System,
Modified for Use
of an Intelligent
Terminal

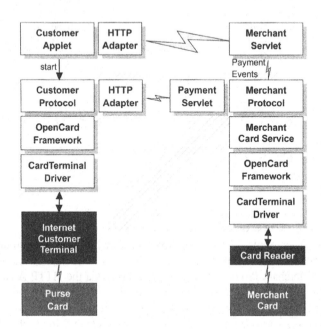

13.2.4
Implementation

In this section, we present a prototype implementation we developed at IBM. Our approach entirely relies on Java technology, both on the client as well as on the server side. Figure 13.10 shows the software stack we chose.

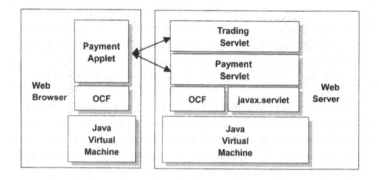

13.2.4.1
The Standard Software

On the client, we need a web browser that supports the relevant sub-set of Java 1.1 that is required for running the payment applet. We decided to use Netscape Communicator 4.5 or higher, but it would also be possible to use Microsoft Internet Explorer or any other Java 1.1 compliant Web browser as well.

On the server, we need a servlet engine that provides a Java 1.2 compliant runtime environment and the Java Servlet 2.2 API (see [SER99]). We decided to use IBM WebSphere Application Server 4.01 or higher, but it would also be possible to use other application servers supporting the Java Servlet API.

13.2.4.2
The Payment Servlet

WebSphere Application Server provides a framework for servlets according to the Java Servlet API v2.2 (see [SER99]) – that supplies base classes for writing own servlets. For example, there is a class named HTTPServlet, from which we derived our payment servlet.

```
...
import java.io.*;
import javax.servlet.http.*;
import javax.servlet.*;
import opencard.core.*;
import opencard.core.service.*;
import opencard.core.terminal.*;
public class PaymentServlet extends HttpServlet {
   SmartCard card_ = null;
   . . .
```

To implement the payment protocol in the servlet, we had to override the methods `init`, `doPost` and `destroy`. As the same mechant card shall be used by the payment servlet for handling all incoming requests, we use the instance variable `card_` to store a `SmartCard` object to be initialized in the `init` method and be used in the `doPost` method.

The `init` method is invoked when the servlet is loaded. The application server loads a servlet at startup, when the first HTTP request for that servlet is received or when the administrator explicitly loads it. A servlet's `init` method has the responsibility to initialize the servlet and allocate all necessary resources so that the servlet is ready to process incoming requests. The following code sample shows a simplified version of the `init` method of our payment servlet.

```
public void init(ServletConfig config) throws
ServletException {
    super.init(config);
    try {
      SmartCard.start();

      CardRequest cr =
        new CardRequest(HaendlerKarteSvc.class);

      card_ = SmartCard.waitForCard(cr);

      MerchantCardService merchantService =
        (MerchantCardService)
        card.getCardService(MerchantCardService.class,
                            true);

      MerchantProtocol merchantProtocol =
        new MerchantProtocol(merchantService);

      serverAdapter_ =
        new PaymentServerAdapter(merchantProtocol);

      card_.beginMutex();
    } catch (Exception e) {
      throw new UnavailableException(
          "Initialization failed: " + e.getMessage());
    }
}
```

The payment servlet does not require any parameters from the servlet configuration; thus we pass the `ServletConfig` object config to the `init` method of the super class `HTTPServlet` and ignore it in due course. Our payment servlet handles incoming payment requests using a `MerchantProtocol` object for interaction with the smart card and a `PaymentServerAdapter` object for receiving and parsing HTTP requests and dispatching them to the appropriate methods of the protocol object. Thus, our `init` method needs to start the OpenCard Framework, obtain a `SmartCard` object for the merchant card, get the appropriate `MerchantCardService` from the `SmartCard` object, create a `MerchantProtocol` object from that card service and create a `PaymentServerAdapter` linked to the protocol object. Finally it calls the `beginMutex` method of the `SmartCard` object to assure exclusive access to the card.

The `doPost` method is called whenever the server receives a HTTP POST request addressed to the servlet. The server passes an `HTTPServletRequest` and a `HTTPServletResponse` to the service method, which processes data read from the input stream obtained from the request object and writes the result to the output stream obtained from the response object. The following sample code shows a simplified version of the service method.

```
public void doPost(ServletRequest req, ServletResponse rsp)
    throws ServletException, IOException {
    DataOutputStream os =
      new DataOutputStream(rsp.getOutputStream());
    DataInputStream is =
      new DataInputStream(req.getInputStream());
    try {
      byte[] data = new byte[is.readInt()];
      is.readFully(data);
      data = serverAdapter_.receive(reqMsg).getContent();
      os.writeInt(data.length);
      os.write(data, 0, data.length);
      os.flush();
    } catch (Exception e) {
      // return empty response to indicate error
      byte[] data = new byte[0];
      os.writeInt(data.length);
      os.write(data, 0, data.length);
      os.flush();
      throw new ServletException(
        "Error processing request: " + e.getMessage());
    }
  }
```

The service method is quite simple, because message parsing and request handling is delegated to the PaymentServerAdapter object referenced by serverAdapter_ and the MerchantProtocol object to which it is linked. The service method only obtains an input stream from the obtained request object and an output stream from the obtained response object, reads the request from the input stream, delegates it to the adapter and writes the result returned by the adapter back to the output stream. The PaymentServerAdapter parses the incoming requests, calls the appropriate methods of the MerchantProtocol to handle these requests and wraps the results into response messages that it returns to the PaymentServerAdapter that sends them back to the client.

The destroy method is called when the servlet is unloaded. This may happen as the result of a serious error or when the administrator explicitly unloads it. A servlet's destroy method has the responsibility to free all resources which are owned by the servlet. The following code sample shows the destroy method of the payment servlet.

```
public void destroy() {
    try {
        card_.endMutex();
        SmartCard.shutdown();
    } catch (Exception e) {
        log("Error shutting down OCF:" + e.getMessage());
    }
}
```

As the init method starts the OpenCard Framework and allocates exclusive access to the merchant card, the destroy method must free the exclusive access by calling the endMutex method of the SmartCard object and shut down the OpenCard Framework.

14 Java Card and OCF

In this chapter, we present a sample Java Card applet together with the basic concepts of on-card programming for Java Cards. We explain the associated off-card programming and show how OCF brings off-card and on-card parts together. You can find a brief introduction to the Java Card platform in Section 2.3.2 "Java Card".

14.1
Developing a Card Applet

The process for developing a card applet is shown in Figure 14.1. There are variations in the tools and in the development environment provided for the Java Cards of the various suppliers. Therefore, your environment might differ in details from what we describe.

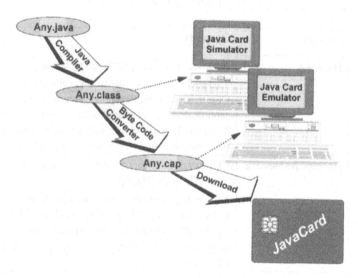

Figure 14.1:
The Process for
Developing a
Card Applet

The code development starts with the creation of a Java source code file. You compile this source file with a standard Java compiler, using in place of the JDK the class libraries of the Java Card Framework. You can test the resulting class file in the Java Card simulation environment on your computer.

In the next step, the byte code converter verifies the class file and optimizes it for the limited resources of a smart card. You can test the resulting cap file in the Java Card emulator on your computer.

Finally, all cap files comprising your on-card application are downloaded into the card. This download can be secured by signing the code and letting the card verify the signatures.

14.2
Inside the Java Card

To better understand what our card applet needs to do and how we drive it from the off-card application, we first take a look at the objects on a Java Card and their life cycle.

14.2.1
The Java Card Framework

The Java Card framework consists of four packages. These packages and their content are listed in Table 14.1.

Table 14.1:
The Packages
of the
Java Card

Package	Contents
java.lang	A subset of the Java programming language. This package contains the fundamental classes Object, Throwable, Exception, RuntimeException, and several specialized exceptions. These fundamental classes differ slightly from their corresponding classes in JDK's java.lang.
javacard.framework	Classes and interfaces for the core functionality of a Java Card applet. This package provides smart card specific interfaces like ISO7816 and PIN, and classes like Applet, AID, and APDU. In addition, it contains the class JCSystem, which corresponds to JDK's java.lang.System.

| javacard.security | Classes and interfaces for the Java Card security framework.
This package provides interfaces for all kinds of keys, and the classes like KeyBuider, MessageDigest, RandomData, and Signature. |
|---|---|
| javacardx.crypto | Extension package containing security classes and interfaces for export-controlled functionality. Interface KeyEncryption and class Cipher. |

14.2.2
Lifetimes of On-card Programs and Objects

Another important distinction between a Java environment on a workstation and the Java Card environment is the lifetime of the applets and of the objects owned by the applets.

The applets installed in the card have a long lifetime. They will terminate only when they are explicitly de-installed. Otherwise, they will stay alive as long as the card is usable.

Lifetime of the applets

The objects created and owned by an applet are allocated in the EEPROM by default and thus persistent. The specification defines a way to create transient arrays but does not define a way to make an object transient. The Java Card system class JCSystem provides makeTransient...Array() methods for Boolean, Byte, Short, and Object. Transient arrays are alive until the card is powered down or the applet is deselected.

Lifetime of the applet's objects

When an applet is installed on the card, its installation method public static install(...) is called. This method should allocate all objects the applet will use, thus making sure during installation that sufficient space will be available for the applet later. Otherwise, an out-of-memory failure should surface already during installation. If the installation was successful, the applet must call one of its inherited register() methods to get its application identifier registered with the Java Card runtime environment.

After an applet has been installed, it can be used by an application. For communicating and working with an applet, the application must select it by sending an appropriate select command, a SELECT APDU with the application ID of the applet. The applet that became selected is called the "active" applet. All APDUs that the application is sending to a card are passed to the active applet. This applet remains active until another applet is selected.

Selecting the active applet

Such change of the active applet causes the deselect() method of the currently active applet being called, followed by select() of the selected applet being called.

process(APDU) Once an applet is active, all APDUs sent to it are causing a call to its method process(APDU) with the APDU forwarded as argument.

14.3
A Sample Java Card Applet

In the following, we want to examine a Java Card applet in detail. This applet will later be called through OCF.

Our simple sample applet is maintaining business card information. It provides methods to read and write this information.

One of the features of the Java language, which many of us can hardly imagine to do without, is the class String. Not having this class on a Java Card, we store all business card information in byte arrays of fixed length, which we call fields. Corresponding to one business card, we make up a record from five fields containing the name, title, address, telephone, and e-mail address.

The applet provides methods to set and get the individual fields. To protect the fields from unauthorized access, the applet does not grant any access until the correct PIN was entered. After the PIN has been verified, it remains valid until the applet is deselected or until the card is powered down.

The card we develop this applet for is the IBM "JCOP10" Java Card, which reflects the Java Card 2.1.1 specification. This card also contains the support for the Open Platform 2.0.1 specification.

Now we start creating the applet. We call it BizCardApplet. To make it a Java Card applet, we derive it from the class Applet in the Java Card framework:

Card applet definition
```
public class BizCardApplet
                          extends javacard.framework.Applet {
```

Selection processing Remember that before we can communicate with our applet to use its services, we need to select it. The off-card part of the application must send a SELECT APDU to the Java Card runtime environment, which then calls the card applet's select() method and subsequently its process(APDU) method with the SELECT APDU passed to it.

Here we encounter another class from the Java Card framework, the class APDU. The APDU was passed to the applet from the off-card part of the application.

In our applet, we do not need to perform any special functions during selection. We merely perform some checks on the APDU and return successful, when the APDU is as expected. Because you will see such APDU checking in other methods, we do not show it here and move on to the process (APDU) method instead.

After our applet was successfully selected, it receives all subsequent APDUs in its method process (APDU). The responsibility of the process (APDU) is to dispatch incoming APDUs to the appropriate methods of the applet. To determine, where to forward the call to, we examine the class and instruction byte of the APDU.

process(APDU)

```
public void process(APDU apdu) throws ISOException {
  byte[] apduBuffer = apdu.getBuffer();

  // Dispatch commands depending on
  // the instruction byte.
  switch ( apduBuffer[ISO7816.OFFSET_INS] ){
    case (byte) 0x01 :
      performCHV(apdu);
      break;
    case (byte) 0x02 :
      getField(apdu);
      break;
    case (byte) 0x03 :
      setField(apdu);
      break;
    case (byte) 0xA4 :
      selectFile(apdu);
      break;
    default :
      ISOException.throwIt(ISO7816.SW_INS_NOT_SUPPORTED);
      break;
  }
}
```

Our sample applet has four methods, which can be called from the off-card application through the appropriate APDU: performCHV(APDU), getField(APDU), setField(APDU), and selectFile(APDU).

Selecting our applet is an operation that can be done without any authentication. For all other methods, our applet requires that the caller is authenticated by entering the personal identification number (PIN).

The applet uses the class OwnerPIN from the Java Card framework, which offers services to update and check the PIN and to reset the counter for unsuccessful authentication attempts:

```
final static byte PIN_TRY_LIMIT = (byte) 10;
  final static byte MAX_PIN_SIZE = (byte)  8;
  /**
   * The OwnerPin must be matched before this applet
   * cooperates.
   */
  private OwnerPIN pin_
          = new OwnerPIN(PIN_TRY_LIMIT, MAX_PIN_SIZE);
```

deselect()

We want to accept the PIN as valid only as long as our applet is active. Therefore we use the method deselect(), which is called by the Java Card runtime environment before our applet loses its active status. In this way, we can reset the PIN when our applet is deselected:

```
/**
 * Actions to be performed if this applet is deselected.
 */
public void deselect() {  // Switching the applet
  pin_.reset();           // .. resets PIN-validated flag
}
```

To feed the user's PIN input to the applet and have the applet check it against its value of the PIN we provide a method of its own, which we call performCHV(...) :

```
private void performCHV(APDU apdu) {
  byte[] buffer = apdu.getBuffer();
  byte lc = buffer[4];
  ...
```

After we have carefully checked all parts of the APDU, we let the OwnerPIN object check the input passed in the APDU's body. On any error, we exit by calling ISOException.throwIt(short) with the appropriate constant defined in the class ISO7816.

```
...

  // Check class byte. Only 0x80 is allowed.
  if (buffer[ISO7816.OFFSET_CLA] != (byte) 0x80)
    ISOException.throwIt(
      ISO7816.SW_CONDITIONS_NOT_SATISFIED);
  // For brevity, the checks for P1 and P2 not shown here ...

  // Check the pin.
  if (pin_.check(buffer, ISO7816.OFFSET_CDATA, lc) == false)
    ISOException.throwIt(
      ISO7816.SW_SECURITY_STATUS_NOT_SATISFIED);
  ...
```

If all went well, we return successfully passing back an APDU with no data. We use the method setOutgoingAndSend(...) of class APDU to do so:

setOutgoing-And-Send(...)

```
...
  // Send the response: Return successfully, passing no data
  apdu.setOutgoingAndSend((short) 0, (short) 0);
}
```

So far we have done housekeeping, input validation and user authentication. Therefore, it is about time now to turn to the main purpose of this applet, storing and retrieving business card data. The way our applet is handling these data is in records that contain fields for the name, title, address, telephone, and e-mail address. To set a field we provide a method setField(APDU):

setField(APDU)

```
private void setField(APDU apdu) {
  byte[] buffer = apdu.getBuffer();
  short lc = (short) ((short) 0x00FF & buffer[4]);
  ...
}
```

setField(APDU) is a private method because it will only be called through the method process(APDU) and not from other objects.

In setField(APDU) we need to determine, what field should be set. Then we extract the business card data from the APDU. You will encounter a new class here, BizCardRecord. We defined this simple class in our application. It contains the fields of business card data together with methods to set and get them.

```
...
// Check class byte. Only 0x80 is allowed here.
if (buffer[ISO7816.OFFSET_CLA] != (byte) 0x80)
  ISOException.throwIt(
    ISO7816.SW_CONDITIONS_NOT_SATISFIED);

// Check P2. This is the field to be read:
//  1 <= field <= 5  (field 1 has index 0)
if ((buffer[ISO7816.OFFSET_P2]) > 4)
  ISOException.throwIt(ISO7816.SW_INCORRECT_P1P2);

// Check if the CHV has already been verified.
if (pin_.isValidated() != true)
  ISOException.throwIt(
    ISO7816.SW_SECURITY_STATUS_NOT_SATISFIED);

// Determine which information to update
BizCardRecord bcRecord = null;

switch (buffer[ISO7816.OFFSET_P1]) {
  case 0x00 : bcRecord = bizCardRecord0_; break;
  case 0x01 : bcRecord = bizCardRecord1_; break;
  default : // Index is out of bounds
    ISOException.throwIt(ISO7816.SW_INCORRECT_P1P2);
}

// Set the field to the value transmitted in the APDU.
bcRecord.setField(buffer[ISO7816.OFFSET_P2],
                  buffer, ISO7816.OFFSET_CDATA, lc);

// Send the response: No data, status word 0x9000.
apdu.setOutgoingAndSend((short) 0, (short) 0);
}
```

In the same way we provide a method getField(APDU), which is retrieving a field of business card information and returning it through the response APDU to the off-card part of the program. get-Field(APDU) is close to setField(APDU), so that we do not list all of its code here. Just the returning part is different, because we need to return data that can not be returned with the method APDU.setOutgoingAndSend(...). Therefore we use the method APDU.sendBytesLong(...) after we prepared to send by calling APDU.setOutgoingLength(short):

setOutgoing-Length(short) and SendBytes-Long(...)

```java
private void getField(APDU apdu) {
  byte[] buffer = apdu.getBuffer();
  ...  // similar to setField(APDU)

  // Le currently
  short le = apdu.setOutgoing();
  apdu.setOutgoingLength(bcField.length);

  // Send the response.
  apdu.sendBytesLong(
    bcField.data, (short) 0, bcField.length);
}
```

Now we have seen all run-time functions of our applet. The bit that remains to be done is the initial installation of our applet. We provide a method install(...). It invokes the constructor of our applet (which we made protected) and then registers the applet to the Java Card runtime:

install(...)

```java
/**
 * Install the applet on the Java Card.
 *
 * @param All parameters are currently ignored.
 *
 */
public static void install( byte[] bArray,
                            short bOffset, byte bLength) {
  BizCardApplet me = new BizCardApplet();
  me.register();
}
```

The constructor allocates all instance data for our applet. To prevent that the applet fails during runtime for lack of memory, the constructor already claims all memory needed for the lifetime of the applet:

```
/**
 * Create a new BizCardApplet.
 */
protected BizCardApplet() {
  super();
  bizCardRecord0_ = new BizCardRecord();
  bizCardRecord1_ = new BizCardRecord();
}
```

Now we are done with developing our sample card applet. To keep things simple, we have completely left out the personalization life-cycle step. Just installing the applets on the card will not produce real world cards. The personal data on the card, including the PINs, are usually set in a personalization step, which invokes personalization methods of the applets. Either the life-cycle management functions specified in the GlobalPlatform [GP01], or custom code can be used to prevent later modification of the personal data.

You may want to review the complete source code. You can find it in the file samples.business.BizCardApplet.java in the sample code archive on http://www.opencard.org/SCJavaBook/.

14.4
Using OCF to Work with Card Applets

The applets on the Java Card are Java objects, in the same way as the objects of OCF and of the Java code using OCF are Java objects. The major difference between these Java objects is that the card applets are on a computer of its own. Conceptually we have to treat the objects on the Java Card as objects on a server.

Using the services of objects on a remote computer is a common situation. Known mechanisms to call the services of remote Java objects are Remote Method Invocation [RMI99] or the Common Object Request Broker Architecture [CORBA99].

Both RMI and CORBA require additional code on the client side as well as on the server side. With the limitations of today's smart cards, we can not afford additional code on this tiny server. Therefore, both mechanisms cannot reasonably be used for the Java Card today. For accessing and using the applets on Java Cards, we need a new concept that minimizes the work to be done by the card.

14.4.1
Card Applet Proxies

The mechanism for using objects from a Java Card involves proxy objects, a standard object-oriented design pattern also applied in RMI and CORBA. We let card applet proxies represent the applets on the card. An application uses the services of a card applet through the corresponding card applet proxy.

Each proxy class has to know the application identifier (AID) of the card applet to communicate with and the protocol for interaction with that card applet. Whenever the application invokes a proxy method, the proxy starts communicating with the card applet on the card and generates some result, which it returns to the application.

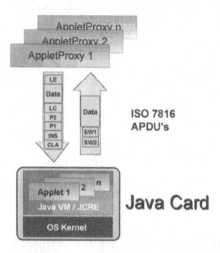

Figure 14.2: All Communication between OCF and the Java Card is through ISO 7816 APDUs.

The communication layer between the proxy and the card is standard ISO 7816 APDUs (see Figure 14.2). This has the advantage that Java Cards can have a high compatibility to other non-Java cards.

Because applet proxies need to communicate with the card and hold knowledge about the card, we can best make them subclasses of the OCF CardService. As specialized card services, before sending APDUs, card applet proxies must allocate a card channel for communication with the Java Card from the card service scheduler – like any other card service.

Applet proxies are special CardServices

Card applet proxies as well as all other card services[1] may be used in multithreaded programs. This means they may be instantiated several times by different threads so that concurrent access by different instances to the card must be serialized. If the card channel has already been allocated by another card applet proxy, the threads of activity of card applet proxies trying to allocate it are blocked until the current owner of the channel releases it.

Card State and Card Applet State   As there might also be several instances of the same card applet proxy class, it must be possible to share the associated card applet's state so that the different proxy instances interact properly. A card channel may hold a card state object. We let this card state object contain a collection of several applet state objects. Each applet state object represents the state of a card applet on the card (see Figure 14.3). If, for example, we have a card applet that simulates a file system, the state would consist of the currently selected directory and information about the access conditions.

Figure 14.3: Card Applets with their Associated Proxies and States

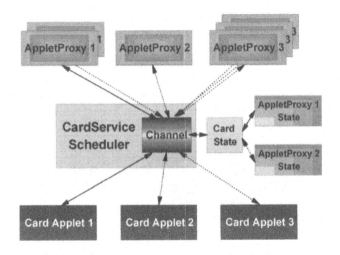

There may be applets without state; their associated proxies don't need a state object (see Figure 14.3). As access to the channel is synchronized and states can only be obtained from the channel, there is no need for additional synchronization of access to states.

Each applet proxy is responsible for creating its associated state object and adding it to the card state. The first applet proxy also needs to create the card state itself.

---

[1] We can assume that most card services for a Java Card are applet proxies, but not all. For example can a generic VisaCashCardService operate on the card, if the card has a compatible applet installed.

Common to all applet proxies is the need to send APDUs to the card and to handle the card channel and the card state. We recommend that you factor out this function common to all applet proxies and place it into a base class, say into the class AppletProxy.

Base class
AppletProxy

In order to send an APDU to a card applet, the card applet must be selected – except if it is the currently selected card applet. To avoid unnecessary selections, the applet proxy services have to keep track of the currently selected card applet. There may exist several instances of applet proxy services for one Java Card simultaneously. Therefore, we must make sure that all these applet proxy services accessing the same card also share the representation of the card's state, which then refers to the currently selected card applet. We are maintaining this information in the card state object. It works out nicely that the card state object is associated with the card channel, for which we have exactly one instance per each physical card.

Controlling the
Selection State

On a Java Card with several card applets, selection of one applet always causes deselection of another applet, potentially causing the deselected applet to lose its state. This potential state loss requires that the state of the associate applet proxy is changed accordingly whenever a card applet – other than the one the proxy is associated with – is selected. We recommend that you again factor out all commonality and place any common state handling it into the common base class of all applet proxies. Even better, you can reuse the code in the new OCF 1.2 package opencard.opt.applet.

Reflecting applet
state changes in
the associated
proxies

14.4.2
Controlling Our Sample Card Applet through OCF

Let us come back to the card applet that we have developed in 14.3. For this applet, BizCardApplet.java, we now create a proxy that we call BusinessCardProxy.java.

Before we dive down into an individual class, let us take an overview of the classes involved (see Figure 14.4).

BusinessCardProxy extends the class AppletProxy. Every AppletProxy has an AppletID, which uniquely identifies its application. AppletProxy does all handling of that applet AID including passing it to the methods communicating with the card. AppletProxy and AppletID are both found in the package opencard.opt.applet.

AppletProxy extends BasicAppletCardService. The main responsibility that we give this base class is to actually send and receive the APDUs. Here we also make sure that the correct receiving

BasicApplet-
CardService

applet is selected before the APDU is sent, and that the PIN is (re-)entered if necessary.

Figure 14.4:
The Off-card
Classes Driving
Our Sample
Card Applet

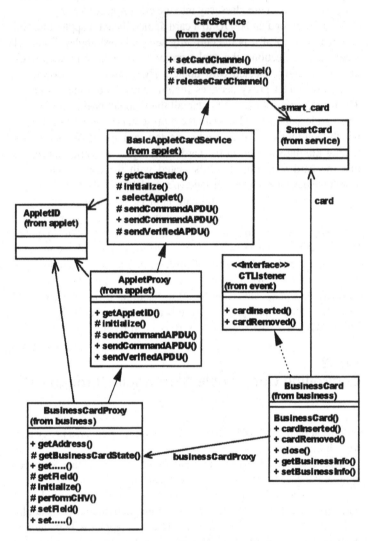

BasicAppletCardService extends OCF's abstract class CardService. Each BasicAppletCardService refers to an AppletID.

BusinessCard   Although the class BusinessCardProxy hides all details of APDUs and card communication, we do not expect that other application programmers use it directly. Rather we create an abstraction that also hides details of card handling (insertion/removal) and offers a true application interface: the class BusinessCard. A business card object listens and reacts to the card insertion and removal events by executing the methods implementing the interface CTListener. In addition, it also maintains a reference to the OCF object SmartCard.

After this overview of the off-card classes and their main responsibilities, we are ready to approach these classes in more detail.

14.4.2.1
Class BusinessCardProxy

Class BusinessCardProxy is responsible for acting as a proxy to the card applet BizCardApplet.

First we define several constants for BusinessCardProxy objects, like return codes and the numbers of the business card entries name, title, and so forth. We also define a command and response APDU as instance data that we can reuse to avoid object creation overhead.

```
public class BusinessCardProxy extends AppletProxy {

    // Return codes.
    protected final static int OK = 0x9000;
    ...
    protected final static int CHV_FAILED = 0x6982;
    ...
    // Field identifiers.
    protected final static int NAME = 0;
    protected final static int TITLE = 1;
    ...
    protected final static int ADDRESS = 4;


    /** Reusable command APDU for getting a field. */
    private CommandAPDU getFieldAPDU = new CommandAPDU(14);


    /** Reusable command APDU for setting a field. */
    private CommandAPDU setFieldAPDU = new CommandAPDU(255);
```

Next, we create public methods to get and set the business card data fields, like getAddress(), setAddress(String), and so forth. These public get/set-methods internally use the protected methods getField() and setField(...):

setAddress(...)

```
public void setAddress(int index, String address)
      throws CardServiceException, CardTerminalException {
   setField(index, ADDRESS, address);
}
```

setField(...)

The methods getField() and setField(...) send an APDU invoking the equally named function of the card applet. Because this demonstrates a typical communication between a card applet and its applet proxy, we will show the entire set method here (see also the corresponding card applet method in section 14.3).

Between the card applet and the proxy, we made the agreement that the class byte to use for this method is 0x80 and the instruction byte is 0x03.

To communicate with the card, we must allocate the card channel – as in every other CardService. Next, we check, whether the PIN has already been entered and is still valid. The proxy's associated state object keeps that information. If necessary, we call the method performCHV (...).

```
protected void setField(int index, int field, String value)
         throws CardServiceInvalidCredentialException,
                       . . .
                   CardServiceException {

    // Class and instruction bytes for the SetField Command
    final byte[] SET_NAME_COMMAND_PREFIX
                   = {(byte) 0x80, (byte) 0x03};
    try {
      allocateCardChannel();

      // Perform Card Holder Verification if necessary
      CardChannel cc = getCardChannel();
      if (!getBusinessCardState(cc).isCHVPerformed()) {
        performCHV(cc, 1);
      }
```

Next, we set all parts of the command APDU. First, we empty our reusable APDU by setting the length to 0. Then we add the class and instruction bytes. Next, we append P1 containing the index what business card entry to set. Then, P2 contains the info, what field of that entry to set.

Last, we append the length and the contents to be set:

```
// Set up the command APDU and send it to the card.
 setFieldAPDU.setLength(0);
 setFieldAPDU.append(SET_NAME_COMMAND_PREFIX);
 setFieldAPDU.append((byte) index); // Entry Index
 setFieldAPDU.append((byte) field); // Field identifier
 setFieldAPDU.append((byte) value.length()); // Lc
 setFieldAPDU.append(value.getBytes()); // Data
```

Now we send that command APDU and analyze the response APDU. Whatever may have happened, finally we release the card channel.

```
    ...
    ResponseAPDU response
      = sendCommandAPDU(cc,
                        BUSINESS_CARD_AID, setFieldAPDU);

    switch (response.sw() & 0xFFFF) {
      case OK :
        return;
      case INDEX_OUT_OF_RANGE :
        throw new CardServiceInvalidParameterException(
                                "Index out of range");
      default :
      throw new CardServiceUnexpectedResponseException(
                                "RC=" + response.sw());
    }
  } finally {
    releaseCardChannel();
  }
}
```

The protected methods performCHV(CardChannel, int) and getField(int, int) are of a similar nature as the method set-Field(...) that we just went through.

You probably have noticed in method setField(...) that when checking if the PIN was already entered, we used a state obtained from getBusinessCardState(CardChannel). Let us have a look at this method. It retrieves the applet's state from the card state. The card state is a hash table containing the states of all card applets

GetBusiness-CardState (CardChannel)

accessed by their application identifier as the key (see Figure 14.3). The search key for our applet is BUSINESS_CARD_AID.

In getBusinessCardState(CardChannel) we assume that the applet state has already been set up during the initialization of this proxy and that the card state has been set up during the initialization of its base classes.

```
protected BusinessCardState getBusinessCardState(
                                CardChannel channel) {
    return (BusinessCardState) ((Hashtable)
            channel.getState()).get(BUSINESS_CARD_AID);
}
```

initialize(...)   As we just said, we rely on proper initialization. Therefore we now create the protected method initialize(...), in which we make sure that the base classes and the card state object are set up properly. First, following standard practice for initialization, we pass the call to our base class (our base class AppletProxy in turn passes the call to its base class BasicAppletCardService).

```
protected void initialize(CardServiceScheduler scheduler,
                        SmartCard card, boolean blocking)
                throws CardServiceException {

    super.initialize(BUSINESS_CARD_AID, scheduler,
                card, blocking);

    ...
```

To set up the applet proxy state, we first allocate exclusive access to the card channel and retrieve the card state from the card channel.

```
try {
    // Allocate the card channel. This gives us exclusive
    // access to the card until we release the channel.
    allocateCardChannel();
    // Get the card state.
    Hashtable cardState = (Hashtable)
                        getCardChannel().getState();
```

Next, we retrieve the state for our applet and applet proxy from the card state. If this applet state is not yet set, we create a new Busi- nessCardState object. We set it to reflect that the PIN verification (or cardholder verification, CHV) has not been successfully done yet.

Next, we put this card applet state object into the card state. Finally, we release the card channel.

```
    // Get the business card applet state.
    // If not already there, create it.
    BusinessCardState state = (BusinessCardState)
                        cardState.get(BUSINESS_CARD_AID);
    if (state == null) {
        state = new BusinessCardState();
        state.setCHVPerformed(false);
        cardState.put(BUSINESS_CARD_AID, state);
    }
  } finally {
    releaseCardChannel();
  }
}
```

Now we have discussed the main parts of our business card applet proxy. You might want to review the entire source, which you find in samples.business.BusinessCardProxy.java, which you get from http://www.opencard.org/SCJavaBook/.

Our proxy's base class AppletProxy is so straightforward that we will not cover it here. Of course, you can find it in the OCF distribution in package opencard.opt.applet.

Moving upwards in the inheritance tree one more time, we find a class that has a few details that we should look at in the following.

14.4.2.2
Class BasicAppletCardService

The main purpose of the BasicAppletCardService is to offer to its derived proxy classes a convenient method to send APDUs to their corresponding card applets. It is a service of this class to determine if a selection command must be issued first, or if the receiving card applet is the currently selected applet. In this way the overhead of unnecessary selection commands is avoided.

All instances of the class BasicAppletCardService associated with the same physical card share a common object of type CardState to ensure a consistent view including keeping the information on the active applet. BasicAppletCardService uses an application identifier for this CardState that can not collide with an application identifier of a real applet and applet proxy:

```
/** This is a pseudo AID for the CardState.
       Normal applets can not have the same AID
       accidentally, because real AIDs consist of
       at least 5 bytes. */
private final static AppletID CARD_STATE_AID
    = new AppletID("SAID".getBytes());
```

Using the proxy state mechanism also for the state of the `Basic AppletCardService` we access the same state object for the same card, no matter how many instances of proxies exist.

The card state object is correctly set up in `initialize(...)` with the same logic that we have used in class `BusinessCardProxy`.

send-
Command-
APDU(...)

The method `sendCommandAPDU(...)` is for the derived classes the primary method to call. We have seen it being called in the method `setField(...)` of `BusinessCardProxy`[2]. Despite of its importance it is short:

```
protected ResponseAPDU sendCommandAPDU(CardChannel channel,
            AppletID appletID, CommandAPDU commandAPDU)
     throws CardTerminalException, CardServiceException
{
  selectApplet(channel, appletID);
  return channel.sendCommandAPDU(commandAPDU);
}
```

select-
Applet(...)

`selectApplet(...)` sends the appropriate selection APDU to the card, unless the card applet that is specified by `appletID` is already active. It does not create and send the APDU directly though. Rather it delegates this to the method `selectApplet(...)` of an object of type `ISOAppletSelector` (instance variable `selector_`):

```
// in selectApplet(CardChannel …, AppletID appletID) …

if ((state.getSelectedAppletID() == null)
    || (!state.getSelectedAppletID().equals(appletID)))
{
   AppletInfo info =
       selector_.selectApplet(channel, appletID);
   ...
```

---

[2] To be very precise, this call went through the method `sendComman-dAPDU(...)` of `AppletProxy`.

After successful selection we must call `appletDeselected()` of the state object of the previously selected applet:

```
AppletID previouslySelectedAID
   = state.setSelectedAppletID(AppletID);

if (previouslySelectedAID != null) {
  Hashtable cardState = (Hashtable) channel.getState();
  AppletState appState = (AppletState)(cardState.get(
                                previouslySelectedAID));
  appState.appletDeselected();
}
```

Now we are done with handling the selection and de-selection of card applets in class `BasicAppletCardService`, the base class of all applet proxies. We have used applet state objects to keep track of the state of the card applet with which they are associated.

Let us look at the applet state for our business card applet now.

14.4.2.3
Class BusinessCardState

For our business card applet we are interested only in one state information. We need to know whether a valid PIN has been entered after this applet became active. This information is stored in the boolean variable `chvPerformed_`. The variable is set to false in method `appletDeselected()`.

Class `BusinessCardState` is short enough that we can show the pure code (with all commentary removed) as a whole:

```
public class BusinessCardState extends AppletState {
  protected boolean chvPerformed_ = false;

  public void appletDeselected() {
    chvPerformed_ = false;
  }
  public boolean isCHVPerformed() {
    return chvPerformed_;
  }
  public void setCHVPerformed(boolean chvPerformed) {
    chvPerformed_ = chvPerformed;
  }
}
```

Now we have seen the applet proxy for our card applet, its base classes, and the state object associated with it.

In our example we do not intend to let an application program use `BusinessCardProxy` objects directly. Instead, we provide as application programming interface a class `BusinessCard`.

14.4.2.4
Class BusinessCard

Class `BusinessCard` is responsible for storing business card information on the card and retrieving it from there. It takes responsibility for all necessary subtasks, such as starting and closing OCF, reacting on card insertion and card removal events, and working with the card applet using a `BusinessCardProxy`.

The techniques used in class `BusinessCard` are not Java Card specific, but standard OCF application programming as we have shown it in Chapter 12. Therefore we do not discuss the source code here. You can find it in `BusinessCard.java`. This file is contained in the complete source code for the business card sample program, which we provide as package `samples.business` in the sample code archive on http://www.opencard.org/SCJavaBook/.

As a historical note, the code has been originally developed and tested with OCF version 1.1.1 as demonstration for the first edition of this book. For OCF version 1.2 several of the classes were promoted into the new OCF package `opencard.opt.applet`. For the second edition of this book the code was tested with OCF 1.2 and with the IBM Java Card "JCOP10" [IBMJC01], which implements the Java Card 2.1.1 specification.

15 Card and Application Management

In this chapter, we give an overview on card management and application management systems. We also describe how OCF can be used to support these systems on client devices. In Section 15.1, we give an overview on card, application, and key management systems and the life cycles of cards and applications. Card management systems, as well as application management systems need to perform card-related actions on various client platforms. In Section 15.2, we show how the OpenCard Framework can be used to support application download to smart cards via the Internet and for application personalization via the Internet.

15.1 Introduction

The tasks related to the management of smart cards and card applications can be categorized in three different domains: management of cards, management of applications, and management of keys. The term *card management* refers to the functions that are required to allow for management of multi-application smart cards in a multi-enterprise environment. *Application management* refers to the functions required for management of applications for multi-application smart cards. *Key management* refers to management of cryptographic keys, key distribution, and security policies.

In a complex smart card system, there are usually three kinds of management systems: Card Management Systems (CMS), Application Management Systems (AMS), and Key Management Systems (KMS). The different management systems within a smart card system may be owned by a single entity in simple systems. In more complex smart card systems, there are several cooperating entities running their own systems: The card issuer owns the card management system and each application provider owns his own application management system. The key management system is usually run in a trust center by a trusted third party. In the following sections we will explain card, application, and key management systems in more detail.

15.1.1
Card Management Systems

Card management systems are used to manage entire smart cards. They allow to issue cards, to handle damage, theft or loss of cards, to keep track of the states of individual cards and of the applications on these cards, and finally to withdraw and replace cards. The life cycle of smart cards spans a number of states that may be very different depending on the approaches chosen by the card issuer and to some extent on design decisions made by the card operating system provider. In this section, we describe a very generic life cycle model with a rather big number of card states. In concrete smart card systems, some of these states may be missing.

- **Pre-Issuance** – this is the state, where only a chip module with the operating system burned in ROM exists. Initialization moves the module to the next state.

- **Enabled** – the data that is common for all cards of a lot has been written to the persistent memory. Personalization moves the chip to the next state.

- **Personalized** – this is the state after personalization, where the modules are embedded in plastic cards and card-individual data is written to the card. The card now contains all data required for first use. Delivery to the cardholder moves the card to the next state.

- **Issued** – the card has been delivered to the cardholder. Use of the card by the cardholder moves it to the next state.

- **Active** – this is the state where the card is actually used by the cardholder. Expiry, loss, theft, damage or blocking moves the card to one of the next states.

- **Lost, Stolen, Damaged, Defective or Blocked** – the card was lost, stolen, damaged, is defective or was blocked by the card issuer. Inactivation moves the card to the next state.

- **Inactive** – usage of the card has been dispensed. Withdrawal moves the card to the next state.

- **Withdrawn** – this state represents the end of the card life cycle, where the card is not usable anymore.

15.1.2
Application Management Systems

Application management systems are used to manage card applications. They allow for provision of card applications during card production and for post-issuance application download as well as tracking of application states and removal of applications. In this section, we describe a very generic life cycle model with a rather big number of application states. In concrete smart card systems, some of these states may be missing.

- **Pre-Issuance** – this is the initial state of an application, where it does not exist on the particular card. Loading the application on the card moves it to the next state.

- **Loaded** – the application has been loaded on the card, but cannot yet be used. Installation moves the application to the next state.

- **Installed** – the application has been installed and is ready to be personalized with card-individual data. Personalization moves the application to the next state.

- **Personalized** – the application has been personalized with card-individual data. Issuing the application to the cardholder moves it to the next state.

- **Issued** – the application has been issued to the cardholder.

- **Active** – this is the state where the application is actually used by the cardholder. Expiry, loss, theft or blocking moves the card to the next state.

- **Lost, Stolen or Blocked** – the card was reported lost or stolen or the application provider blocked usage. Inactivation moves the card to the next state.

- **Inactive** – usage of the application has been dispensed. Withdrawal moves the card to the next state.

- **Withdrawn** – this state represents the end of the card life cycle, where the card is not usable anymore.

15.1.3
Key Management Systems

Key management systems are used to manage cryptographic keys within a smart card system. They allow for generation of keys and secure distribution of keys across the system. Key Management Systems track the keys in the system and enable their controlled replacement.

Keys are needed by card management systems, application management systems, and by individual smart cards and smart card applications. Card management systems need keys for personalization or for blocking/unblocking of smart cards for example. Application management systems need keys for loading new applications on smart cards, for installing and personalizing applications, as well as for blocking or unblocking of applications. Finally, smart card applications themselves usually need keys for protecting sensitive operations.

15.2
Using OCF for Card and Application Management

In this section we describe how the OpenCard Framework can be used to perform administrative tasks required for card and application management. The card life cycle can be subdivided into three major phases: The card issuance phase, the card usage phase, and finally the disposal of the card. Usage of OCF in the card issuance phase would be possible, but usually card initialization and personalization is done in closed factories using proprietary hardware and software. Usage of OCF is particularly advantageous when performing card or application management tasks during the usage phase in a smart card's life cycle.

While traditional smart cards did not allow for adding or removing applications in the usage phase, today's advanced smart cards offer this possibility. They provide the technical prerequisites that are needed on the card side - now there is a need for an infrastructure that allows for usage of these features and makes download of applications via the network possible. In this chapter, we describe an architecture that can be used to implement card and application management functions and we present two concrete examples – post-issuance application download and decentralized personalization of an application.

15.2.1
Example

An example where post-issuance application download and person-alization are required is the following scenario: A customer of a bank has a smart card that hosts a purse application and a home banking application. While doing home banking, he realizes that now his bank also offers online brokerage with smart cards and he wants the brokerage application on his card. He clicks on the link to the application management system for the brokerage application and the application download applet is displayed in the browser. First, it creates a new application directory with appropriate files for the brokerage application on the card. Then, the application download applet lets the card compute an asymmetric key pair and retrieves the public key from the card. It sends the public key together with parameters entered by the cardholder to the brokerage key management system for certification, receives the certificate, and stores it on the card. From now on, the customer can use his card to digitally sign orders instead of using transaction numbers.

15.2.2
Security

Each of the actions performed during application download needs to be appropriately secured, e.g. by usage of security domains associated with application providers. A security domain contains cryptographic keys that are owned by the application provider. Examples for security domains are GlobalPlatform security domains on Java Cards or application directories that contain key files on file system cards. Installation of a security domain on a card usually requires a key owned by the card issuer. Once a security domain for an application provider has been installed, only the keys of the application provider are needed for further actions: Application code and data can be downloaded using the application provider's keys that have been installed on the card with the security domain. Figure 15.1 shows an example of a protocol that may be conducted between a client that wants to download an application to the card, the card issuer's card management system, and the application provider's application management system on a high level.

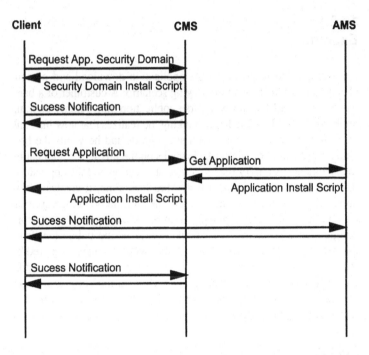

First, the client needs to check whether the application provider's security domain is already present on the card. If this is not the case, the client requests the download of the appropriate security domain and obtains an install script from the card management system, i.e. a sequence of card commands that must be exchanged with the card to install the security domain. After successful installation of the new security domain on the card, the client notifies the card management system.

After installation of the security domain, the card is ready for download of the application itself. The client requests the application download from the application management system. As a response, the client receives an application install script, i.e. a sequence of card commands that need to be exchanged with the card to install the application on the card. After successful download of the application, the client notifies the application management system and the card management system.

15.2.3
Architecture and Technology

One approach to implement card and application management functions is a three-tier architecture as shown in Figure 15.2.

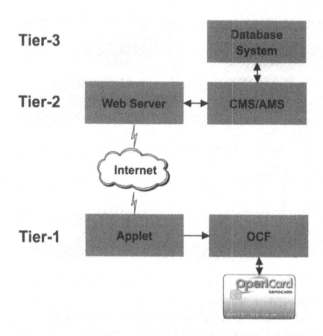

Figure 15.2:
Infrastructure for
Decentralized Card
Administration and
Personalization

Tier-1 consists of these devices where card or application management tasks shall be performed, like personal computers, network computers, ATMs, set-top boxes or any other smart card enabled device connected to a network. Tier-2 consists of application servers hosting card and application management software. Tier-3 consists of database systems that are used to trigger and track actions performed on Tier-2 and Tier-1 and to provide the required data.

Standard Internet technology can be used to implement a three-tier system like this. At Tier-1, a Web Browser can be used for running the required management applets. The management applets can use the OpenCard Framework to access smart cards. At Tier-2, a Web Server with an integrated application server can be used to provide the required HTML pages as well as for running servlets that provide the connection to Tier-3. At Tier-3, database servers can be used to manage data required for card and application management.

Figure 15.3:
A Possible
Software Setup
for Web Based
Card and
Application
Management

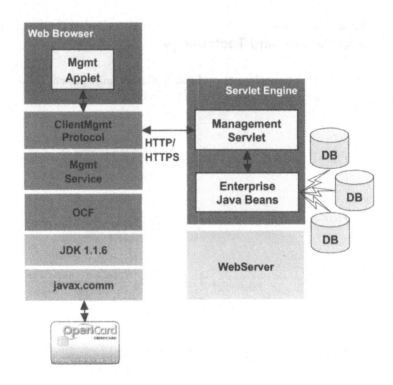

Various products may be used as browser, web server, application server, and database server. In most cases, the browser that is used is either Netscape Communicator or Microsoft Internet Explorer. Possible Web Servers are IBM HTTP Server, Apache, Netscape Enterprise Server or Microsoft Internet Information Server. There are also several servlet engines available on the market, also some web servers come with built-in servlet support. We prefer IBM WebSphere Application server, because it does not only provide full servlet support but also supports Enterprise Java Beans (EJB) as well as various enterprise connectors and is available on virtually every platform from Windows NT/2000/XP over Unix to S/390 mainframes.

15.2.4
Post-Issuance Application Download

Application download to smart cards always depends on the particular card operating system of the card. In this chapter, we discuss post-issuance download of applications to smart cards with two different kinds of card operating systems: File system oriented smart cards and Java Cards with GlobalPlatform (see Chapter 2).

15.2.4.1
Post-Issuance Application Download
to File System Cards

Applications on file system cards, as defined in ISO 7816 and EMV, usually consist of an application directory (ADF) that contains several application files (AEFs) and – if required – key files and password files. If there is a directory file (EF_DIR) on a file system card, applications may have entries in that file. Thus, downloading an application to a file system card in general consists of the following steps:

1. Creation of a new application directory (ADF) under the applications unique application identifier (AID).

2. Registration of the new application directory in the directory file.

3. Creation of data files, key files, and password files in the new application directory.

4. Writing initial data to the data files, writing initial keys to the key files, and writing initial passwords to the password files.

For each of the above steps, certain access conditions need to be fulfilled. Usually, creating the application directory, adding an entry to the directory file, creating the key file inside of the application directory, and writing initial keys to that file require keys owned by the card issuer. Once these steps have been performed, more files inside of the application directory may be created and be written to using application keys.

Regarding application download, one problem with file system cards is that most older card operating systems have not been designed for download of applications via networks. Often, the secure messaging mechanisms implemented on these cards require exchange of a random number for each protected or encrypted command that has to be sent to the card. If this is the case, it is not possible to prepare a sequence of commands on the application management system server, pre-calculate the appropriate MACs on the server and send the whole sequence to the client. Instead, each command to be sent to the card with a MAC requires communication with the server.

15.2.4.2
Application Download to GlobalPlatform Java Cards

Applications on Java Cards that support GlobalPlatform are represented by a card applet. Downloading an application to a GlobalPlatform Java Card consists of the following steps:

1. Loading the applet on the card
2. Installing the applet
3. Personalizing the applet

GlobalPlatform has been designed to support application download via the Internet. It allows for establishing a session key between a security domain on the Java Card and the server. The server can prepare the entire command sequence for loading the applet on the card using that session key for encryption and protection of the individual card commands and can then send this sequence to the client in one step. The software on the client can receive the prepared command sequence and send it to the card command by command.

15.2.5
Post-Issuance Application Personalization

After an application has been installed on a card, it needs to be personalized to add card individual data to the application files. This may be immediately after application installation in the case of post-issuance application download or long after the application has been installed in the case of an application that had been pre-installed at card issuance and that was inactive. For personalization, data from the card and additional data to be entered by the cardholder requesting the application as well as data from databases of card issuer or application provider may be required. Once the required data has been gathered, it needs to be sent to the application provider who needs it for generating the personalization data set. The rest of the procedure depends on the type of smart card that is used.

For smart cards that allow usage of one random challenge for a sequence of commands – like Java Cards for example – the application management system can generate personalization scripts, which are sequences of personalization commands. It embeds the required data in personalization Command APDUs, signs, and encrypts parts of these APDUs using keys that match the keys of the application security domain on the card. The personalization script can then be sent to the client that sends all Command APDUs in the script to the smart card one after the other. Figure 15.4 shows this scenario.

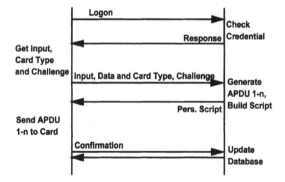

Figure 15.4: The Simplest Case of Post-Issuance Application Personalization.

However, Command APDUs cannot be aggregated in scripts like described above for smart cards that use a challenge-response protocol per command – like older file system oriented cards for example. In this case, a communication between the client and the server must take place for each piece of data to be written to the card, because the server needs a new challenge from the card for each command APDU to be prepared. Figure 15.5 shows this case.

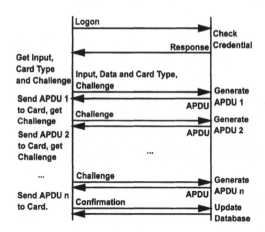

Figure 15.5: Post-Issuance Personalization for a Card that Requires Challenge-response per Command

16 OCF for Embedded Devices

In this chapter, we present a compact version of the OpenCard Framework for Embedded Devices (see [OCFE01]) that is intended for use in embedded devices that do not have extensive resources like PCs and do not require the full flexibility of Open Card Framework. For example, OCF for Embedded Devices has been adopted as a smart card API for software in set-top boxes by the Digital Video Broadcasting (DVB); Multimedia Home Platform (MHP) Specification 1.1.

In Section 16.1, we present a categorization of devices in different profiles and position the OpenCard Framework and the OpenCard Framework for Embedded Devices against these profiles. In Section 16.2, we present the high level structure of OCF for Embedded Devices, some important differences to OCF and the prospective footprint of OCF for Embedded Devices.

16.1
Device Profiles

There are a big variety of pervasive computing devices on the market with very different capabilities, e.g. mobile phones, screen phones, personal digital assistants, intelligent card terminals, payment terminals, wearable computers, and intelligent car radios. It is not reasonable to address the full range of devices with a single framework because they are just too different. We see three classes of devices to which we will refer as high-end, medium, and low-end pervasive computing devices. The most relevant criteria for our classification are the installed memory and the Java language subsets available on these devices. Table 16.1 gives a brief characterization of the three profiles.

On big terminals, the full OpenCard Framework can be used. It was originally developed for use on Personal Computers, Network Computers, and Workstations, but it is compact enough to fit in high-end devices like screen phones and kiosks. The OpenCard Framework provides support for multiple card readers that may have multiple slots as well as many convenience functions that in some cases can save work for application programmers.

Table 16.1: Device Categories

	Big Devices	Medium Devices	Small Devices
RAM	> 1024 KB	256-1024 KB	< 256 KB
ROM	> 1024 KB	256-1024 KB	< 256 KB
Java Subset	Personal Java	Embedded Java	Embedded Java
Threads	Yes	Yes	No
Comm.	TCP/IP, SSL	TCP/IP, SSL	WAP or similar
Examples	Screen Phones, Kiosks, Wearable Computers, Telematics units	Intelligent Card Terminals, Set Top Boxes	Small Payment Terminals, Mobile Phones

On medium devices, a more compact version of the OpenCard Framework is required. It must suit the memory and language restrictions of these devices, that means the footprint of the class files must be small as well as the dynamic memory consumption and only language features which are supported in Embedded Java environments may be required. The prototype of the OpenCard Framework for Embedded Devices was developed with these restrictions in mind. The features needed for these devices are implemented in OCF-compatible manner, but given the constraints of these devices, all functions that are not absolutely necessary are missing. This results in a very low footprint of only about 25 K.

The memory and language restrictions that apply to low-end devices are still being discussed. What seems to be clear by now is that a footprint of 25 K may still be too much for low-end pervasive computing devices. Here a subset of the OpenCard Framework for Embedded Devices that only contains the minimum set of classes, which is required for communication with the card, may be used. It doesn't provide the event and service layer, thus the footprint can be as low as 7 K. If required, the event layer may be added, resulting in additional footprint of about 3 K.

The sizes given here were obtained by compiling to the standard class file format without debug information. Further reduction by converting the classes to a different format – for example something similar to the CAP format used for Java Card applets – is still possible.

16.2
OCF for Embedded Devices

As mentioned in the previous section, the full version of the Open-Card Framework is not adequate for medium and low-end terminals. It has been designed to run on Personal Computers, Network Computers, Workstations etc. and thus has features which are not needed in a terminal environment: automatic configuration from property files, multiple card terminal support, dynamic attachment and detachment of card terminals for example.

The concept of the OpenCard Framework for embedded devices is to provide subsets of the OpenCard Framework with functionality reduced to the essential features required *inside* of terminals. One subset is intended for low-end terminals and only contains a minimal subset of the original OpenCard Framework classes. The other subset offers more features but still is much smaller than the full Open Card Framework. The Figure 16.1 shows which OpenCard Framework packages these subsets span: The subset for low-end devices only contains classes at the terminal layer, while the subset for medium devices additionally contains classes on the event and service layer. As the subset for small devices is a subset of that for medium devices, all applications for the low-end subset also run on the medium subset.

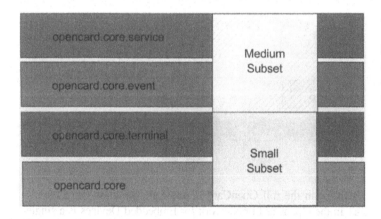

Figure 16.1: The Subsets of the OpenCard Framework for Embedded Devices

16.2.1
Differences between OCF and OCF for Embedded Devices

The generic architecture of the OpenCard Framework has been adapted for terminals, where only one card reader with one or more slots or transceivers exists. Another important change to the architecture was the introduction of strict layering. All dependencies from the terminal package to the event package have been removed. As a result, the terminal package can be used alone if desired.

The following picture gives a rough overview on the architecture of the OpenCard Framework for Embedded Devices. Arrows indicate dependencies of classes on other classes. The classes with thick borders and the mark (S) are singletons i.e. there is exactly one instance of these classes [GAM95]. The boxes with dotted borders depict interfaces.

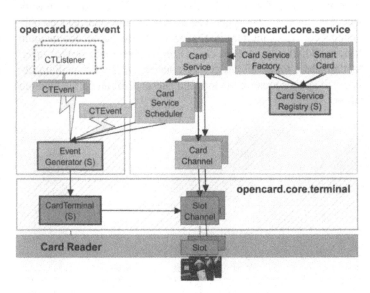

Unlike in the full OpenCard Framework, the class CardTerminal in the OpenCard Framework for Embedded Devices is a singleton that represents the single card reader of the embedded device. As there is exactly one CardTerminal instance, which can always be obtained by calling the appropriate static method the CardTerminalRegistry does not exist in OCF for Embedded Devices. The card reader of the device in which OCF for Embedded Devices runs may have one or more slots. The number of slots may be queried and

SlotChannel objects for a slot with a given number can be obtained from the CardTerminal singleton. A SlotChannel represents a connection to a smart card in a slot rather than a slot; there can be at most one SlotChannel per slot with an inserted smart card. In contrast to the full OpenCard Framework, where the Slot class still exists as a deprecated class for backward compatibility, there are no objects that represent slots in OCF for Embedded Devices.

Like OCF 1.2, OCF 1.2.2 for Embedded Devices has an Event-Generator that detects card insertion and card removal events using a method of the CardTerminal singleton, generates appropriate CardTerminalEvents and multicasts these events to all registered CTListeners, i.e. explicitly registered applications or automatically registered CardServiceSchedulers.

When an application receives a CardTerminalEvent resulting from card insertion, it can obtain a SmartCard object using the static method SmartCard.getSmartCard(). The application can then use the new SmartCard object to obtain a CardService object.

When the user removes a card, the associated CardServiceScheduler - which is a CTListener - will be notified by the EventGenerator and closes all SmartCard objects, the CardChannel, the SlotChannel associated with the card and finally itself.

Although there are significant internal differences between the full OpenCard Framework 1.2 and the OpenCard Framework for Embedded Devices 1.2.2, the differences from an application's or card service's point of view are minimal:

- Applications cannot rely on automatic configuration of card service factories from a property file when using OCF for Embedded Devices. Instead, they must explicitly register the required factories with the CardServiceRegistry.

- An application must provide a class implementing the interface CHVDialog to the used card services if a card holder verification is required. OCF for Embedded Devices provides no default CHV dialog because there is no common AWT for embedded devices.

- Card services that are relying on the secure cardholder verification feature of the full OpenCard Framework must be slightly changed. OCF for Embedded Devices doesn't provide this feature since it runs *inside* of terminals.

- Card service factories using the deprecated customization feature for CardChannels must be changed so that they use the state objects associated with CardChannels instead.

16.2.2
Footprint Statistics

In this section we provide footprint statistics on the prototype of OCF for Embedded Devices 1.2.2 developed at IBM. We list the footprint of each class and package as well as the total footprint of the medium subset and the low-end subset.

To get an idea what footprint a pure Java driver for the built-in card reader of a card terminal might add, we implemented a pure Java driver prototype for the Gemplus GCR 410, which turned out to require 7 K.

The footprint of card services will be very different, depending on functionality. It may be between 1 and 5 K for simple card services with small functionality. Card services with a rich functionality may have a footprint of 10 to 20 K. The size of the very simple pass through card service that only routs given APDUs to the card is about 1 KB for example.

The numbers below were obtained by using JDK 1.2's javac compiler with the option -g:none, which generates class files without debug information.

Table 16.2:
Footprint
Statistics of OCF
for Embedded
Devices

OCF for Embedded Devices 1.2.2 Implementation	25 KB
OCF for Embedded Devices 1.2.2 Terminal Layer	7 KB
OCF for Embedded Devices 1.2.2 plus GCR410 Driver	32 KB
OCF for E.D. 1.2.2 Terminal Layer plus GCR410 Driver	16 KB
Java Driver for GCR410 including T1 Protocol	6 KB

Part IV
Appendices

A The Card

In this appendix, we provide information on the smart card that comes with this book. In Section 1, we describe the card and its basic features. We also provide information on the card family to which this card belongs. In Section 2, we explain the file structure on the card. Finally, in Section 3, we explain how the OpenCard Framework can be used to access the card.

A.1
The IBM MultiFunction Card

The IBM MultiFunction Card belongs to the kind of smart cards that are most widely used today – file system oriented cards. The data on file system cards is organized in directories and files. For each directory and for each file, access conditions can be specified for several access modes like READ, UPDATE, INCREASE, DECREASE, CREATE, DELETE etc. In addition to unsecured access to a file, a file system smart card can allow access to files and directories only if the specified access conditions like card holder verification, external authentication, secure messaging or encryption are satisfied by the application.

The card that comes with this book is an IBM MFC 4.1, which is the entry-level version within the IBM MFC card family. It is a file system card with additional increase and decrease commands that can be used to implement counters on the card. It uses the DES or Triple DES algorithm for protecting data. The MFC 4.1 has an improved file system, an extended command buffer and is available with 2, 4, 8 or 16 kb of EEPROM.

The flagship of the IBM MFC family is the MFC 4.3. This card has a cryptographic coprocessor and does not only support the DES algorithm, it also supports RSA and DSA for generating and verifying digital signatures. A special feature of this card is that it can even generate key pairs on the card.

A.2
The File Structure on the Card

The file structure on the card that comes with this book is very simple to be easily understandable. It contains three application directories: The first directory belongs to the loyalty application example in Chapter 9. The second directory belongs to the Internet Broker Demo that is available on the OpenCard web site and is described in Chapter 10.

The third directory belongs to the Business Card Demo that is also available on the web site http://www.alphaworks.ibm.com/ as part of the OCEAN package. Figure A.1 shows an overview of the file structure.

Figure A.1:
The File Structure
of the Card that
Comes with this
Book

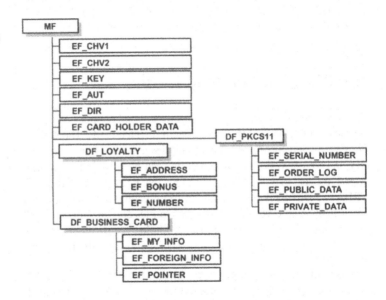

The files EF_CHV1 and EF_CHV2 hold passwords and unblock passwords for these passwords along with initial and current retry counters. These passwords are used to protect files on the card against access without authorization by the cardholder. The file EF_KEY holds cryptographic keys and related retry counters for use for external authentication (see Section 4.2.1), secure messaging, and encryption (see Section 4.2.3). In our example, EF_KEY holds a single key that is used as a global administration key. The file EF_AUT holds a key to be used for internal authentication (see Section 4.2.2).

The file EF_DIR holds directory information about the applications on the card. The file EF_CARD_HOLDER_DATA contains information about the cardholder, like name and address for example. Finally, the application directories DF_LOYALTY, DF_PKCS11, and DF_BUSINESS_CARD contain smart card application data for the Loyalty Sample Program, the Stockbroker Demo and the Business Card Demo mentioned above.

The listing below gives a detailed description of the file structure on the card. For each directory, the file identifier and the access conditions for creating and deleting files are specified. For each elementary file, the file identifier, access conditions for read and update and the initial content are specified. File identifiers are two-byte values that are specified as hexadecimal values. The access conditions used on the card are:

■ *Always*
The access condition *Always* means that access is possible by simply sending the appropriate command APDU.

■ *Cardholder Verification 1/Cardholder Verification 2*
Cardholder Verification 1 and *Cardholder Verification 2* mean that the first password or the second password respectively must be provided to the card with the VERIFY command before sending the access command to the card.

■ *Protected with Key 0*
Protected with Key 0 for CREATE, DELETE and UPDATE means that a Message Authentication Code (MAC) must be appended to the appropriate Command APDU before sending it to the card. For READ, *Protected with Key 0* means that the card will return the data with an appended MAC that is calculated with key 0.

■ *Enciphered with Key 0*
The access condition *Enciphered with Key 0* for CREATE, DELETE and UPDATE means that a MAC must be appended to the appropriate Command APDU and that the resulting APDU must be enciphered with Key 0 before sending it to the card. For READ, it means that the card returns data appended by a MAC and in enciphered form.

■ *Never*
The access condition *Never* means that access is possible under no circumstances.

When reading the listing below, please keep in mind that it is only intended as a simple example to be used by demos and sample programs and should not be taken as a template for designing real-life file system layouts.

Directory MF (0x3F00)

AC Create: Protected with Key 0
AC Delete: Protected with Key 0

File EF_CHV1 (0x0000)

File Type: Transparent
Size: 23 bytes
AC Update: Cardholder Verification 2
AC Read: Never
Data --
0x01,   // Activation
0x00,   // Way to present
0x00,   // Key Number in relevant EF_KEY
"password",   // Password
0x03,   // Initial attempt counter
0x03,   // Remaining Attempts
"unblckpw",   // Unblock Password
0x01,   // Initial Attempt Counter
0x01   // Remaining Attempts

File EF_CHV2 (0x0100)

File Type: Transparent
Size: 23 bytes
AC Update: Enciphered with Key 0
AC Read: Never
Data --
0x01,   // Activation
0x00,   // Way to present
0x00,   // Key Number in relevant EF_KEY
"password",   // Password
0x03,   // Initial Attempt Counter
0x03,   // Remaining Attempts
"unblckpw",   // Unblock Password
0x01,   // Initial Attempt Counter
0x01   // Remaining Attempts

File EF_KEY (0x0001)

File Type:	Variable (2 records)
Size:	32 bytes
AC Update:	Never
AC Read:	Never

```
Data Record 1 -------------------------------------
0x00,                 // Key Number
0x06,                 // Algorithm ID (DES)
0x03,                 // Attempt Counter
0x00,                 // Key version
0xFFFF,               // Key usage counter RFU
0x1031323437383B3E    // Key (odd parity per byte)

Data Record 2 -------------------------------------
0x05,                 // Key Number
                      // Note: Key 5 is used for RND
                      // number generator
0x06,                 // Algorithm ID (DES)
0x03,                 // Attempt Counter
0x00,                 // Key version
0xFFFF,               // Key usage counter RFU
0x0123456789ABCDEF    // Key (odd parity per byte)
```

File EF_AUT (0x9F03)

File Type:	Variable
Size:	16 bytes
AC Update:	Enciphered with Key 0
AC Read:	Never

```
Data Record 1 -------------------------------------
0x00,                 // Key Number
0x06,                 // Algorithm ID (DES)
0x03,                 // Attempt counter
0x00,                 // Key Version
0xFFFF,               // Key usage counter RFU
0x0123456789ABCDEF    // Key with odd parity
```

File EF_DIR (0x2F00)

File Type:	Linear Fixed, Record Length 40
Size:	3 * 40 bytes
AC Update:	Protected with Key 0
AC Read:	Always

```
Data ----------------------------------------------
```

```
0x61,                    // Application Template 1
38,                      // Length of contained data
0x4F,                    // Application identifier tag
9,                       // Application ID length
0xD276000022,            // Application ID: RID
                         // assigned to IBM
0x00000060,              // Application ID PIX PKCS11
0x50,                    // Application label tag
16,                      // Application label length
"PKCS#11 token    ",     // Application label
                         // No Application Pref. Name
                         // No App. Priority Index
0x52,                    // Command to Perform
7,                       // Command to Perform Length
0x00, 0xA4,              // MFC Select
0x00, 0x00, 0x02,        // P1, P2, P3
0xC110,                  // File id of Application DF
0x61,                    // Application Template 2
33,                      // Length of contained data
0x4F,                    // Application identifier tag
9,                       // App. Identifier  length
0xD276000022,            // Application identifier: RID
0x00000001,              // Application identifier: PIX
0x50,                    // Application label tag
11,                      // Application label length
"SCT LOYALTY",           // Application label
                         // No Application Preferred
                         // Name
                         // No Application Priority
                         // Index
0x52,                    // Command to Perform
7,                       // Command to Perform length
0x00, 0xA4,              // MFC Select
0x00, 0x00, 0x02,        // P1, P2, P3
0x1000,                  // File id of Application DF
                         // No Directory Discretionary
                         // Template
0x0000000000,            // Padding to multiple of 40
0x61,                    // Application Template 3
33,                      // Length of contained data
0x4F,                    // Application identifier tag
9,                       // Application ID length
0xD276000022,            // Application identifier: RID
0x00000002,              // Application identifier: PIX
```

```
0x50,                    // Application label tag
13,                      // Application label length
"BUSINESS CARD",         // Application label
                         // No Application Pref. Name
                         // No App. Priority Index
0x52,                    // Command to Perform
7,                       // Command to Perform length
0x00, 0xA4,              // MFC Select
0x00, 0x00, 0x02,        // P1, P2, P3
0x0815,                  // File id of Application DF
                         // No Directory Discretionary
                         // Template
0x000000                 // Padding to multiple of 40
```

File EF_CARD_HOLDER_DATA (0xC009)

```
File Type:      Transparent
Size:           64 bytes
AC Update:      Cardholder Verification 1
AC Read:        Cardholder Verification 1
Data ----------------------------------------------
"IBM PvC Smart Card Solutions",
0x0D, 0x0A,
"scard@de.ibm.com"
```

Directory DF_LOYALTY (0x1000)

```
AC Create:      Protected with Key 0
AC Delete:      Protected with Key 0
        File EF_ADDRESS (0x1002)
        File Type:      Transparent
        Size:           66 bytes
        AC Read:        Cardholder Verification 2
        AC Update:      Protected with Key 0
        Data ----------------------------------------
        "Old Orchard Road",
        0x0D, 0x0A,
        "Armonk, New York", 0x00
        File EF_BONUS (0x1003)
        File Type:      Transparent
        File Size:      4 bytes
        AC Read:        Cardholder Verification 1
        AC Update:      Cardholder Verification 1
        Data ----------------------------------------
        0x00000000
        File EF_NUMBER (0x1004)
```

```
            File Type:      Transparent
            Size:           8 bytes
            AC Read:        Always
            AC Update:      Never
            Data -----------------------------------------
            0x40E20100
```

Directory DF_PKCS11 (0xC110)

```
AC Create:      Cardholder Verification 1
AC Delete:      Cardholder Verification 1
```

File EF_SERIAL_NUMBER (0xC001)

```
            File Type:      Transparent
            Size:           16 bytes
            AC Update:      Never
            AC Read:        Always
            Data -----------------------------------------
            "0123456789ABCDEF"
```

File EF_ORDER_LOG (0xC002)

```
            File Type:      Linear Fixed, Record Size 20
            Size:           5 * 20 bytes
            AC Update:      Cardholder Verification 1
            AC Read:        Cardholder Verification 1
            Data -----------------------------------------
            "11111111111111111111",
            "22222222222222222222",
            "33333333333333333333",
            "44444444444444444444",
            "55555555555555555555"
```

File EF_PUBLIC_DATA (0xC100)

```
            File Type:      Transparent
            Size:           1000 bytes
            AC Update:      Always
            AC Read:        Always
```

File EF_PRIVATE_DATA (0xC200)

```
            File Type:      Transparent
            Size:           1000 bytes
            AC Update:      Cardholder Verification 1
            AC Read:        Cardholder Verification 1
```

Directory DF_BUSINESS_CARD (0x0815)

```
AC Create:      Always
AC Delete:      Always
```

```
File EF_MY_INFO (0x0816)
File Type:        Transparent
Size:             400 bytes
AC Update:        Cardholder Verification 1
AC Read:          Always
```

File EF_FOREIGN_INFO (0x0817)
```
File Type:        Transparent
Size:             1200 bytes
AC Update:        Always
AC Read:          Cardholder Verification 1
```

File EF_POINTER (0x0818)
```
File Type:        Transparent
Size:             2 bytes
AC Update:        Always
AC Read:          Always
```

A.3
Accessing the Card

As mentioned above, the card that comes with this book is an IBM MultiFunction Card Version 4.1 with 8 kb EEPROM size. This card is supported by the reference implementation of the OpenCard Framework that is available on http://www.opencard.org/. To access this book's card, you need to make the following entry in the opencard.properties file:

```
OpenCard.services =
com.ibm.opencard.factory.MFCCardServiceFactory ...
```

This entry specifies the factory that can provide the appropriate card service for the IBM MFC cards (including MFC 3.5, MFC 4.1 and later) known to the OpenCard Framework.

B Useful Web Sites

Dallas Semiconductor's IButton
http://www.ibutton.com/

The IButton is a security module in form of a ring. Its programming interface is very close to the Java Card specification.

On this web site, you can order your IButton including accessories on-line. The 1-Wire for Java™, the latest development tool for the IButton supporting OCF, is also available for download.

Gemplus
http://www.gemplus.com/

Gemplus is one of the leading providers of smart cards and smart card readers.

This web site contains information about smart cards in general and about products from Gemplus of course. You can also order smart cards like Gemplus' GemXpresso online.

Gemplus Developers
http://www.gemplus.com/developers/

This web site contains the latest information for developers, like a forum, latest trends, and current drivers. It also provides access to OpenCard CardTerminals and CardServices for hardware from Gemplus.

GlobalPlatform

http://www.globalplatform.org

Visa and other companies from the smart card and finance industry founded GlobalPlatform. This organization continues the development of the Open Platform technology, originally started by Visa.

IBM

http://www.ibm.com/pvc/

IBM Pervasive Computing provides a wide range of technology and solutions for pervasive computing and smart cards. IBM is committed to open standards and has developed the OpenCard Framework reference implementation in close coordination with other members of the OpenCard Consortium.

On this web site, you can find an overview of the technology and solutions IBM offers in the area of pervasive computing and smart cards.

Java Card Forum

http://www.javacardforum.org/

The Java Card Forum is the group working on the Java Card specification.

On this web site of the Java Card Forum, you can find the list of its members, its charter, information on the membership, minutes of recent meetings, and technical documents.

Mondex

http://www.mondex.com/

This is the web site of Mondex, the organization behind the Mondex electronic purse. Here, you can find information how Mondex works, which devices are available to be used with Mondex and how it can be used for payments over the Internet.

Multos

http://www.multos.com/

On this web site, the Maosco consortium provides information about its Multos smart card operating system, the companies behind Maosco, and how you can obtain implementation and application licenses. Developers find technical manuals, technical bulletins, as well as training modules.

OpenCard

http://www.opencard.org/

OpenCard Framework provides a Java application-programming interface to smart cards. It is supported by the OpenCard Consortium, which was founded by members from the IT industry, smart card industry, and payment systems industry. The OpenCard Framework reference implementation is publicly available free of charge.

On this web site, you can find the current version of OpenCard Framework with source code, binaries, documentation, and samples. The OpenCard Consortium also maintains a discussion list for interested parties.

PKI Survey

http://home.xcert.com/~marcnarc/PKI/

On this web page you can find excellent links to information on public key infrastructure (PKI) and cryptography.

PC/SC

http://www.pcscworkgroup.com/

The PC/SC workgroup specified an interface to smart cards in a Windows environment. Microsoft offers an implementation of this interface for the current versions of the Windows operating system.

On this web site, you can find the PC/SC specifications.

Proton World

http://www.protonworld.com/

ERG, American Express, Banksys, and Visa founded Proton World in 1998. Proton World is now owned by ERG and provides the Proton electronic purse scheme.

On this web site, you can find a description of Proton, a list of current projects, and recent press releases.

Smart Card Central

http://www.smartcardcentral.com/

On the Smart Card Central web site, you can find a wide variety of smart card related information, like industry news, links to companies in the industry, a list of smart card books, links to technical documentation, and a discussion forum.

Schlumberger

http://www.slb.com/smartcards/

Schlumberger is a leading smart card provider.

On this web site, you can find information about Schlumberger products and solutions.

Visa

http://corporate.visa.com/mc/facts

Visa International is the leading credit card organization with over 21.000 member financial institutions. Visa has founded the Open-Card Consortium and other industry organizations. Visa developed VisaCash and the Visa Open Platform specification.

In the 'Media Center' section of Visa's web site, you can find and download information about Open Platform, VisaCash, and other Visa technologies.

C Bibliography

[AES01] *Specification for the Advanced Encryption Standard (AES)*, FIPS 2001,
http://csrc.nist.gov/publications/fips/fips197/fips-197.pdf

[Ala02] Aladdin Knowledge Systems Ltd, 1999 http://www.aks.com/etoken/

[Ampel98] Andre Ampelas, *Calypso – contactless transport pass with a contact electronic purse – 4 European citites (Constance, Lisbon, Paris, Venice)*, Proceedings of the CardTech/SecureTech, 1998

[BEY98] Hans-Bernhard Beykirch, *Chipgeld – Wie die GeldKarte funktioniert*, 1998, in iX, Hannover, http://www.ix.de/ix/artikel/1998/12/148/

[Booch97] Grady Booch, Jim Rumbaugh, and Ivar Jacobson, *Unified Modeling Language User Guide*, Addison Wesley, December 1997,
http://www.awl.com/cp/uml/uml.html.

[CEPS00] CEPSCO, *Common Electronic Purse Specification*, 2000,
http://www.cepsco.com/

[Chamb99] Brian Chambers, *Octopus – The Hong Kong Contactless Smartcard Project* (Contacless smart card in a mass transit application, operations started October 97), Proceedings of the CardTech/SecurTech, 1999

[Chen00] Zhiqun Chen, *Java Card™ for Smart Cards: Architecture and Programmer's Guide*, Addison-Wesley 2000

[COR89] Thomas H. Cormen, Charles E. Leiserson, Ronald L. Rivest, *Introduction to Algorithms*, MIT Press, 1989

[CORBA99] OMG CORBA, http://www.corba.org/

[DIE99] The Internet Society *The TLS Protocol Version 1.0*, 1999,
http://www.faqs.org/rfcs/rfc2246.html

[DIF76]   W. Diffie and M.E. Hellmann, *Multiuser Cryptographic Techniques*, Proceedings of AFIPS National Computer Conference, 1976, pp. 109–112.

[EPSO02] European ePayment Systems Observatory, 2002, http://epso.jrc.es/purses.html

[GAM95]   Erich Gamma, Richard Helm, Ralph Johnson, John Vlissides, *Design Patterns – Elements of Reusable Object Oriented Software*, Addison-Wesley Publishing Company, 1995

[GP01]   *GlobalPlatform Card Specification 2.1*, June 2001, available from http://www.globalplatform.org/

[GUT98]   Guthery, Scott B. & Jurgensen, Timothy M. , *Smart Card Developer's Kit*, Macmillan Technical Publishing, Indianapolis, USA, 1998

[IBMJC01] IBM Java Card, http://www.zurich.ibm.com/JavaCard

[IBtn02] Dallas Semiconductor's iButton, 2002, http://www.ibutton.com/

[ISO02]   International Organization for Standards, 2002, http://www.iso.ch/

[Jain99] Anil K. Jain, Ruud Bolle and Sharath Pankanti, *Biometrics – Personal Identification in a Networked Society*, luwer Academic Publishers 1999

[JC00]   *Java Card 2.1.1 Platform Specification*, 2000, http://www.javasoft.com/javacard/

[JCF02]   Java Card Forum, http://www.javacardforum.org/

[JCM98]   *JNI – Java Native Interface*, http://java.sun.com/products/jdk/1.1/docs/guide/jni/

[JNI98]   *Java ™ Communications API 2.0*, http://www.javasoft.com/products/javacomm/

[KOB87]   N. Koblitz, *Elliptic Curve Cryptosystems, Mathematics of Computation*, v. 48, n. 177, 1987, pp. 203–209

[MER78]   R.C. Merkle, *Secure Communication Over Insecure Channels*, Communications of the ACM, v. 21, n.4, 1978, pp. 294–299

[MIC01]   Microsoft Software Development Kit for Java 3.1 Documentation http://www.microsoft.com/java/

[MIC99]   Microsoft Smart Card for Windows, 1999 http://www.microsoft.com/smartcard/

[MIL86] V.S.Miller, *Use of Elliptic Curves in Cryptography, Advances in Cryptology* – Crypto '85 Proceedings, Springer-Verlag, 1986, pp. 417–426

[MNDX02] Mondex Electronic Cash, 2002, http://www.mondex.com/

[MUL02] Multos, http://www.multos.com/

[NET01] *Netscape Object Signing, Establishing Trust for downloaded software*, http://developer.netscape.com/docs/manuals/signedobj/trust/owp.htm

[NET97] *Preventing Subversion of Public Helper Methods*, http://developer.netscape.com/docs/manuals/signedobj/capabilities/

[NIS94] National Institute of Standards and Technology, NIST FIPS PUB 186, *Digital Signature Standard*, U.S. Department of Commerce, May 1994

[OCC99] OpenCard Consortium, 1999, http://www.opencard.org/

[OCF99] *OpenCard Framework Programmer's Guide*, 1999, http://www.opencard.org/

[OCFE01] *OpenCard Framework for Embedded Devices Specification 1.2.2*, 2000, http://www.opencard.org/download/docs/1.2T/ocfembeddedspec.zip

[PCSC02] PC/SC Workgroup, http://www.pcscworkgroup.com/

[PGP02] The International PGP Homepage, 2002, http://www.pgpi.com/

[PRO02] Proton World, 2002, http://www.protonworld.com/

[RAN00] W. Rankl, W. Effing, *Smart Card Handbook, 2nd edition*, John Wiley and Sons, 2000

[RIV78] R.L. Rivest, A. Shamir, and L.M. Adleman, *A Method for Obtaining Digital Signatures and Public-Key Cryptosystems*, Communications of the ACM, v. 21, n. 2, Feb 1978, pp. 120–126

[RIV79] R.L. Rivest, A. Shamir, and L.M. Adleman, *On Digital Signatures and Public-Key Cryptosystems*, MIT Laboratory for Computer Science, Technical Report, MIT/LCS/TR-212, Jan 1979

[RMI99] *Java ™ Remote Method Invocation*, http://java.sun.com/products/jdk/rmi

[SCH96] Bruce Schneier, *Applied Cryptography*, Wiley, 1996

[SER99] James Duncan Davidson, Danny Coward, *Java Servlet Specification v2.2*, Sun Microsystems, 1999

[Smith97] Richard E. Smith, *Internet Cryptography*, Addison Wesley 1997

[TOW02] Towend, Robin C., *Smart Card News: Finance: History, Development & Market Overview*, 2002,
http://www.smartcard.co.uk/articles/finance.html

[UML97] *Unified Modeling Language Version 1.1*,
http://www.rational.com/uml/resources/documentation/

[VIS02] Visa International, 2002, http://www.visa.com/

[ZKA99] *Schnittstellenspezifikation für die ec-Karte mit Chip, GeldKarte Internet-Kundenterminal, Version 3.0*, 1999

D Glossary

- **AES** – Advanced Encryption Standard, standardized by NIST is the successor of the DES algorithm.

- **APDU** – Application Protocol Data Units are messages exchanged at the application level of communication stacks. In context with smart cards, APDUs are the messages exchanged between card readers and smart cards.

- **Applet** – A small program that can be downloaded to and executed on a client. In this book, the term applet is used both for programs running in web browsers as well as for programs running on Java Cards.

- **Authentication** – a sequence of actions proving the *authenticity* of an entity to a second entity.

- **Card Applet** – A Java application that is stored and executed on a Java Card. A card applets inherits from the class Applet of the Java Card Framework. Card applets have no dependencies on Java's AWT.

- **Card Reader** – a device that can be used to communicate with a *smart card*.

- **Card Terminal** – a device including a *card* reader plus some additional components like displays or PIN pads.

- **Command APDU** – An *APDU* sent from a card terminal to a *smart card*.

- **Contact Plate** – the metal plate covering a smart cards chip that is contacted when the card is inserted into a card reader.

- **Cryptographic Protocol** – A protocol that employs a sequence of cryptographic operations to authenticate entities or transmit information.

- **DES** – Digital Encryption Standard, invented by IBM and standardized by NIST, is the most well known widely used symmetric cryptographic algorithm.

- **Digital Signature** – encrypted digital fingerprints of data, ensuring data integrity and authenticity

- **DSA** – Digital Signature Algorithm, a public-key algorithm that – unlike *RSA* – is only intended for digital signatures, standardized in the Digital Signature Standard (DSS).

- **EEPROM** – Electrically Erasable Programmable Memory. This is the typical persistent storage medium used in smart card chips.

- **EMV** – This acronym from the three initial letters for Europay, MasterCard International, and Visa International is often used in the smart card industry to refer to "EMV'96: ICC Specifications for Payment Systems".

- **External Authentication** – *cryptographic protocol* proving the authenticity of an external entity to the smart card.

- **Hash** – a digital fingerprint of data. Hash algorithms are often used in conjunction with *Digital Signatures*.

- **ICC** – Integrated Circuit Card, a synonym for chip card.

- **Initialization** of smart cards – in mass production of smart cards, this is the first step where data common for all cards of a lot is written to the cards.

- **Internal Authentication** – *cryptographic protocol* proving the authenticity of a smart card to an external entity.

- **ISO 7816** – The International Standard Organization's standard relevant for smart cards.

- **Java Card** – a *smart card* that has the capability of running *Java* programs using a restricted command set and library on-card.

- **Java Card Framework** – Applets on a Java Card use the Java Card Framework as standard programming interface.

- **Java Card Runtime Environment (JCRE)** – The execution environment for Java Card applets.

- **JVM** – Java Virtual Machine. The execution environment for Java programs. The JVM interprets the Java byte code. The JVM also enforces security restrictions for the executed code.

- **Memory Card** – a credit card sized plastic card with a memory chip.

- **Off-Card Code** – Code outside of running in *card terminals* or computers.

- **On-card Code** – Code running in a *smart cards* processor. See also Off-Card Code.

- **OpenCard** – standard for smart card access on *Java* platforms.

- **PC/SC** – standard for smart card access on Windows platforms.

- **Personalization** of Smart Cards - in mass production of smart cards, this is the step where card individual data is written to the cards.

- **PKCS** – The Public-Key Cryptography Standards are a series of standards initiated by RSA to foster interoperability of cryptographic systems. Especially PKCS#11 and PKCS#15 are relevant for smart cards.

- **Privacy** – the property of not being readable by an enemy.

- **Private-Key** – Private-Keys are used in public-key cryptosystems to generate digital signatures or decrypt messages. Private-keys must be kept in secret to assure that only the owner can use them.

- **Public-Key Algorithm** – asymmetric cryptographic algorithm, where one key is revealed to the public and one key is kept in private. *Public keys* are used for encryption of data or validation of digital signatures while *private keys* are used for decryption of data or generation of digital signatures.

- **Public-Key** – Public-Keys are used in public-key cryptosystems to verify digital signatures or to encrypt messages. Public-keys are usually published so that anybody can use them.

- **RAM** – Random Access Memory

- **Response APDU** – An *APDU* sent back by a smart card after receiving a *command APDU*.

- **ROM** – Read Only Memory

- **RSA** – Most important *asymmetric cryptographic algorithm*. The acronym stands for the inventors Rivest, Shamir and Adlemen.

- **Secret Key** – A key for a symmetric algorithm, that needs to be kept in secret to assure security of the system in which it is used.

- **Servlet** – A small java program that can be deployed and run on an Java-based application server.

- **Smart Card** – a credit card sized plastic card with a computer chip.

- **Symmetric Cryptographic Algorithm** – cryptographic algorithm, where the same key is used for encryption and decryption. Examples are *DES* and IDEA.

- **Tamper Proof** – Tamper proof devices are built so that they loose all stored information when somebody tries to tamper with the device.

E Index

3

3-tier architecture 215

A

AAM 33
Abstract Syntax Notation (ASN) 27
acceptance device 69
access condition 30, 244
access conditions 277
access control 17
access modes 275
addCTListener(...) 204
address line 21
Administration System 42
Advanced Encryption Standard 55
AES 55
AID 31, 76, 234, 243
anonymity 39, 40
answer to reset (ATR) 26, 76, 77, 79, 95
APDU 24–26, 87, 120, 234
applet 233–34, 236–42
applet proxy 243–45
appletDeselected() 253
AppletProxy 245
Application Abstract Machine (AAM) 33
Application Access 148
application identifier (AID) 31, 76, 234, 243
application management 94
Application Protocol Data Unit (APDU) 24–26, 87, 234
application provider 93

application selection 79
ApplicationManagement-CardService 97
approval of cards and terminals 78
Architecture Overview 93–100
ARPAnet 35
asset protection 90
association 92
asymmetrical key 44, 46
ATR 26, 76, 77, 79, 95, 120
attacks 21
authentication 15, 36, 43–46

B

Bank of America 42
beginMutex() 150
benefits 13, 15–16
biometric identification 72–73
BizCardApplet 247
BizCardRecord 240
Booch 92
browser security 188
building access 15
bulk encryption services 80
BusinessCard 247, 254
BusinessCardProxy 245, 247–51
BusinessCardState 253–54
byte array 236
byte code converter 234

C

cap file 234
card acceptance device (CAD) 69

Printed in the United States
By Bookmasters